POUND
FOR
POUND

ALSO BY HERB BOYD

Heroes of America: Martin Luther King, Jr.

Down the Glory Road: Contributions of African Americans in United States History and Culture

Black Panthers for Beginners

African History for Beginners

Former Portuguese Colonies: Angola, Mozambique, Guinea-Bissau, Cape Verde, São Tomé and Príncipe

EDITED BY HERB BOYD

The Harlem Reader: A Celebration of New York's Most Famous Neighborhood from the Renaissance Years to the 21st Century

Race and Resistance: African Americans in the Twenty-First Century

Autobiography of a People: Three Centuries of African American History Told by Those Who Lived It

Brotherman: The Odyssey of Black Men in America—An Anthology (co-editor Robert Allen)

POUND FOR POUND

A Biography of

Sugar Ray Robinson

HERB BOYD
WITH RAY ROBINSON II

Amistad

An Imprint of HarperCollins *Publishers*

Dedicated to the memory of Edna Mae Robinson

A hardcover edition of this book was published in 2005 by Amistad, an imprint of HarperCollins Publishers.

POUND FOR POUND. Copyright © 2005 by Sugar Ray Robinson Properties and Licensing. All rights reserved. Printed in the United States of America. No part of this book may be used or reproduced in any manner whatsoever without written permission except in the case of brief quotations embodied in critical articles and reviews. For information, address HarperCollins Publishers, 10 East 53rd Street, New York, NY 10022.

HarperCollins books may be purchased for educational, business, or sales promotional use. For information, please write: Special Markets Department, HarperCollins Publishers, 10 East 53rd Street, New York, NY 10022.

First Amistad paperback edition published 2006.

Designed by Renato Stanisic

The Library of Congress has cataloged the hardcover edition as follows:

Boyd, Herb.
    Pound for pound: a biography of Sugar Ray Robinson/Herb Boyd with Ray Robinson II.—1st ed.
        p. cm.
    Includes index.
    ISBN 0-06-018876-6
     1. Robinson, Sugar Ray, 1920–1989. 2. Boxers (Sports)—United States—Biography.
I. Robinson, Ray. II. Title.

GV1132.R6B69   2004
796.83'092—dc22
[B]

ISBN-13: 978-0-06-093438-5 (pbk.)
ISBN-10: 0-06-093438-7

06 07 08 09 10 BVG / RRD 10 9 8 7

ACKNOWLEDGMENTS

A biography of Sugar Ray Robinson required a corps of reliable and inexhaustible cornermen and -women. I should note at the outset my indebtedness to the unpublished memoir of Edna Mae Robinson. Ed Summer, who devoted many hours by her side, gave me a lengthy manuscript she had written. She had worked on it for several years and it was more than three hundred pages. Each attempt she made to get it published was met with rejection; among her notes and memorabilia—and she kept everything—are several rejection letters from editors who expressed deep regret that her manuscript, though well done, was "not what we are looking for at this time."

It was just what I needed. I read the manuscript and found it more than adequate for a beginning writer, and then Summer told me about Edna Mae's condition. There was no way I would be able to plumb additional information from her, because she was in the advanced stages of Alzheimer's disease. But he promised to set up a meeting so I could visit her, if I wanted to. The visit was without any worth, other than to see how such a ravishing beauty had so totally disintegrated, and was as hopelessly dependent as Sugar was in his final years. On several occasions I went by the apartment and just sat with her, and there were times when she would make a remark that seemed to have no meaning. I thought things would improve once her son came to town from California to visit. But together we would sit, and Ray II would put on videotape of her on some television show with Sugar, and it didn't seem to mean anything to her. As she herself had said about her life with Sugar—so many wonderful moments, but no way to relive them, no way to thrill again to how gorgeous she was, no way to recapture the astounding glamour she radiated wherever she went.

Complementing Edna Mae's manuscript were the memories of her son, Ray Robinson II. Sugar Deuce, as I call him, searched his yesterdays and divulged an array of gems, many of which have been processed and interwoven throughout the book. Also in my corner were three women to deal with various facets of completing this match with Sugar. My wife, Elza, was an irreplaceable sparring partner with whom I grappled over tone, mood, and perspective. Marie Brown, my agent, was like my manager/ trainer, making sure I got the right deal and the right encouragement to go the distance. And then there was my cut lady—my editor, Dawn Davis—who rescued me when I was on the ropes, applied the salve and sutures to a tattered text, and pushed me out into the ring once again. Of course, neither she nor my other handlers are responsible for the outcome of this match.

Many years ago, it had been my mother who introduced me to Sugar. When I was growing up, there were three men I knew she admired—Nat "King" Cole, Billy Eckstine, and Sugar Ray

Robinson. I appropriated all of them. Jim Fitzgerald, Manie Barron, Carol Mann, and Ed Summer were among the first promoters of this bout, and I was blessed to have their faith and support. Back in the hood there were Clinton Edwards, Johnny Barnes, Jules Allen, Robert Van Lierop, Malik Edwards, Delilah Jackson, Sylvia Dixon, Percy Sutton, Sigmund Wortherly, Hilly Saunders, Jackie Tonawanda, Roger Simon, Reverend Dino Woodard, Bill Haley, Mel Dick, James Booker, Charles Dudley, Joe Bostic, Sr., Howie Evans, Herbert Wright, Sondra Kathryn Wilson, Sharon Howard, Kelly Howard, and Claude Sharrief, all of whom in their special ways helped me get back into the ring of this project and to see it through.

Langley Waller adopted me at the very start of all this, and has been unflagging in his ringside assistance.

It is to Waller and his ilk, who saw Sugar in the flesh, that this book is dedicated. I hope there are enough flashes of the past to remind you of Sugar's greatness and the joy he brought. Though I may not have cornered and nailed him like I wanted to, I think you will appreciate this encounter. Let us hope that I've done no worse on paper than his opponents did in the ring.

—*Herb Boyd*

I want to completely acknowledge my former wife, Celeste Robinson, who supported the vision of this book, and my children, Ray Robinson III, CoCo Robinson, D. D. Robinson, Tal Mario Robinson, and Zoe Grace Robinson, who are the result of the dream of my Mom and Dad! One World, One Race—HUMAN!

—*Ray Robinson II*

CONTENTS

CONTENTS

FOREWORD

It was in the mid- to late 1950s in Harlem, on a Saturday afternoon at a Malcolm X rally that drew more than twenty thousand spectators, that I met the man called "Sugar." Sugar Ray Robinson was born in Georgia, nurtured in Detroit, and developed as a boxer in New York City. He had incredibly fast fists and feet, and matchless pugilistic skills in the ring.

I was Malcolm's lawyer then. But after meeting the Sugar Man, I represented him on two occasions on matters of not great monetary consequence to him or to me; however, it was of some emotional consequence to Mr. Robinson. In the first instance, I was his lawyer in an incident involving an itinerant car washer who left a scratch on the Sugar's beautiful pink Cadillac. An unforgivable, but uncollectable sin.

When Sugar was seeking to get his tavern and businesses on

the New York City Visitor's Bureau schedule of important places to see, I successfully represented him.

Sugar Ray Robinson, then and always, had enough celebrity, glitter, and glamour wattage to match all the neon that glowed from his array of businesses on Seventh Avenue. The Sugar Man was a most radiant personality.

Herb Boyd has done a superb job of capturing Ray Robinson's life and ring prowess, particularly those stirring bouts with Jake LaMotta, Gene Fullmer, Kid Gavilan, and Carmen Basilio. For many boxing authorities, Sugar was "pound for pound" the greatest fighter to ever lace on gloves. And Herb Boyd has amassed enough information and woven a sufficiently detailed and informative story to confirm this fact.

Because of my limited relationship with Sugar Ray, I didn't get a chance to know his wife, Edna Mae, in any substantial way, but her life—from what we can glean in these pages—was a remarkable one as well. Together, there was a time when they were an indomitable couple, dominating the social scene and providing Harlem with its own touch of royalty.

In the seamless weave of their lives, we are able to relive the community's promise in the forties and fifties, when Sugar Ray's pink Cadillac was symbolic of an evanescent prosperity. Those were the years when Sugar Ray's glory was inextricably linked to Harlem's fortunes, and we reveled in the ascent of those moments, just as we mourned their demise.

When I, with a large body of help from Congressman Charles Rangel, placed time, money, and energy of my own, my family, and my company—Inner City Broadcasting Corporation—into the rehabilitation of the Apollo Theater in the early 1980s until 1992, some of the intent was to revive a community that had slumped considerably after Sugar Ray's enterprises were no longer available to inspire. In fact, the Apollo and Sugar Ray can be compared in the sense that each was, for a while, a singular lodestar that drew millions of visitors to Harlem. And during those years in which they existed simultaneously, the allure was undeniable. Thanks, Charlie Rangel; thanks, Harlem; thanks, Sugar Ray and Lady Edna Mae.

How wonderful it is to experience, once more, some of Harlem's halcyon times in this marvelous book. It not only depicts a man and a community, but a man and a woman, two star-crossed lovers who found it difficult to live together and apart. I was also thrilled to learn of the close companionship between Sugar Ray and Joe Louis. The similar trajectories of their lives gives the book an extended, and engrossing, leit-motiv.

But above all else, this book is Herb Boyd's biography of a great fighter, a boxer who compiled an incomparable record as an amateur and as a professional. In my lifetime, I have seen a number of fighters come along who have anointed themselves "Sugar," but there was only one Sugar Ray, and Herb Boyd places him back in the ring, back in the spotlight that he relished—and that relished him. Pound for pound, the Sugar was the best, and page for page this book matches his poetry in motion, his powerful punches—his fascinating and fulsome life.

—*Percy Sutton*
    Chairman emeritus, Inner City Broadcasting
    Corporation, and cofounder & CEO, Synematics, Inc.

PROLOGUE

"Do I remember Sugar Ray? Indeed I do. Watched him fight Duran and Tommy Hearns . . ."

"No, I mean Sugar Ray Robinson, the original Sugar."

This was typical of the exchanges that occurred between men in their forties and me when I asked them if they had ever seen Sugar Ray fight. When the same question was posed to older men, men in their sixties and seventies, they knew exactly which Sugar Ray I was talking about. Then would come a flood of memory—Graziano, Basilio, Gavilan, Maxim, and the slugfests with LaMotta. "Pound for pound," they would conclude, "Sugar Ray Robinson was the greatest fighter to ever step into the ring. He had it all: speed, power, endurance, savvy, and style. There will never be another like him."

. . .

When literary agents Jim Fitzgerald and Ed Summer and editor Manie Barron took me to lunch to talk about my writing a biography of Sugar Ray Robinson four years ago, I was very excited, though a bit apprehensive. Sugar Ray Robinson had a special place in my memory, and I wasn't sure I wanted to tamper with it or know any more about him than what I had read and seen of him in countless films, to say nothing of the Friday-night fights on television sponsored by Gillette Blue Blades. The first time I heard his name, which reminded me of Detroit's Sugar Chile Robinson, who was a child prodigy at the piano, I was hooked.

Much of what I heard of Sugar Ray's legend was very familiar. Whenever he returned to fight in Detroit, particularly at the Olympia, right around the corner from one of the many places I once lived in the city, I longed for a chance to see him entering or leaving the arena. A gang of us, mainly there to see what dimes we could earn watching the cars, would cluster near the arena's back exit, hoping to see Sugar Ray. It never happened.

Before my mother's hard work and good fortune commanded enough money to get us out of a basement apartment on Detroit's North End to within two blocks of the border at Eight Mile Road, she had a roomer who used to box. Sonny was an aspiring welterweight, and he would take the time to show me how to ball my fists and hold them up to protect myself. He taught my brother and me the proper way to execute a jab—the slight twist, the locked elbow. To keep our opponents from taking our jaws off, he showed us how to tuck them down under our shoulders, and to keep them that way as we extended a stiff jab.

Sonny rarely missed a Friday-night fight on NBC, and it was with him that I first listened to Don Dunphy and Bill Corum on radio as they did a blow-by-blow account of Sugar's fight with Kid Gavilan. I was amazed at how fast Dunphy could call a fight, the words flying out of his mouth as he tried to keep up with Sugar's rapid punches. You could tell when Sugar had the other fighter in trouble because Dunphy's voice would become even more dramatic and the roar of the crowd even more intense. One night, after what Dunphy described as a brutal exchange of punches, Corum came on the radio and said, "It wasn't a very interesting round," which baffled us and caused us to wonder if he had fallen asleep at some point. When the fight was over, and the decision went to Sugar, Sonny, my brother, my mother, and I cheered. I was only nine and I guess I cheered because Sonny had told us that he had met Sugar and that he used to live not too far from him in Detroit's Black Bottom.

This was my introduction to Sugar Ray Robinson, and from that fight onward I looked for his picture in the newspapers and in the magazines my mother would bring home from the people's houses where she worked as a domestic. When my brother and I went to camp the next summer, we both were part of the boxing tournament; like me, my brother had absorbed all the lessons Sonny had taught us, and the championship bout was between us. But we decided we were not going to fight each other. After some prodding we were finally forced to fight, and after we both danced around the ring like miniature Sugar Rays they gave me the decision, I think because I was able to stay away from my brother's windmill blows. That summer at camp in upstate Michigan was the first and last time I ever put on boxing gloves. I didn't like the idea of being punched squarely on the nose, no matter the prize. My brother felt the same, and we shifted our childhood passion to baseball. But Sugar remained my hero.

One of the reasons he was my hero was that he always seemed to win. And everyone loves a winner. When we moved from the North End to the "suburbs" of Detroit, we also acquired a front lawn, a backyard, a driveway, and a television set, with tinted cellophane taped across the screen to give us the illusion of color television. Now, rather than listening to Sugar Ray's bouts, we could watch them, and no fighter was ever more suited for television than Sugar. Everything about him was immediately telegenic—from his flashy style to his radiant smile. Dunphy's colorful descriptions on radio were marvelous, but now we could see what was happening. The advent of televised fights put the golden age of boxing on the tube and into the living rooms and dens of millions of fans, making Sugar a household name.

One of Sugar's most memorable televised fights was in 1952 against Rocky Graziano. We had a houseful of folks that night and, naturally, we were all pulling for Sugar to win, which of course he did. By this time I had begun to read more and more about Sugar, particularly in the *Detroit Times*. It seems that Detroit still made claims on him, though he moved from the city when he was eleven. From the articles I learned that he used to hang out at the Brewster Center, where he would carry Joe Louis's bags. In fact, the idea that both Joe Louis and Sugar Ray had their roots in Detroit and had come to the city from the South gave me additional reasons to admire them, since we shared the same migratory pattern. My mother brought my brother and me to Detroit in 1942 from Alabama, exactly ten years after Sugar had moved on to Hell's Kitchen in New York City.

By the time I moved to New York City in 1960, Sugar's career was in decline. His enterprises were closed or being closed and no longer significantly vital to the Harlem community, which was fast becoming the prototype of a squalid ghetto, and a place that even Sugar had begun to avoid. This meant avoiding his fans. James Baldwin, like others who grew up in Harlem, had experienced these conditions. "The people in Harlem know they are living there because white people do not think they are good enough to live anywhere else," the author observed in an often published essay, "Fifth Avenue Uptown," before concluding, "No amount of 'improvement' can sweeten this fact. Whatever money is now being earmarked to improve this, or any other ghetto, might as well be burnt. A ghetto can be improved in one way only: out of existence."

• • •

When Sugar's last great fight, with Gene Fullmer, took place in 1961, I was dealing with the Army and the draft. Boxing was the last thing on my mind. I was living in Bedford-Stuyvesant and working at a brake factory in Canarsie when I read about his loss to Fullmer. From then on, I preferred my *memories* of Sugar: when he was picture-perfect, an untarnished icon, a stylish symbol of black manhood, and my idol. Rather than see him defenseless and humiliated by second-rate fighters, I stored my Sugar away, way back to the late forties when he was at the top of his game.

It was within the roped square that Sugar gathered his iconic power, and it was this aura that captivated millions, placing him in a pantheon of athletic greats. But the swift feet of the ring master often turned to clay when he stepped from the pedestal.

CHAPTER 1

FROM RED CLAY TO BLACK BOTTOM

Sugar Ray Robinson on the page is almost as elusive as he was in the ring. In the opening chapters of the autobiography that he completed with the assistance of *New York Times* sportswriter Dave Anderson, Sugar states that he was born May 3, 1921, in Detroit's Black Bottom. While the date of his birth is accurate (though it is listed as 1920 in *Ring* magazine, boxing's bible), the location he gives is contradicted by a birth certificate that cites Ailey, Georgia, as his place of birth. Whoever filled out the certificate—and it could have been Sugar's father, Walker Smith, Sr.—was only barely literate, since colored was misspelled "colerd." He was named Walker Smith. His mother's name appears to be Lelar, though in his book Sugar refers to her as Leila; her maiden name was Hurst. According to the certificate, Walker, Sr., is twenty-eight and a farmer and Lelar is twenty-three and a domestic. Gene Schoor, who wrote a biography of Sugar Ray Robinson in 1951, notes that Mrs. Smith was born August 25, 1900, which would have made her twenty-one at the time of Sugar's birth, and was one of sixteen children. Walker, Jr., was the couple's third child. And "Junior" would be the name Sugar would answer to as a boy. [1]

In his autobiography, Sugar writes that his parents were from Dublin, Georgia, which is about 130 miles northwest of Savannah. Both of his older sisters, Marie and Evelyn, were born on a farm not too far from Dublin. In 1980, Walker Smith's funeral announcement states that he arrived in Detroit in 1916; Schoor reported 1917. If either is true, then he must have gone back and forth for the children to be born in the South, or he came alone and his wife came later. This region of Georgia at that time, mainly within Montgomery County, was well-known for three things: cotton, the Ku Klux Klan, and lynching. During the post–World War I years, particularly 1919, the year Evelyn was born, at least ten black soldiers were lynched, half of them in Georgia. According to author Donald L. Grant, "Many of the demobilized black veterans continued to wear their uniforms, sometimes because they had no other clothes and sometimes because they were proud of their service. Many whites reacted savagely to this practice." Countless numbers of black soldiers who had gone abroad to make the world "safe for democracy" returned home with a newfound spirit of freedom, only to be brutally reminded by the Klan and other white residents that nothing had changed. And to drive this point home, the Klan torched several black churches and lodges, burning them to the ground. [2]

With the cotton infested with boll weevils and the membership of the Klan increasing with each lynching, black farmers had few alternatives but to seek better opportunities elsewhere. Sugar's aunt and her husband were among the migrants who moved north to Detroit looking for a better life. They found a place to live and settled in an area known as Black Bottom. This sector on the city's east side was an outgrowth of the restrictive covenant that confined the movement of African Americans. It contained the most dilapidated houses and received the least services. Even so, it was an improvement over where its residents had lived before. Sugar's aunt and uncle notified Walker, who followed them, gaining employment almost immediately as a ditch digger. "Pop was a wiry little guy," Sugar recalled in his autobiography, "five foot seven and a hundred and fifty pounds, with a dazzling smile that lit up his dark brown face. And he was strong." Much of Walker's strength—and certainly his fatigue—came from wielding a shovel, digging out cellar shells for buildings. Resourceful and hardworking, he was soon behind the wheel of a shiny new black Ford Model T, tooling about town and "styling," like sashaying while driving, just as his son would do years later in flashier automobiles: Cadillacs and Lincolns.

His father's tastes for luxury notwithstanding, he managed to purchase train tickets for his wife and children to join him in Detroit. This act alone distinguished him from so many fathers who, once out of the grip of American apartheid, never looked back or gave a thought to those they left behind. Sugar wrote that he made the trip to Detroit in his mother's womb, coming into the world a few weeks after their arrival. If they left Georgia shortly after he was born, that might account for his recollection that he was born in Detroit, not Ailey, Georgia. Or given Sugar's penchant for invention, this was just another example of his remaking himself, his way of recalling his life the way he wanted it to be, not as it was. Blurring dates, events, even people came as easily, and was probably as necessary, to him as sidestepping a blow or counterpunching opponents with a wicked left hook.

The Smiths' home on Canfield, just north of Black Bottom, and near Paradise Valley, was typical of the small homes in the area. It was a two-story yellow brick house, neat but not pretentious. The neighborhood's citizens, many of them recent migrants from Alabama, Georgia, and Mississippi, had begun coming to the city in droves since 1914, shortly after Henry Ford announced the possibility of earning five dollars a day in his automobile plants. The population increased astronomically, from 5,000 to 120,000, between 1910 and 1930. There were jobs for them in the factories, but mainly they were the hardest, most dangerous, lowest-paying, and most unskilled ones. But the majority of these new arrivals were not deterred by the onerous work, since they were used to spending long days under a blazing sun picking and chopping cotton. They were more deeply concerned about the restrictive covenant that kept them confined residentially in what was no more than a two-mile-square ghetto. Like Coleman Young, Detroit's first black mayor, who came to Detroit with his family from Tuscaloosa, Alabama, in 1923, residents knew practically every nook and cranny in the Bottom. Despite squalor and all of the inconveniences and hardships that segregation bred, there were also endless possibilities for those with a little spunk and savvy, which Young had in spades. In his autobiography, *Hard Stuff,* he wrote: "With all of the little enterprises we had going on, our family was never indigent. We did particularly well during Prohibition, which can be said for all of Black Bottom and Paradise Valley. I never saw such prosperity in the black community—hell, in the city—as there was then." [3]

Sugar's recollection of the enclave was far less flattering: "Black Bottom was made up of wooden houses, mostly two-story, on flat, dusty streets."

By now, Walker was working two jobs to take care of his family and to keep gas in his car. To his ditch-digging job he added cement mixing. Leila, who was a husky woman with a round, café au lait–colored face, found employment as a chambermaid at the fabulous Statler Hotel on Washington Boulevard. She never dreamed that her son would one day reside there as an honored guest.

When the couple was not at work, they spent time together in Walker's car riding around town or dancing and drinking the night away at one of the many nightclubs in Paradise Valley. This section of the city, north of Black Bottom, stretched from Warren to Jefferson, though the hub of activity was near Gratiot, a main thoroughfare, around Adams and St. Antoine, where during that decade the 606 Horseshoe Lounge and the Plantation Club were among the city's liveliest spots. Sugar was about nine years old in 1930 when the joints were jumping in the Valley and in the Bottom. Practically every bar along Hastings Street, the area's main and most colorful drag, was alive and jumping with the blues and jazz. The Plantation Club, one of the Smiths' favorite haunts, was located in the basement of the Norwood Hotel on Adams Street. At this elegant club the pair could sport their finest garb, sip champagne, and watch first-class floor shows featuring such performers as the Duke Ellington Orchestra, the Count Basie Band, and vocalist Savannah Churchill.

Walter Norwood, a numbers man, was one of several enterprising black businessmen who took advantage of the city's segregation. Another was nightclub owner Sunnie Wilson, dubbed the honorary mayor of Paradise Valley during these spirited times and who at one time had lived on Canfield near the Smiths. He recalled his first years in the community: "When I first came to Detroit (in 1927), I thought the city would be filled with black businessmen," he said in his memoir. "Initially, I was quite disappointed because I believed these black northerners had more know-how than my southern friends in Columbia, South Carolina."[4] But after a few years in the Bottom, he noticed the change, and was able to enumerate place after place owned or managed by blacks. Coleman Young's father was a very successful tailor, and there were funeral parlors, beauty salons, barbershops, and small grocery stores throughout the neighborhoods under black ownership. Anyone coming of age at this time could not help but be a frequent patron at one of Barthwell's Drug Stores, where they would enjoy delicious milk shakes and sundaes.

Both Walker and Leila drank their share of whiskey and gin, according to Sugar, and this cut considerably into their meager earnings, precluding any successful investments or entrepreneurial endeavors. Their drinking was also a source of contention between them and, from Sugar's perspective, pushed them apart. The decisive break occurred in 1927. One day Walker got up early, went to work, and when he came home that evening Leila and the children were gone. They had returned to Georgia to live with Leila's mother. After leaving the children with her mother, Leila returned to Detroit and to a new job as a seamstress at General Linen and Supply, Sugar remembered. (This may have been the Supreme Linen and Laundry Company owned by Fred Allen, a close associate of Sunnie Wilson's.) Located at 700 East Alexandrine, the company was a thriving business, and by the early thirties Allen was on the brink of building an empire. His dream came to an abrupt halt after he began to infringe on territory controlled by white gangsters. Union opposition was fierce, and Allen's audacity and business venture ended one day when he arrived at work to find one of his employees drowned in a washing tub. [5]

Leila worked there long enough to earn the money she needed to return to Georgia a year later to bring her children back to Detroit. Thousands of black women, working as domestics in the city and the suburbs, had followed a similar practice in reclaiming their children from relatives who had helped them during a critical moment of instability. It's possible to detect a little regret in Sugar's memories of leaving the country to return to the Bottom, which he characterized as "bleak." Farm life agreed with Sugar, and he seemed to even welcome the chores that put him in touch with nature and a menagerie of animals. To placate her glum son and to keep him out of mischief, Leila gave him a quarter when he was seven and told him to go and join the Brewster Center. The quarter was dues money for a month. Sugar was soon a "gym rat," spending hours in the sprawling, two-story building at 637 Brewster between St. Antoine and Hastings that had opened only a few weeks before Sugar began attending on a regular basis. The facility had a swimming pool, a basketball court, Ping-Pong tables, and every conceivable game to keep his busy and adventurous mind occupied. Oddly, Sugar expressed no real interest in boxing, though he was blessed with quick feet and fast hands.

"The first time I ever showed my mother I was fast with my hands was when there was a fellow about twenty years old visiting in our flat," he told a newspaper reporter. "I was seven. This fellow got to sparring with me and I slapped him on the side of the face. He got mad and everybody in the room was amazed, but not my mother. She just laughed and said, 'Play with a puppy and he'll lick your mouth.' This made everybody else laugh, especially the man that got slapped." One day at the gym he watched as boxers worked out in the ring; he was so fascinated that he was unable to go on about his business. He was even more fascinated by a big young man who could turn a speed bag into a blur of motion and who stalked his opponents without expression. "You know who that big kid is?" someone asked Sugar, and then quickly answered his own question, "That's Joe Barrow." Within a few years, Barrow would change his name to Louis, and the powerful young giant would become the heavyweight champion of the world.

"Joe Barrow was the big hero in the neighborhood," Sugar recalled. He had demolished nearly all the amateur fighters he met, knocking them out without breaking a sweat. Barrow lived only a few blocks from Sugar, so it was easy for Sugar to keep tabs on him, to wait outside his idol's house and to grab his boxing equipment and carry it for him. According to Joe, "Little kids on my block followed me around all the time. There was one kid in particular who seemed to know my schedule. He'd be there, Johnny-on-the-spot, asking to carry my bag. I felt embarrassed and silly and proud, but anyway I let him carry it to Brewster Center for me. When he moved to New York, I missed him. He was a real nice kid. His name was Walker Smith. Later they changed his name to 'Sugar' Ray Robinson." [6]

Like Sugar, Joe was a son of the South, born in Alabama. He landed in Detroit along with his stepfather, Pat Brooks, and eight siblings in 1926. They lived in an eight-room house on Macomb Street before moving to a tenement house on Catherine Street. By the time Joe was a teenager, he was working on a horse-drawn wagon, delivering fifty-pound blocks of ice. After his deliveries he would head straight to the gym, and Sugar would be there waiting for him. The same routine was followed each day when Barrow completed his workout and headed home: Sugar would be right there to tote Joe's bag and to badger him about boxing, begging him to show him a few punches.

Never an enthusiastic student, Sugar couldn't wait for the bell to ring signaling the end of the school day so that he could hustle over to the center. When he wasn't at the center, he could be found on a playground, showing off his ability to walk on his hands. It was nothing for him to walk a whole city block on his hands, and he did it several times to amuse Joe. Once while walking in this manner, he cut his hand on a piece of glass. Rather than tell his mother about the accident, he kept it from her until the next day. By then his middle finger had swollen to twice its size. A doctor told his mother that the finger might have to be amputated, but she refused to consider such an alternative. Another doctor informed her that the finger was infected all the way to the bone and that scraping it might be sufficient. It was, but it would cost her twenty-five dollars, a hefty sum on her meager salary of ten dollars a week. She borrowed the money, and Sugar's finger was treated.

While playing baseball, which was Sugar's favorite sport (the Detroit Tigers were his favorite team), he received another injury that would mark him for life. "One day a fastball hurled by a burly pitcher caromed off the worn mitt and slammed into his face. That is the only kayo on [Sugar's] record. He was quickly revived, and a few stitches were taken in his lip." [7]

To help make ends meet, Sugar delivered the *Detroit News,* sometimes assisted by his older sisters. If Sugar paid much attention to the contents of the papers he sold, it was most likely to the sports pages. There's little chance he kept abreast of political events or labor conflicts, even at the Ford Motor Company, where security forces and the Dearborn police killed five unarmed hunger marchers in 1932. But he must have noticed the increased number of blacks moving into the Bottom, many of whom had their dreams bashed immediately, since the Depression limited employment opportunities. The only businesses flourishing in the Bottom were the numbers racket, bathtub gin distilleries, and other illegal enterprises. Leila was lucky to earn the ten dollars a week from her work at the laundry, but soon she began to think about greater opportunities farther north. So when a friend of hers in New York City wrote to her of being able to make a better living there, she didn't hesitate. "Children," she announced suddenly one week, "pack your bags—we're moving." On the Sunday following Election Day in 1932, with Franklin Delano Roosevelt the president-elect, the family boarded a bus to New York City for a new deal.

CHAPTER 2

STREET DANCER FROM HELL'S KITCHEN

Arriving at the bus station in downtown Detroit for their departure to New York City, Leila Smith and her children, with their cardboard suitcases, could have been mistaken for a group of vagabonds. In preparation for the long bus ride, Leila had prepared a good supply of bologna sandwiches. Two pieces of Silvercup bread with a smear of Hellmann's mayonnaise or mustard spread across a thin slice of bologna was the nutrition for thousands during the Depression, and for millions even such a meager meal was not possible. Sugar said his knickers were patched and his sisters' dresses were faded, but they were clean. In Buffalo, Leila wanted something hot, and when she went to purchase a cup of soup, Sugar took the opportunity to strike up a conversation with the bus driver, who, upon learning they were headed for New York City, gave him a quarter for good luck. Later, Sugar gave the quarter to his mother, which she added to the fifty cents she had in her pocketbook.

In the winter of 1932, the Smiths settled into their three-room flat at 419 West 53rd Street, between Ninth and Tenth Avenues. This section of the city was known as Hell's Kitchen, and the several blocks occupied mainly by blacks were an atoll surrounded by Italians and the Irish. (The black population was concentrated in Harlem.) Sugar would learn quickly it was not safe to venture outside the enclave, unless you were ready to fight or fast enough to outrun the gangs of white toughs who preyed upon little "niggers" like Sugar. On several occasions, Sugar, seeking a free lunch at the nearby Salvation Army office, was cornered outside his zone and had to use his wits to avoid getting his "black ass kicked," as he recalled. But a good meal, he'd apparently decided, was worth the risk of getting his nose bloodied or his lips busted.

The always industrious Leila soon secured work as a seamstress at a linen-supply company. It was similar to the job she had in Detroit, but it paid two dollars more a week. Even so, with the rent twenty-three dollars a month, it was barely enough to feed and clothe her children. Somehow, though, she managed to squirrel away a few cents to purchase a bottle of gin every Saturday night, and to pay for dancing lessons for Sugar and Evelyn. Sugar's imitation of Bill "Bojangles" Robinson, the best tap dancer of the day, convinced his mother to spend fifty cents a week for his lessons—both to invest in his talent and to keep him out of mischief. But the lessons, at the Roy Scott Studio, around the corner from his home on Ninth Avenue, came to an abrupt halt when Leila discovered that neither Sugar nor Evelyn was going to the studio, but rather spending the money on candy. Because it was Sugar's idea, he got two whippings—one for him and one for Evelyn.

With no more money coming from his mother, Sugar resorted to making a little change dancing outside theaters on Broadway and Times Square. Improvising around the one step or two he had learned at the studio, Sugar joined several other young black dancers who'd gather at the theaters to entertain patrons who would go outside to smoke and mingle during intermission. When the dancing was over one day, outside the Alvin Theater, Sugar was the lone dancer, and the doorman asked him if he would like to perform for a smoker. He had no idea what a "smoker" was, but it was an opportunity and he leaped at it. A smoker, he was to learn, was an informal gathering of young men that usually featured female dancers. Sugar did his Bojangles routine, for which he earned two dollars. After the performance he hurried home to give the money to his mother. When he told her how he had earned it, she took it and told him: "It's about time you paid me back for all that cheatin' you did on dancing school."

To fill in the slow days when dancing wasn't bringing in the money, Sugar made a few dollars collecting driftwood along the docks of the Hudson River, which was only a couple of blocks from his home. He would chop up the driftwood and stuff it into bushel baskets. A junk dealer gave him twenty-five cents for each bushel. The man never told him what he did with the wood, and Sugar never asked. Maybe he sold it to artists; there were several notable sculptors who used driftwood during the Depression to make furniture and even to construct inns. Alternatively, it could have been stored and used as kindling during the winter. What the man did with the driftwood didn't

concern Sugar. Nor did the future boxer express any keen interest in what was going on inside nearby Madison Square
Garden, where one day he would be a headliner. He was only
interested in exploring the city, which with its tall buildings and
endless motion stood in stark contrast to Detroit's downtown
section. He found himself moving from one landmark to the
next, including the Empire State Building. A trip up the elevator there sickened his stomach, and it would be his first and last
elevator ride. For the rest of his life, he would climb the stairs,
no matter what floor his destination.

CHAPTER 3

A HOME IN HARLEM

After moving several times, often to larger places, the Smiths finally settled in an apartment with just enough space for four, six blocks from a brownstone where the magician/escape artist Harry Houdini had lived from 1904 till his death in 1926. For a while, Sugar himself proved to be an escape artist, as he cleverly avoided the roughnecks in his new neighborhood.

One pleasurable site for Sugar was Dave's Vegetable and Meat Market, right around the corner on Seventh Avenue. Almost daily, a hungry Sugar would dash by the market, grab a piece of fruit, and vanish down the block. One day neither his feet nor his hands were fast enough to elude Dave. Rather than punish the little thief, Dave offered him a job delivering groceries. "It pays three-fifty a week," Dave told him. Sugar couldn't believe his good fortune, and promised to arrive early the next morning, ready to work.

For Sugar to get a job bordered on the miraculous, especially in Harlem, where the unemployment rate for blacks was almost four times that of whites in New York City. Blacks in the city constituted about 20 percent of the people on welfare or receiving aid for dependent children, though there is no indication that the Smiths were ever on relief. [1]

Along with his pay, Sugar was able to pick up additional change whenever Bojangles came to town and appeared at the Tree of Hope or the "Wishing Tree," which was located on Seventh Avenue between 131st and 132nd Streets, near the Lafayette Theatre. Black performers believed the tree to be the purveyor of good luck to those who stood beneath its branches. "It was their totem pole of hope. More than that, the immortal Bojangles Bill Robinson used to pay a weekly visit to the tree, which had been there when he was a kid with dreams of greatness. Young Sugar and the other boys would wait for Bojangles. When he arrived, he would have the kids dance for him, rewarding the best ones with a handful of coins. It was no contest. Sugar always won. With his natural grace and lithe, limber body, he would tap his way to a perfect imitation of the grinning Bojangles." [2]

Sugar did not grin, though, when he was provoked by the neighborhood bullies. One day while they were playing a game of racing from sewer to sewer, about a twenty-five-yard dash, "Shake" (Samuel Royals), the fastest kid on the block, challenged him to a race. [3] When Sugar won the race, Shake challenged him again. Sugar told him he didn't want to race anymore because he was too tired. The boy offered another sort of challenge to the fatigued Sugar, and threw a punch at him. Sugar showed Shake that he was just as fast with his fists as he was on his feet, and bloodied Shake's nose. Soon, he had a reputation both as a fast runner and a hard puncher. Then he learned the fine art of defense, at the Police Athletic League.

A PAL supervisor, Benny Booksinger, heard about Sugar's talent and invited him to participate in one of his tournaments, held in a "boxing ring" whose perimeters were marked off by orange crates. In Sugar's first bout with gloves on, he won a three-round decision. The loser's big brother stepped in front of Sugar and demanded the next fight. Booksinger [4] was coaxing them on when, out of nowhere, Leila appeared. All the while she had apparently been watching the matches from their apartment window. She pushed Sugar out of the makeshift ring, turned to Booksinger, and commanded he get off the block and leave her son alone. Booksinger didn't move fast enough, and Leila slapped him. He never came around again, but he knew how to find Sugar—and Sugar knew how to be found. He became a regular in Booksinger's bouts.

Sugar at thirteen stood about five feet eight inches and weighed around eighty-five pounds. Lean as a whippet, he won all of his fights except one. His one loss was to a tough Irish kid named Billy Graham, who would one day be a top welterweight contender. Although they never fought as adults, they had several common opponents, including Carmen Basilio and Kid Gavilan, and Graham held his own against both of them. Sugar's early neighborhood bouts didn't mean much in terms of money or prestige, but he began to turn heads with his ability after he defeated a boy who was considered the best in his weight division. Boxing was now Sugar's passion, and it took up most of his time. His interest intensified when a classmate at Cooper Junior High School, at 116th and Madison Avenue, convinced him to stop by the Salem Crescent gym, located in the basement of the Salem Methodist Church on Seventh Avenue at 129th Street.

Back in those days, bootleg fights were matches in which boxers were paid under the table. They were quite common. One of the fighters told Sugar the bouts were staged in upstate New York, New Jersey, and Connecticut. For the payoff, each fighter was given a watch, then had it bought back from him. If a boxer won, he was given fifteen dollars for the watch; if he lost, he got ten. To participate, Sugar was told, he had to do road-work—laps around Central Park—as well as workouts at Salem under the guidance of George Gainford. Gainford, who had a growing reputation as a trainer, had fought under the name of Kid Ford as a middleweight back in the late twenties. Like any good coach or manager, Gainford could give a boxer the once-over and determine almost immediately if he had what it took to be a good fighter. Sugar had never done roadwork and didn't know who Gainford was, but he understood the value of the money. No further inducement was necessary. After several months fighting with Booksinger, he was ready.

CHAPTER 4

THE CRESCENT'S STAR

Sugar was nearly fourteen in March 1935 when a riot raged through the streets of Harlem. A Puerto Rican youth, a year older than Sugar, was caught stealing at the Kress department store on 125th Street and was subsequently beaten to death by the store manager. Mobs quickly gathered on the street corners of Harlem. Mayhem was inevitable, and it exploded, and for one furious night 125th Street was torn apart—it was, according to Adam Clayton Powell, Jr., the first race riot started by black people. When it was over, three blacks were dead. Some two hundred stores were plundered and looted, and property damage was estimated in the millions of dollars. Sugar never said where he was during the riot, but it's a good bet he was in the basement of the Salem Methodist Church, working up a sweat pounding a punching bag, or doing hundreds of sit-ups to toughen his still developing stomach and back muscles, or above all, absorbing the sage advice of William "Pops" Miller, who had managed and trained middleweight champion Theodore "Tiger" Flowers in 1926. Miller was the dean of the Salem Crescent gym's coaching staff, and he taught Sugar the combination punches that would make him so formidable with his fists.

The boxing team at Salem was managed by Peter J. White, and George Gainford and Miller were the top trainers. Each night the fighters trained in the basement gym, encouraged by the church's pastor, Reverend Cullen, whose adopted son was the famous poet of the Harlem Renaissance, Countee Cullen. "The church was open to the boys of the community and even though the boys were rough, the congregation tolerated them because they believed it was better to have them under good and wholesome supervision rather than on the street," wrote Linda Reynolds in her history of the church based on Reverend Cullen's memoir. Among the team members were Gus Levine, Danny Cox, Cedric Harvey, Spider Valentine, Buddy Moore, Junior Burton, and Coley Wallace, who eighteen years later, in 1953, would portray Joe Louis in a movie based on the Brown Bomber's life.

"I knew a lot of the fighters that came out of Crescent," said Sigmund Wortherly, a former boxer and ring authority. "Spider Valentine was every bit as good as Sugar Ray; they had similar styles. He was trained by the great Al Smith, who was also my trainer. Smith was a legend in the Harlem boxing circles and he has not received the recognition he deserves. Yeah, Sugar was good but there were several fighters around at that time who could take him out." [1]

When Sugar came under the wing and the close scrutiny of Gainford, he was told to add a few pounds, to drink more milk, and to "put some meat on those bones" (at that time, Sugar weighed only a little over one hundred pounds). Gainford's reputation as the kingpin of amateur boxing in Harlem was legend. Never much of a fighter himself, he knew exactly what it took to become a Golden Gloves champion, and when he barked out his commands he loomed even larger than his hulking six feet two, two hundred and fifty pounds of pure intimidation. Each time he heard Gainford's powerful voice or had to endure his imposing presence, Sugar would tremble. A native of Charleston, South Carolina, Gainford had come with his parents to the United States from British Guiana, now Guyana. He was a no-nonsense guy who expected his orders to be followed without any back talk. But talking back to him was the last thing on Sugar's mind.

As a tiny flyweight (a boxer under 112 pounds), Sugar fought other PAL fighters his age and weight. When Sugar began boxing, he adopted a flailing, windmill style of moving his arms, but Gainford gradually developed him into a more polished boxer, adding technique to Sugar's natural speed, balance, and endurance. During this period, while Sugar was processing Gainford's lessons, developing a snappy jab and a solid two-punch combination, his idol, Joe Louis, was destroying every opponent he faced in his climb to the top of the heavyweight ranks. Sugar would later recall Louis's encounter with Max Schmeling on June 19, 1936, at Yankee Stadium in the Bronx, forty some blocks uptown and across the Harlem River. Just about everybody in Harlem had their radio on that sultry evening, tuned to the fight. "I was outside, sitting on our gray cement stoop," Sugar wrote in his autobiography, "listening to all the radios around me, but I couldn't believe what I was hearing. My man Joe couldn't stay away from Schmeling's right hand."

Sugar and the rest of Harlem—and millions of Americans—were stunned to hear that Louis had been knocked out by the German. It was his first defeat as a professional fighter.

Sugar was so devastated by his hero's defeat that he took all of the equipment Gainford had given him to the pawnshop and hocked it for three dollars. When Gainford's nephew told him what Sugar had done, the trainer demanded that Sugar return the equipment to him. Eventually, after getting reports that Gainford was looking for him, Sugar returned to Crescent and begged for a second chance. Only after severely chiding him did Gainford relent and allow him to return to the gym. Leila dropped by the gym one day after hearing her son was learning to box. She confronted Gainford and told him that she didn't mind her son spending time at the gym because it kept him off the streets and out of trouble, but that there would be no fighting.

Both Gainford and Sugar kept this bargain for several months, with Sugar just tagging along to the bootleg fights. But when a promoter of fights in Kingston, New York, informed Gainford that he needed a flyweight for one of his bouts, Sugar begged the trainer to give him a shot. Gainford hesitated for a moment or two, and then gave his consent. There was another problem, however. Sugar didn't have the required AAU card, certifying his amateur status. Gainford remedied this situation by giving the promoter one of several cards he carried in his wallet of fighters in his stable at the Crescent. The one he offered belonged to a fighter named Ray Robinson, who had stopped boxing.

As he was about to enter the ring, Sugar—now Ray Robinson—was half terrified and half excited at the prospect of being the center of so many people's attention. It would be like performing outside the Alvin Theatre, he told himself, while mumbling a silent prayer. Gainford slapped three sprays of water from a sponge over his head as if he were anointing him. Sugar had no idea that this would be the beginning of a ritual that would be carried out before each of his fights in the future.

After three frantic rounds, Sugar was declared the winner by a unanimous decision. This bout had been an easy victory. Gainford pointed out to him that some would not be so easy. But the young man had no thought about rough fights to come; he just wanted to enjoy this one—and get the gold watch that he was promised. As per the custom, Sugar gave the watch back to the promoter and received his fifteen-dollar payment in return. For the first time in his life, Sugar had real money in his pocket. But how would he explain this windfall to his mother? He knew that if he told her, it would end the possibility of future fights, and he was eager to return the following week. Luckily for Sugar, his sister Marie agreed to hide the money.

Meanwhile, over the course of several weeks, Sugar continued to pile up victories and money. Boxing and training were soon consuming most of his waking hours; either he was working the bags at Crescent, jogging around the north end of Central Park, or hanging out at Grupp's Gym—where the legendary Jack Dempsey learned how to throw a double left hook off a jab—on 116th Street Street near Eighth Avenue (Grupp's was the premier gym in the city until it was supplanted by Stillman's, which was located on 125th Street near Seventh Avenue before moving to its final, more famous location on Eighth Avenue between 54th and 55th Streets). Even before he was sixteen, Sugar was beginning to demonstrate his skill on the speed bags and in skipping rope, which at first he disdained, believing jumping rope was for girls. At Grupp's "College," as Sugar called it, the professors of the "sweet science" were such ring veterans as Kid Norfolk, Panama Joe Gans, and the indomitable Harry "Black Panther" Wills, whom Jack Dempsey refused to fight. They, along with Soldier Jones, who would be a mainstay in Sugar's camp during his professional career, supplied the bantering remarks that were history lessons of the fight game, and Sugar was all ears. From Wills he learned the importance of balance. Jones gave him lessons in basic anatomy. He would take his finger and swab a bit of sweat from Sugar's body and taste it. If it was salty, he would smile. "When it's not salty," he told Sugar, "it means you're stale." Gans, Wills, Norfolk, Jones—the black "professors"—and an old Irishman named Kelly were like surrogate fathers to Sugar, teaching him the manly art, but Gainford was "Big Daddy," or "The Emperor."

Gainford delivered the lectures in strategy and psychology. Once Sugar was slated to fight a pug with loads of scar tissue, a flat nose, and cauliflower ears, and he was leery of him. But Gainford explained that the reason the opponent appeared so menacing was because he had been beaten so many times. If he were any good, Gainford told Sugar, he wouldn't be so scarred and battered. Sugar won the decision without breaking a sweat.

Sugar's skill and precision were improving at such blinding speed that he was matched in just a few weeks against seasoned amateurs, including one tough Italian named Willie Papaleo. Sugar beat him in a close decision in a bout in Hartford. That fighter would later be called Willie Pep, and would rule the featherweight ranks for years.

Sugar's next big fight was against another unbeaten bruiser, from Canada. The bout was set for Watertown, New York, a stone's throw from the Canadian border. Sugar and Gainford had just been released from a night in jail, having been detained when someone had accused Sugar of being a professional because he had defeated Papaleo. Sugar's status was verified after a call to the AAU the next morning. But the fight was delayed a week as Gainford negotiated for more money. The delay also allowed the anticipation of the fight to build, and for Sugar to catch up on his homework, though by now he had practically stopped going to classes.

But finally the bout was held. Concerned about being cut in the face, which would certainly be noticed by his mother, who still didn't know he was boxing, Sugar quickly moved to put the Canadian on the defensive. The tactic worked, and a blistering left hook dropped his opponent for the full count. It was the first time Sugar had ever scored a knockout.

When it was over, as Sugar was leaving the ring, a sports-writer told Gainford: "That's some sweet fighter you've got there." A woman at ringside heard the comment and added: "As sweet as sugar." In the paper the next day, the sportswriter called him Sugar Ray Robinson, and "Sugar" was born. From that day forward, he had a moniker that, like the Babe's, was distinctly his. Now, the Crescent had a real luminary, a true star.

CHAPTER 5

THE MAN WITH
THE GOLDEN GLOVES

In 1939, the pinnacle of amateur boxing was the Golden Gloves tournament. Like minor league baseball in relation to the majors, the tournament, which began in Chicago in 1923, was the stepping-stone to the big time, to the big bucks. While the bouts were held in several of the major cities, the best crop of fighters tended to come from Chicago, Philadelphia, Detroit, and New York City. (For years there had been a bitter rivalry between the Windy City pugs and the stylish boxers from the Big Apple.) Winners of regional matches would fight the other regional winners, bouts from which national champions were crowned. To fight for a tournament championship was the dream of every amateur fighter, and it was a plateau that Sugar felt he could easily reach. And indeed, everybody in the basement of Salem Methodist Church knew that in Sugar they had a fighter of great promise.

Hearing about promising fighters was nothing new for the great trainer Ray Arcel, so he was only mildly interested when Gainford invited him up to check out his latest prospect. Arcel had seen all of the great fighters from the 1920s on. In his career, he would train such champions as Benny Leonard, Barney Ross, Tony Zale, Kid Gavilan, and Ezzard Charles. When the genuine article came along, Arcel didn't have to take a second look; he'd know right away. "George and I were good friends," Arcel recalled in an interview with writer Ronald K. Fried. "I said, 'What? You got another bum you want me to look at, George?' He says, 'Come on up and look at this guy. This guy's gonna make me a millionaire.' I went up there, and I saw a *fighter*. I said 'You got something . . . Where d'ya build *this*?'" [1] He would get an even longer look at Sugar at the Golden Gloves tournament.

As always, there were a number of promising young amateur fighters on the bill, including Spider Valentine and Sugar Ray Robinson from the Crescent gym. Unfortunately for Valentine, he was matched in the same 118-pound featherweight division with a now heavier Sugar, his best buddy. Other than this dilemma, Sugar entered the tournament having overcome many personal problems. One of the major changes in his life had come to him quite suddenly when his girlfriend Marjie jolted him with the news that she was pregnant.

He couldn't believe that his affair with Marjie had reached such a point. For several months he had admired her from afar. She lived in the neighborhood, and she had no idea how often he imagined being with her. After ignoring his attempts to sweet-talk her, she gave in one evening and they began to date, often snuggled up in a 1928 Ford, one of the cars Gainford used to transport his boxers to the bootleg bouts.

Sugar had all but stopped going to school, since he was doing so well on the boxing circuit—having accumulated close to a thousand dollars, which he was still giving to Marie to stash away from his mother's prying eyes. Marjie, or Marjorie Joseph, was a gorgeous, dark-skinned beauty with long legs, and Sugar loved to go out dancing with her at the Savoy and other ballrooms where there was a live band. Sugar was as nimble on the dance floor as he was in the ring, and Marjie was one of the few women who could match him step for step in the lindy hop or jitterbug.

Eventually, she surrendered her virginity, and it was the beginning of many afternoon sessions on her couch. A few months later, Marjie told Sugar she'd missed her period. The inference was wasted on him, since he had no idea what she was talking about. When she made it plain, he was momentarily stunned, as if he had been hit by an uppercut. Hearing the news, Leila was equally shocked, and began to arrange a marriage. Her parents agreed. The marriage would give the baby a name, though Sugar was not to live with Marjie.

"When my mother told me I would have to marry (her), I began crying," Sugar told a reporter from *Time* magazine. "She screamed at me and said, 'Junior, if you don't marry, you're going to get a record against you. You'll go to prison and that'll be on your record for the rest of your life. You got to get married.' I agreed." Sugar had no idea she was underage. On September 25, 1939, Ronnie (Smith) Robinson was born. (Sugar, in his autobiography, remembered the year as 1938.) The marriage was annulled shortly thereafter.

. . .

A few weeks before the eighteen-year-old Sugar was to enter the Golden Gloves tournament, his picture appeared in the *Daily News* as part of the promotion for the event. His mother saw the photo and almost collapsed. By way of explanation, Sugar gave her the stack of money and watched as she ran her hands through the bills of various denominations, a smile slowly replacing her scowl. It must have crossed her mind that it would take her almost a year to earn comparable money on her job sewing at the Champion Coat and Apron Company. "I guess it's all right, but if you start to get cut up, I'll have to ask you to stop," she said. "Don't worry about that," he replied. His secret out, Sugar no longer had to hide his money from his mother.

Sugar felt good that all his secrets were now out in the open. No longer was he worried about Marjie, the marriage, or hiding the fact that he was boxing full-time. Earlier he had settled the issue of attending school—he had officially dropped out, much to his mother's dismay. She had been convinced by Dr. Vincent Nardiello, then affiliated with the New York State Boxing Commission and Madison Square Garden, that Sugar would probably never be much of a student but could be a world-class fighter. She acceded. Sugar's mind was clear now to focus on winning in his first Golden Gloves tournament.

Langley Waller was familiar with the contests and had witnessed the progress of many top fighters through the amateur ranks who'd gotten their start as Golden Gloves titleholders. Like Dr. Nardiello, he felt that Sugar had all the skills needed to win a championship. "It was at the Salem Crescent gym that I first met Sugar Ray in 1939," said Waller, who had been brought to New York City from Chicago by the owners of the *Amsterdam News,* Dr. P. M. H. Savory and Dr. C. B. Powell, to do the engraving work for the paper. "Dan Burley, a writer for the *Amsterdam News,* took me there to meet him. He was then training for the Golden Gloves, so he wasn't a professional yet. But you could see right away that he was bound for greatness." [2]

Sugar's friend Spider would be the recipient of this emerging greatness during their match for the New York title. They had both romped over their opponents, and now the two friends would have to face each other for the Golden Gloves featherweight title. He had mixed feelings about fighting his best pal, but when the bell sounded they tore into each other like bitter strangers. Sugar soon cornered Spider with a flurry of punches. A furious left hook stopped his friend in his tracks, and he crumbled to the canvas. Looking at a helpless Spider, Sugar leaned over and picked him up. The referee waved him off, at the same time chiding him for assisting his opponent. Similar admonishments came from Harry Wiley, who had replaced Gainford in Sugar's corner, Gainford having stepped aside because he trained both Sugar and Spider. "Next time you knock him down, let the referee pick him up," Wiley said, wiping the sweat from Sugar's brow.

The next round witnessed a fully recovered Spider, and he slugged it out with Sugar, neither of them giving any ground. At the end of three rounds, Sugar was declared the winner. Just four years after he'd started boxing, he was a Golden Gloves champion, and he glowed in the spotlight, bowing to spectators in each sector of the arena. His fans and friends tried to leap into the ring with him, chanting his name and jostling each other for a chance to touch their hero.

A week later, Sugar would experience exultation again when he won the Golden Gloves Eastern finals and then, two weeks later, the twelfth annual Intercity title at Chicago Stadium, before a sellout crowd of twenty thousand. Going into the fight, all the talk had been about Bill Speary, a classy boxer out of Philadelphia, but when it was over Sugar was the new rage. Throughout his career, Chicago Stadium would be a good-luck charm for him. The program for the event, which included his photo and praised his skills, listed his age as nineteen and his birthplace as Virginia. They were wrong on two counts, but right about his talent.

. . .

In 1940, Hollywood produced *Golden Gloves,* starring Robert Ryan, in which a crook bribes a professional fighter to join the ranks of a sportswriter's newly established boxing league. In contrast to that fictitious plot, Sugar's bouts were real. And one year after his first Golden Gloves victory, a year older and ten pounds heavier, he went through the lightweight division without a hiccup, winning the Golden Gloves title again. And this time he didn't have to face Spider, who, in 1940, matched Sugar's feats by winning the Eastern finals and the Intercity featherweight belts.

With two Golden Gloves titles in successive years—one as a featherweight and one as a lightweight—Sugar began to seriously consider turning pro. An invitation to participate in the Olympics would have been the only temptation to delay such a decision, but the advent of World War II precluded that possibility.

From 1936 to 1940, Sugar won all of his eighty-five amateur contests, sixty-nine by knockouts. It was time to stop taking all the blows for little or no payoff. If he was going to get hit, he pondered, then why not get paid for it? And there was another reason to quit the amateur ranks and earn some money: The landlord had given the Smith family a dispossess notice—either they come up with the back rent immediately, or they would find their belongings outside on the sidewalk. Luckily, Sugar had a stash to take care of the arrears, but the landlord was tired of the family's delinquent payments, and asked them to pack their things and move. They found an apartment at 264 West 117th Street that was within walking distance of the Crescent gym.

Although their new home was a bit of an improvement over their previous apartment, it was still a long way from the big house that Sugar now fantasized buying for his mother. To make that dream come true, Sugar would have to keep to Gainford's demanding regimen, sharpen his skills, and gain the confidence to overcome foes no matter how menacing they appeared, and no matter their reputation. As a fighter, he knew, he must not show fear or feel the least bit intimidated. During the walk home from working out at the gym, pondering his prospects of turning professional, Sugar often created his fantasies, plotting a way to get Curt Horrmann [3] to manage him, having seen Horrmann pursue Buddy Moore, the promising heavyweight on their team. It was widely known that Horrmann, whose fortune was the product of a brewery he owned on Staten Island, was interested in managing a topflight boxer. Whenever he came around the gym, cruising up to the church in his sixteen-cylinder maroon Packard, sporting his English-tailored suits, and handing out twenty-dollar tips like they were dimes, Sugar watched him with envy.

In many ways, Horrmann was as elegant and imposing as St. Thomas the Apostle, a huge neo-Gothic, Roman Catholic church on the corner of St. Nicholas Avenue and 118th Street, just around the corner from where Sugar lived. Somehow, Sugar mumbled to himself, he had to get the rich man to notice him, to pull his eyes from Buddy Moore. Horrmann knew all about success, and Sugar believed he had the Midas touch, the pathway out of the squalor that engulfed his neighborhood, with its alarmingly high incidence of crime, infant mortality, and syphilis. Horrmann was the key to escape from a vicinity where more than 25 percent of the residents were on relief. All around him, as he trudged home from the Crescent, was the evidence of unrelieved poverty; beggars on the verge of starvation, rats scampering from dilapidated building to dilapidated building.

While he wanted a nice place for his mother, one that was a long way from the ghetto, he knew that he aspired to the finer things for himself as well. He often dreamed about being the best boxer in the world, with enough money to buy some of the apartment buildings where he and his family had to pay rent. Rather than taking his clothes to somebody else's cleaners, Sugar dreamed of owning one. And why not a barbershop, a restaurant, a clothing store? He was tired of handouts, of payments made under the table because of his amateur status. These payoffs were much too small and irregular; he needed the big paydays to match his big dreams.

In Gainford, Sugar knew he had the best trainer in the business. Now, for his manager, he set his sights on Horrmann, a man of exceeding wealth who could lead him from the Golden Gloves to a gold mine as a professional.

CHAPTER 6

PUNCHING FOR PAY

While the United States sought ways to prop up democracy in Europe and simultaneously to avoid getting involved in the growing conflict, Sugar Ray Robinson prepared for his first professional battle at Madison Square Garden, against club fighter Joe Echeverria. With Gainford in his corner, and Horrmann as his new manager, Sugar's adrenaline was soaring. It didn't take Horrmann long to recognize the talent Sugar possessed. He knew that the small amounts of money he gave Sugar to sustain him at the start of their relationship would bring in huge dividends in the future.

Echeverria turned out to be an immobile pinata, and Sugar knocked him out in the second round on October 4, 1940. Except for a knot of boosters, dressed in blue and white jackets, a few monogrammed with "Crescent Gym," there were few spectators to witness his debut as a pro. "But the next time I fight here I'm going to fill this place up," Robinson muttered to himself as he waved to friends in the Garden's ringside seats. "In those days you didn't get a fight on any Garden card unless you had a number of fights before that, and a good manager. Sugar Ray Robinson turned pro on the undercard (a preliminary match) of a world title fight in Madison Square Garden. True, it was only a four-rounder, but still, he would not have gotten that berth had he not been a topflight amateur," said noted boxing historian Herb Goldman.

Sugar's take from the fight was $150, far more than he earned, off the books, as an amateur, and he was surprised when manager Horrmann said he could keep it all. It was a sizable sum during a period when the annual median income for a Harlem family barely exceeded two thousand dollars. Since it was Sugar's first payday as a pro, Horrmann and Gainford decided to forgo their usual percentages. They could see the future hurricane of dollars.

In one easy fight, Sugar told his friends, he had pocketed the equivalent of three months' rent for a three-room apartment on St. Nicholas Avenue. [1] Already he was earning more than the jazz musicians he idolized at Minton's Playhouse in the Cecil Hotel, which was near his home and just across the street from St. Thomas the Apostle Church, whose architecture Sugar admired. Sugar could boast that he earned per fight more than Dizzy Gillespie, one of the stalwarts at Minton's, made per arrangement, though it wouldn't be long before the twenty-two-year-old trumpeter's career matched Sugar's in its acceleration to the top.

After disposing of Echeverria, Sugar was so caught up in the euphoria that he forgot that his idol, Henry Armstrong, was also on the undercard. Armstrong, known as "Hammering

Hank," was the welterweight champ. But Sugar knew Armstrong had his hands full with a tough Croatian named Fritzie Zivic. After his victory over Echeverria, Sugar rushed back to the arena with his entourage to see Armstrong in the main event against the rugged Zivic. At times the two fighters stood at the center of the ring and battered each other mercilessly. Sugar winced with each punch Armstrong took, and there were quite a few, causing him to lose the fifteen-round decision. "I want Zivic," Sugar told his mother, who had come to see her son's professional debut. She voiced her objection, pleading with him not to pursue a fight with him. "He'll gouge your eyes out," Sugar remembered her telling him. But Sugar was determined to avenge his hero's setback, and continued to pester Gainford to get the match.

The pestering gradually became an obsession. Gainford heard so much about Zivic that he had trouble keeping Sugar's concentration on his next fight, scheduled for Savannah. This would be Sugar's first trip back to the state where he was born. While still an amateur, Sugar had handily whipped a white fighter from Georgia, and now that both were pros, the loser wanted a rematch. There was one problem, however. In Georgia and other places in the South, blacks and whites, whether amateur or professional, were not allowed to fight each other. So, to get a measure of revenge, the white fighter's promoter contacted the toughest black fighter in the state to challenge Sugar. He was a deaf-mute named Silent Stafford. Four days after he had vanquished his first professional opponent, Sugar outpunched Stafford, knocking him out in the second round. Sugar didn't dally too long in Savannah. Joe Louis, now the heavyweight champion, had invited him to train with him at Greenwood Lake back East. They hadn't been together since Louis had won the title over James Braddock in 1937. Louis had been on a mission since his loss to Schmeling in the summer of 1936, and Sugar kept tabs on each of his friend's victories over the next four years. When Louis avenged his loss to Schmeling in 1938, Sugar was ecstatic. He was equally overjoyed when the heavyweight champ beat "Two Ton" Tony Galento and twice conquered the tough Arturo Godoy. Sugar's excitement was uncontained when he learned later that Horrmann had arranged for him to be on the same schedule of bouts with Louis in the Brown Bomber's defense of the crown against Red Burman at the Garden. This was certainly a step up in his professional career.

The area around Greenwood Lake, half of which is in New Jersey and half in New York, was picturesque and serene. Pine trees filled the sloping valleys and thickly covered the Ramapo Mountain range. There was no Highway 87 then, as there is now, so the trip from New York City took more than two hours, winding through many small towns in New Jersey. Most people ventured there to fish; the lake was known for its enormous basses. But while Louis was out at the lake, his trainer, Jack "Chappie" Blackburn, saw to it that he worked out in a rowboat in order to strengthen his arms. He required the same of Sugar. Blackburn, as Louis knew, was a taskmaster when it came to training. He had come by it honestly during his own career, one that included matches in which he more than acquitted himself against such all-time greats as Joe Gans and Sam Langford. "Blackburn was a stern trainer, and he looked the part," Barney Nagler observed in *Brown Bomber,* his biography of Louis. "A bony face, marked by a scar on the left cheek and set off by beady eyes that peered out of angular slits, he appeared as an instrument of discipline. Usually taciturn, he was informative and kindly where Louis was involved. He knew boxing as a serious business and instilled in his pupil an early devotion to the course . . ." [2] It could have been Melville describing Queequeg, the harpooner, in *Moby Dick*.

Although Louis was in his "Bum of the Month" phase, where his competition was notable for not being notable, Blackburn still made sure he prepared him rigorously, as if he were going up against a top contender. Sugar got the same treatment, and this included hours of roadwork, a nutritious diet, and plenty of rest. In his autobiography, Sugar recalled: "I was up at dawn with Joe for roadwork. At that hour, the lake was even more beautiful. The morning mist was hanging over the lake and the sun was creeping up over the mountains, and the little boy from Brewster Center was really in his heaven, running on the road with Joe Louis. We ran every morning together, Joe and me, with a car crawling along a few yards behind us. In the car was a New York City detective hired by Mike Jacobs, the promoter of the Twentieth Century Sporting Club, to be with Joe before a big fight. Also in the car was Jack Blackburn." [3] The only break from the routine came in the late evening. That's when Sugar would rush to sit at a card table and relax.

• • •

When Sugar returned to the Garden with Louis on the last day of January 1941, he won a six-round decision. George Zengaras was the victim of the Greenwood Lake roadwork. Louis did him one better, knocking his opponent, Burman, out in the fifth round.

By the end of February Sugar had a match slated for his hometown of Detroit. Naturally, the city still made some claims on him, and all the local newspapers gave him a big buildup.

The gossip and fanfare attending Sugar's match against Gene Spencer was reported in the local press in banner headlines such as "Local Boy Returns Home After Making Good in the Big Apple" and "Former Detroiter Headlines at Olympia." Given the publicity, Sugar's father heard about the fight and gave his son a call. They hadn't seen one another in the eight years since Sugar had left Detroit, and made plans to see each other after the fight. Perhaps eager to spend some time with his father, Sugar made short work of Spencer, putting him out of his misery in the fifth round.

His father took him to the old neighborhood, and they drove by some of the places where they used to live. Black Bottom, in Sugar's opinion, was just as wretched as ever. By this time, there was a little more action outside the Bottom, in a city that was now called the "Arsenal of Democracy." The automobile plants had been converted into manufacturers of war machinery; instead of Fords, Chryslers, and Cadillacs tumbling out of the factories, tanks rumbled off the assembly lines.

Sugar's rendezvous with his father was short, because Gainford had Sugar on a tight leash, lest he fall in with the wrong crowd and disrupt his training schedule. Before they said their good-byes, however, Sugar's daddy put the bite on him for a few dollars. The son almost relished the opportunity to show his father how successful he was. It wouldn't be the last time Pop, as Sugar called him, would come looking for a handout. It was a clear case of the derelict father taking advantage of his famous son, but apparently this didn't bother Sugar, though it mightily upset his mother when she heard about it. Sugar looked forward to fighting in Detroit or nearby; it gave him a chance to see his father, whose love and affection he still sought.

• • •

Big paydays and reminiscing with his father made Detroit doubly attractive for Sugar, but Philadelphia was soon just as rewarding, since it was closer to New York City and there were several influential promoters on the scene promising lucrative dates. One of Sugar's first major fights was set for July 21, 1941, in Philadelphia against Sammy Angott at Shibe Park, which would later be renamed Connie Mack Stadium. Angott was not going to be a walk in the park; he had a reputation of being a real battler, and indeed the title he held as National Boxing Association lightweight champion was indicative of that ability.

However, Sugar was told that this wouldn't be a title bout; Angott, though confident he could take Sugar, didn't want to risk losing his crown. It was agreed that they would fight over the 136-pound limit for lightweights, thus making it a nontitle bout. Gaining weight was always difficult for Sugar, so to get a few pounds on his frame before the official weigh-in Gainford ordered him to stuff himself with bananas and milk. He was advised not to move his bowels until after the weigh-in. Promised a six-thousand-dollar purse, Sugar was prepared to hold his bowels even during the fight. When told of the amount, he put a call in to his mother and told her that if he won this fight she would never have to work again.

Sugar's preparation for a fight followed a set routine. To keep his skin tough, he didn't shave on the day of the fight. There was tea and toast for breakfast. There was quiet meditation and an afternoon nap. His evening meal consisted of a steak, which he consumed a couple of hours before the fight. Later, prayer sessions with his trainers would be added, along with light workouts to build up a sweat. When he arrived in the dressing room, he could expect that his trainer had unpacked his bag, spread a clean linen sheet over the rubbing table, and laid out clean woolen socks. Neatly folded were the boxing trunks, sometimes white, sometimes purple, with either Trager or Everlast emblazoned at the center of the waistband. His boxing shoes were usually freshly laced and spit-polished. Then came the rubdown with Gainford's special oils and massage to relax the muscles. A few minutes were spent going over the strategy for the fight, and then, after a little pounding of the flat pads worn on the hands by the trainer, Sugar was ready for the walk to the arena.

Angott's name should have been "Ingot," or "Anvil"; throughout the sluggish ten rounds he was like a cast-iron barnacle, clinging to and clutching Sugar. When the decision was announced, Sugar was glad to have won and even gladder to be rid of the human anchor. Angott proved to be a tough customer throughout his career, and in 132 fights only the fabulous Beau Jack was able to knock him out. "Angott was a real good boxer," Sugar told a reporter at *Sport* magazine, "and Fritzie Zivic was a real good fighter. There's a difference." Sugar considered himself a good boxer, not a fighter.

Sugar also considered himself a good and dutiful son, always attentive to his mother's needs and feelings. He couldn't wait to tell her about his recent victory and the money he had earned. When he arrived home, his mother was up waiting for him. "No use of me going to bed," she said with a smile. "I don't have to get up early." [4]

Indeed, she would never work another day in her life, and moreover, Sugar had enough money to move her into a new and nicer four-room apartment at 940 St. Nicholas, at the rate of sixty-three dollars a month; get her some new furniture; and purchase his first car—a 1941 blue Buick convertible. He had won twenty-one straight bouts and was already being touted as the "uncrowned lightweight champion." To solidify what the sportswriters claimed, he needed a major bout at the Garden, not more preliminary fights.

With a promoter such as Mike Jacobs manipulating things, Sugar didn't have to wait long to see his name lit up on the Garden's marquee. On September 19, he stepped into the ring with Maxie Shapiro, then right out of it less than nine minutes later. It was an easy main event for Sugar, much easier than his next encounter, with a young lady sporting long legs, lustrous hair, and an incandescent smile.

CHAPTER 7

SUGAR RAY AND EDNA MAE

On *June 16, 1941, Sugar* was once again in Philadelphia, pulverizing Mike Evans's head and putting him away in the second round. Thus far, it had been a very busy and successful year for him, with an impressive string of twelve victories, including seven first-round knockouts. In only the second year of his professional career, Sugar had lived up to even the most glowing reports of his ring prowess. Sugar was not one to look too far down the road, anticipating a fight or a particular opponent, but there was a real test waiting for him at the end of October: Fritzie Zivic. Sugar's training sessions became strenuous. His body was soon as taut as a piano wire, and he was as focused as he could be. There would be no distractions—except one.

The workouts leading to the bout with Zivic were grueling, but there were moments when he needed to tone down the adrenaline and to allow his steel-coiled tension some relaxation.

Such a moment of release happened one hot day in the summer of 1941 at Lido Pool, not far from Coogan's Bluff and the Polo Grounds.

Often after a hard workout Sugar would go to the pool, more to take a dip and cool off than to swim, though he was smooth off the diving board and an adequate swimmer. One day, to get the attention of a gorgeous young lady with a pair of amazing legs, he pushed her in the pool. She was furious as she climbed out of the water. Her long shiny black hair heavy with water, she glared at Sugar, took his measure, and stormed off in a huff. (Sometime later, when asked to recount the incident, Sugar said he dived into the pool and apologized.) There was no way she could have known that this gentle shove for recognition would one day evolve into physical abuse. Nor could she have predicted the glamorous high life they would lead as the Prince and Princess of Harlem.

"That walk of hers was something else," Sugar recalled. Later, some of the Sugar's gang told him that the pretty lady's name was Edna Mae Holly, a dancer at the Cotton Club and other popular nightspots in Harlem. Sugar made a mental note when informed that she was currently performing at the Mimo Club on 132nd Street. A week later, accompanied by his usual rowdy entourage, Sugar invaded the club and took a table near the stage. For the next several weeks, the club would be Sugar's nightly haunt, though Edna Mae, still bristling from the shove and splash, kept him on a string, playing him like a yo-yo. Her continued rejection of his advances only fueled Sugar's determination. At last she relented, and the aggressive Sugar, just as he did with opponents in the ring, took full advantage of her dropped guard.

Dining, dancing, and romancing Edna Mae throughout the summer did not interfere with Sugar's ring domination. During this phase, he recorded his longest string of consecutive knock-outs, nine in a row beginning with Gene Spencer in Detroit in February and ending with Pete Lello in New York City in July. Edna Mae attended some of these fights, and Sugar often threw her a kiss while the referee was raising his other hand in victory.

Their courtship continued when Sugar went to Greenwood Lake to train for his fight against Zivic, who had battered Henry Armstrong into submission the year before. "All that year," Sugar said, "I had thought about Zivic every so often and about how someday I wanted to humiliate him for Henry." [1] Sugar would call Edna Mae every night "just after bed check at the camp," Edna Mae wrote in her unpublished memoir. "I guess you can say that was the beginning of our love story." On some of the calls, which caught Edna Mae between shows at the Mimo Club, Sugar would serenade her as though he were Billy Eckstine or Herb Jeffries, crooning "I'm just a prisoner of love," his voice still soft and mellow and without the nasality it would acquire in the later stages of his life.

Before Sugar's star rose and he was anointed the "pound for pound" best boxer on the planet, that accolade could have described Armstrong. In several ways, Sugar was just a taller, faster replica of Armstrong, as Muhammad Ali would represent a larger, stronger, more powerful version of Sugar. A measure of Armstrong's character and stamina surfaced very early when the boy, born Henry Jackson, had to fend for himself following the deaths of his father and mother. In 1929, he was seventeen years old, living with his grandmother, and working for the railroad company in St. Louis, but rather than ride the handcar that picked up workers for the ten-mile trip to their destination, Armstrong chose to run. One day he read an article about the Cuban fighter Kid Chocolate making seventy-five thousand dollars for a half hour in the ring, and felt he could do the same. He teamed up with a trainer named Armstrong, adopted his surname, and compiled an enviable amateur record, winning all but four of his sixty-two fights. (It was fairly common in those days for a fighter to accumulate a large number of amateur fights before embarking on a professional career.)

Armstrong, like Sugar, had more amateur fights than most boxers of his day had professional bouts, and one is left to wonder what impact this might have had on the two men's longevity in the ring. Armstrong's beginning as a pro was not as auspicious as Sugar's, but by 1936 he had dethroned the California and Mexican world featherweight champion, Baby Arizmendi. They had fought twice before, with Armstrong being cheated out of his victories both times. Entertainer Al Jolson, famous for smearing burnt cork on his face and singing "Mammy," witnessed the third fight, bought his contract, and became his manager. Under Jolson's front man, Eddie Mead, Armstrong won all twenty-seven of his bouts in 1937, twenty-six of them by knockouts. Then his managers concocted a plan for him to hold three championships in different weight classes simultaneously. Step one for "Hammering Hank," as he would be universally called, was a breeze, as he stopped the world featherweight champ, Petey Sarron, in the sixth round. Unable to get a match with the lightweight belt holder, Lou Ambers, Armstrong leaped to the welterweight division to challenge the champ, Barney Ross. Doing this required making the weight, which meant he had to put on twelve pounds. With a regimen of beer and glass after glass of water at the weigh-in, he had the added pounds. But it was a good thing that rain delayed the fight, Armstrong told the press, "because one punch in the belly and the ring would have been flooded." By the time the rescheduled fight occurred, he was twenty-seven pounds lighter than Ross. It was a lopsided fight, and Armstrong mercifully carried the fatigued champ the last four rounds. Now Armstrong had two belts, and within ten weeks a date was set for a showdown with Ambers for the light-weight title.*

The contest with Ambers was furious, and Armstrong spit so much blood on the canvas that the referee warned him to stop or he was going to have to halt the match. Rather than spit any more blood from his busted lip, Armstrong asked his cornermen to remove his protective mouthpiece, and for the last five rounds of the fight he swallowed his blood. At the end of the bout, Armstrong had achieved his mission—for the first and last time, one fighter held three championships at once. And, even more astounding, he came close to winning a fourth one, but his 1940 match with middleweight champion Ceferino Garcia was ruled a draw. The glorious run came to an end with two defeats to Zivic, and it was the last one, in which he was kayoed in the twelfth round, that was the source of Sugar's lust for revenge.

*About the various weight divisions, something more should be said. It was not easy for Armstrong to meet these requirements without losing strength and stamina. In the days when Sugar and Armstrong were taking on all comers, there were only eight weight divisions. (Today there are seventeen, including the recently added cruiserweight, super-middleweight, light-middleweight, light-welterweight, super-bantamweight, and minimum-weight.) The smallest of the fighters were considered flyweights (112 pounds); when Sugar began as an amateur, this was his weight. Then there were bantamweights (118 pounds), featherweights (126 pounds), lightweights (135 pounds), and welterweights (147 pounds). Many ring authorities feel that it was as a welterweight that Sugar was at his best. Others argue that it was as a middleweight (160 pounds) that he was truly incomparable. When he took on Joey Maxim for the light-heavyweight (175-pound) title, the opinion among many was that Sugar didn't take enough time to beef up or to fight less talented light-heavyweights before taking on the champion. Moreover, the weight differential between a middleweight and a light-heavyweight is the greatest of the lower divisions, fifteen pounds. Back in the day when Joe Louis wore the crown in the heavyweight (190-pound) division, there were no limitations, and that, for the most part, remains the standard today. So, for Armstrong and Sugar to make those weight adjustments—often within weeks—was absolutely phenomenal, and only the very best could have done this successfully at such a high level of competition.

Sugar's showdown with Zivic was set for Halloween night. Joe Louis, in a column in the *New York Post* written with a reporter, predicted that Sugar would win in a decision over Zivic. "Robinson will probably be bobbing around Zivic jabbing that snaky left hand of his into Zivic like a rapid-fire rifle," he wrote. "I think Robinson's youth and speed will turn the trick for the Harlem flash." Edna Mae was again at ringside, and recalled the fight: "They battled on fairly even terms for most of the bout but Sugar was clearly ahead . . . and took the win in ten." Just as the Brown Bomber had predicted.

Hammering Hank had been avenged, and Sugar was fifteen thousand dollars richer. After the fight, a large suite at the Hotel Theresa, Harlem's most prestigious hotel, was the site of the big victory party, Sugar's first. A member of his coterie was sent to fetch Edna Mae from the Mimo Club. Once more the fighter and the nightclub dancer were planning to meet—to the chagrin of Sugar's mother, who wanted something better for her son than a cabaret dancer, and to the disgust of Edna Mae's aunt Blanche, who felt that a fighter was below the station of a young woman from such a prominent and highly educated family.

As Sugar had heard repeatedly from Edna Mae's guardian— her mother died of tuberculosis when Edna Mae was three— "Edna Mae is the fourth generation of college-bred members of our family, which includes doctors and lawyers. And her great-grandfather came out of slavery and graduated from Harvard, studied for the ministry, and was the first Negro to be consecrated a bishop in the United States: the Right Reverend James Theodore Holly, an Episcopal bishop." Holly was the first black Episcopal bishop in America. Edna Mae, who was born in Miami and attended Hunter College, had followed the family tradition of getting a higher education.

Blanche almost had it right. The Holly family tree is not a simple chart of genealogy. Edna Mae's great-grandmother, Emma Webb, gave birth to a daughter, Lucia, who was fathered by a married white man, her employer. "Emma had left to keep anyone from learning about the child, but the news reached her employer's ears," Edna Mae noted. "It seems it didn't stain a white man's honor or his life to father a black woman's child. It was dealt with as a necessary evil, tolerated and then ignored."

Later, Emma would marry a Mr. Poitier and they would have three children, the youngest of whom was Reggie, who would father Sidney Poitier. "He was my cousin and so was Lincoln Perry, later to be better known as Stepin Fetchit, the actor, who was the exact opposite of the image he projected through his movies," Edna Mae wrote.

Edna Mae's grandmother, Lucia, would first marry Erskine Edden, and four children came from this union, including Vernon Rose, Edna Mae's mother. Lucia's second husband was Alonzo Potter Burgess Holly, the son of Bishop Holly; he studied four years in England and subsequently took a medical degree from New York Homeopathic College. [2] Dr. Holly was divorced and had children, one of whom, James Theodore Holly, Jr., would later marry Vernon Rose, Edna Mae's mother.

Another Holly of future prominence was Ellen Holly, Edna Mae's younger cousin, a critically praised actress who would be among the first blacks to appear in a regular role on the television soap operas. The bishop was her great-grandfather. "My maternal Uncle Bill's father-in-law was William Stanley Braithwaite, one of the extolled poets of the [Harlem Renaissance]," Holly wrote in her autobiography, *One Life*. She had a small role in Spike Lee's *School Daze* in 1988.

If Edna Mae chose not to elucidate to a great extent on her

most famous relative, others, including a contemporary of her great-grandfather's, the venerable Alexander Crummell, did. Crummell extolled the virtues of Reverend Holly and remarked on the contributions he made to black nationalism. No one spoke more fervently about emigrating to Haiti in the 1850s than Reverend Holly, the essence of which was published in 1857 and dedicated to Reverend William C. Monroe, rector of St. Matthew's Church in Detroit. Arguing for the inherent capabilities of black people and their civilized progress, with an emphasis on the Haitian revolution, he wrote: "I have summoned the sable heroes and statesmen of that independent isle of the Caribbean Sea, and tried them by the high standard of modern civilization, fearlessly comparing them with the most illustrious of men of the most enlightened nations of the earth, and in this examination and comparison the Negro race has not fell one whit behind their contemporaries." [3]

· · ·

While Edna Mae could boast of a lineage with an abundance of accomplished men and women, Sugar had only his prestige as a boxer to offer. He was also blessed with a gift of gab that had often bailed him out of sticky situations. Now his words would get him around the barrier of class and pedigree, and nail the alluring lady. He tactfully sweet-talked and charmed Aunt Blanche, and then set out to convince Edna Mae to give up show business. Soon, the two lovers were inseparable, careening through Harlem in Sugar's manager's car or his own, sharing drinks at the swanky Smalls' Paradise, where the waiters zipped about on roller skates, or holding hands during long walks in the Catskill Mountains when Sugar was in training. "We saw each other as often as we could with his busy fight schedule," Edna

Mae said. "He carried me with him on as many trips as could be arranged; they included Philadelphia, Washington, and Baltimore, and when I could not go he'd manage to get George's car and come to my house, pick me up, and we'd drive through Central Park, which was only a few blocks from my house. We'd go into small restaurants to eat sandwiches or Chinese food. He'd use these warm loving outings to assure me of his love before leaving me."

• • •

On October 30, the day before Sugar edged Zivic, the U.S. destroyer *Reuben James* was torpedoed and sunk off the coast of Iceland by a German submarine. It was the first American warship to be sunk in the emerging war, and over a hundred lives were lost. A little over a month later, on December 7, the Japanese attacked Pearl Harbor, sinking four battleships and incapacitating several others. Overall, some nineteen ships were damaged and 2,388 military personnel and civilians lost their lives. For two months, as the nation grieved and geared up for war, there was a lull in Sugar's fight schedule. Still, a number of fight fans desired a return match between Sugar and Zivic, and the bout was arranged for sometime near the top of the new year. Meanwhile, Sugar took it easy, spending much of his free time with Edna Mae.

By 1942, Sugar was back in action, dispatching with relative ease a roster of forgettable fighters. The fighters may not have been ranked contenders, but they couldn't be taken for granted, and Sugar had to be focused, though like many Americans he was occasionally distracted by the war raging in the Pacific, where the Japanese were demonstrating their military might, taking one island after the other—Manila, Bataan, Corregidor.

Meanwhile, Sugar and the Brown Bomber were on similar paths of conquest with their gloves on, though their personal lives took divergent paths. While Louis, with an incredible number of romantic liaisons to account for, was divorcing Marva Trotter, Sugar was contemplating marriage to Edna Mae, wooing her with expensive gifts like a $650 mink coat.

"Edna Mae was simply gorgeous," recalled Delilah Jackson, who has diligently chronicled Harlem's entertainment history for several decades in such local publications as the *Amsterdam News* and *The Beacon*. "All the men would stare and whistle at her when she walked down the street. She was every black man's dream, with her light skin, long black hair that hung down her back, and beautiful legs. I knew many a man who would have thought they were in heaven to have her by the arm, strolling down 125th Street. The way she sashayed, throwing her shapely hips, she knew she was something special. I guess she had every reason to be vain. You could tell by the expression on her face that she just loved people noticing her. When I was with her, she loved to show off her legs. Even when she performed almost nude at Connie's Inn in 1932, when she was about sixteen or seventeen, she was proud of her body. She used to show me pictures of her dressed in nothing at all. I have to admit she had a fantastic body. But she also had class, culture, and sophistication." [4]

Like most young men in Harlem, Clint Edwards, a photographer who followed Sugar's career with a passion, was dazzled by Edna Mae's beauty, but he was not so blinded that he couldn't, at the same time, appreciate Sugar's magnificent aura. He saw them as much on the streets as he saw them at the arenas. "There was no one like Sugar Ray," he began. "Just about everything about him was unique. His style, the way he walked, the clothes he wore, the car he drove—all of that set him apart from the rest of us. He was always sharp as a tack. No matter where he went, there was a bunch of onlookers . . . Sugar would walk down the street in a colorful suit with a silk shirt, a mean hat, and his shoes were always shining. I know he had his own tailor, because you couldn't buy the kind of clothes he wore off a rack, no way. And he was as arrogant as he could be. He was bad and he knew it." [5]

Sylvia Dixon, longtime Harlemite, recalls how "when they walked down the street together, they were like the prince and princess of Harlem. They were a matchless pair. In a way, they might have been meant for each other. It was like one was trying to outshine the other, and the light they created together was absolutely radiant. Whenever they walked into a room, all eyes focused on them. They seemed to reflect each other in so many ways; they were mirror images. And depending on the situation, they took turns soaking up the spotlight, reveling in that moment of attention. I don't think they ever tired of this, though in time they seemed to have tired of each other. But while they were young and riding high, they were a unique duo. It's a wonder they never made a movie together; I'm sure it would have been sensational, even better than Harry Belafonte and Dorothy Dandridge. Sugar Ray and Edna Mae—their names even rhymed. To some degree they were star-crossed lovers, like Romeo and Juliet, but that was part of their appeal, part of their magnetism. There may never be a couple like them again. They were . . . well, Sugar and Spice." [6]

. . .

On the return engagement with Zivic, on January 16, Sugar gave his foe a lesson in fisticuffs. He picked him apart with snappy jabs and crushing combinations that kept his slender opponent off balance. Sugar's dominance was so overwhelming that even his mother, who often discussed what he did wrong in the ring, had to praise him. She was even more full of praise when she learned that her son had pocketed another big purse from the fight.

Now that Sugar was beginning to make more money, he attracted elements of the underworld who sought to horn in on his good fortune. But it was not these menacing outsiders who thought nothing of showing Sugar that they were brandishing arms who worried him; it was the insiders, including Horrmann, his manager, who Sugar felt wasn't getting the best deals on fights. Horrmann's tendency to cave in to promoters during negotiations perturbed Sugar. Rather than demand what Sugar requested, he would make up the difference out of his own deep pockets. If the promoter welched on paying Sugar the con-tracted amount, Horrmann wouldn't complain but instead would pay Sugar himself. This was no way to do business, charged Sugar, who even at twenty years of age was already showing an entrepreneurial sensibility. When he finally reached the breaking point, he borrowed ten thousand dollars from Mike Jacobs and bought his freedom from Horrmann. What had begun as a promising relationship was over before it had had a chance to mature. Sugar put a different spin on the break several years later in *Sport* magazine: "The way I understood it from his sister, who came to me to talk about it," Sugar claimed, "his fam-ily thought he was spending too much time running around the country with me. Maybe they didn't like the idea of his being a fight manager at all, I don't know." [7]

Gainford thought he was in line to take over, but Sugar had other plans—he would become his own manager, keeping Gainford as his trainer. During Sugar's amateur days, Gainford took the lion's share of the bootleg payoffs, believing his fighters should be satisfied with whatever he paid them. Sugar no doubt remembered this when he denied Gainford the opportunity of becoming his manager. He would never underestimate Sugar again.

Nor would any of the promoters. They found Sugar to be just as tough at the bargaining table as he was in the ring. Like an independent film director, Sugar reserved the rights of final cut; he would determine what the bottom line was. This was the attitude he evinced in preparation for a fight with the number one contender, Jake LaMotta, the "Raging Bull." LaMotta, a rugged Italian-American from the Bronx, had compiled a fairly impressive record, though it was marred by four defeats. Even so, he was a powerful puncher who never took a step backward in the ring, plodding forward, his fists up by his head like horns. Moreover, he was a colorful crowd pleaser. He had gathered a reputation for his ability to deliver numbing body punches, but he could also take them. The Bull had never been knocked off his feet.

Before taking on the Bull, Sugar had a few household matters to finalize. At the start of his professional career, Sugar had promised his mother a new house, and he lived up to that vow right after ending his relationship with Horrmann. "I paid eighty-five hundred dollars for a big brick ten-room on 238th Street in the Riverdale section of the Bronx," he wrote in his autobiography. And before they moved in, another three thousand dollars were spent redecorating it. With the house purchased and ready to live in, Sugar had two other goals to accomplish: goring the Bronx Bull and corralling Edna Mae of Harlem.

CHAPTER 8

THE MATADOR AND THE BULL

Sugar had three warm-up matches in the summer of 1942
before his fall date with the Bull. There was a return bout with
Angott "the ingot" at the Garden, who once again went the distance but was tagged with another loss, and quick knockouts of
Ruben Shank and Tony Motisi in August. The nation may have
been experiencing a rationing of sugar, but the other Sugar was
on a rampage, sharpening his jabs into lethal banderillas, his
left hook into a potentially deadly sword to the Bull's hefty
neck. Months before the contest, sportswriters were hyping the
fight as a classic showdown between a highly skilled boxer and
a puncher with an iron jaw. This fight was important to both
twenty-one-year-old boxers: The winner was almost guaranteed to move into contention for a title fight. LaMotta, like
Sugar, was on a winning streak, twice besting Jimmy Edgar, a
Joe Louis protégé.

In his autobiography, LaMotta remembered the fight as occurring in the last week of September, but it actually took place October 2 in the Garden. Sugar's memory was a little faulty too. He said LaMotta outweighed him by ten pounds; however, several accounts list LaMotta as fifteen pounds heavier. But there is no disputing the outcome—Sugar tore into the Bull like a piston, wearing him out with a crisp barrage of punches; in Sugar's words, "My arms got weary from throwing so many punches." After hundreds of smashes to his body and head, the Bull was still standing, still snorting, as he collapsed on the ropes, spouting imprecations. At the end of ten rounds of crisp punching from both fighters, the verdict was announced: Sugar had won his thirty-sixth consecutive fight as a pro, twenty-seven of them by knockouts. LaMotta had suffered his fourth defeat, and massive blows to his ego.

Now that Sugar had conquered the Bull, the mob circled him like a flock of vultures. There were rumors they had already seduced LaMotta and fixed one of his fights. If Sugar was on the take in his match against Al Nettlow, it wasn't evident during the fight. On December 14, 1942, "Sugar . . . was supposed to carry Al Nettlow for the full ten rounds of a fight in Philly," Nick Tosches recounted in *The Devil and Sonny Liston*. "But in the third round, when Nettlow hit him with a nasty right, Ray lost his temper, hit him with a left hook, and Nettlow was counted out. That night, Ray went to the newsstand where mobster Frankie 'Blinky' Palermo hung out, and he tried to explain what had happened. 'It was an accident,' he told Blinky. 'I just happened to catch him.' "[1] If Tosches is right, the fight was fixed and the reputed mob leader let Sugar slide. But it would not be the last time Palermo tried to reel him in.

Despite his being voted the fighter of the year by *Ring* magazine, there was no title shot on the horizon for Sugar. He was angry, and he took his beef to Mike Jacobs, boxing's top promoter, whose office was on the sixth floor of the Brill Building in Tin Pan Alley, above Jack Dempsey's restaurant on Broadway. In a couple of years the Alley, where many of the nation's most popular songs were born, would be on the ropes, knocked out by Bill Haley and the Comets and the coming of rock and roll. Sugar was ready to send Jacobs to a similar oblivion, demanding a title bout with Red Cochrane, who had defeated Zivic for the welterweight crown a year earlier and was now in the Navy. Jacobs informed Sugar that Cochrane was not available, and that before long, neither would he be. "Any day now you'll be getting your Army induction notice," Jacobs promised. Sugar asked him how he knew. "I *know,*" Jacobs said slyly. [2] Even so, Jacobs continued, there was still time left to squeeze in a couple of bouts. Sugar felt somewhat better when told that a return match against LaMotta in Detroit was his, if he wanted it. He wanted it. And so did thousands of Sugar's fans—and his father—in Detroit.

The Olympia Stadium, on the west side of the city at Grand River and McGraw, was jam-packed on February 5, 1943, the noise almost unbearable. When Sugar was introduced the decibel level went up another notch. LaMotta, because he had fought so often in the city, most recently in a technical knockout victory over Charley Hayes, who had never been on the canvas, also received a booming welcome. No fighter in any weight class could take as much punishment as the Bull and still remain on his feet, although Sugar came close, having never been knocked out at this stage of his career. That LaMotta had never been floored while absorbing more than thirty thousand punches during his career was a fact that he and his face would wear with lasting pride and honor.

For seven rounds the contest was very even, with each fighter getting and giving his share of effective punches. But in the eighth round the Bull landed a blow to Sugar's solar plexus that took all the air out of him and sent him sailing through the ropes. As Sugar struggled to regain his feet, referee Sam Hennessy reached the count of eight. Sugar barely made it back off the ring's apron before he'd have been counted out. His out-of-shape body was now even more out of shape, and for the two remaining rounds it was all he could do to dance away from the Bull's rushes. Since his last fight with LaMotta, Sugar had done too much celebrating, dancing, and carousing with his friends to have ever been accused of taking his return match with the Bull seriously. The lackadaisical training and the nightlife had defeated Sugar long before he got in the ring with LaMotta. Sugar ended the fight on his feet, but his self-esteem and pride were flat on the floor. There was no place to hide when he heard that LaMotta, a three-to-one underdog, was the victor. All of Sugar's sweet triumphs could not assuage the embarrassment of this setback in his hometown. Facing his friends and his father afterward was the most difficult chore of his short life.

Fortunately, he wouldn't have to wait too long to get a chance to atone for his miserable showing. A tune-up fight against Jackie Wilson at Madison Square Garden back in New York on February 19 was pretty routine, and Sugar had no trouble taking a decision from him. Sugar was on a mission to reclaim his dignity, and he wasn't about to let anything get in his way. Not even the likes of Frankie "Blinky" Palermo, the shady underworld character many believed was in cahoots with mobsters who fixed fights, could distract Sugar once he made up his mind.

For the third time, Sugar and the Bull were going to enter the ring to settle their feud. Each had won a bout; the rubber match was set for Detroit's Olympia on February 26, and hundreds of disappointed fans were unable to get into the sold-out arena. This would be Sugar's third fight of the month, which is absolutely astounding when you consider today's scheduling, in which a ranked contender rarely fights more than once a year. Sugar and LaMotta didn't relish fighting each other, but they had little choice, since most of the top-ranked fighters avoided them, thus forcing them to oppose one another in order to get decent gate receipts. Despite his recent defeat against the Bull, the press favored Sugar. Throughout the days leading up to the fight, LaMotta complained about the lack of press he was getting and all the hype Sugar was receiving. Several stories had even quoted Sugar about his impending tour of duty in the military (Jacobs, as it turned out, was right: Sugar had been called to service). LaMotta was sick of hearing about the "brave boy off to fight for his country."

Unlike their previous match, Sugar trained hard for the fight, and won a ten-round decision, though LaMotta claimed he won. LaMotta's complaints were vociferous: "I didn't lose it, he got the decision. . . . You can ask anyone who was there . . . or you can read the newspaper stories," he would recount in his autobiography.

• • •

Sugar had only a few hours to enjoy the victory. The next day, February 27, as Jacobs had threatened, he was inducted into the Army.

CHAPTER 9

FROM SILK TO OLIVE DRAB

At the Whitehall Street center near the lower tip of Manhattan, draftees and recruits were asked to strip down to their drawers. Walking up and down halls with nothing on but your shorts was nothing new for Sugar. But he was eventually asked to pull them all the way down for a full inspection. Even more disconcerting than the invasion of his privacy was the call to attention by his original name. "Walker Smith," a drill sergeant barked, and Sugar fell into the ranks with the other raw troops, then boarded an olive-drab bus that was bound for the Holland Tunnel and on to Fort Dix, New Jersey.

Fort Dix was a sprawling place where the numerous barracks blended with the greenish uniforms. From this location, a soldier was usually deployed to Europe, if overseas orders were cut. Between each row of plain buildings were exercise grounds that Sugar would become well acquainted with in due time. Making reveille was never a problem for a boxer used to getting up at the crack of dawn. Nor was he that unnerved by the early morning calisthenics. He thought of Greenwood Lake and trotting through clumps of pine trees, sometimes trailing Joe Louis, sometimes leading the way. Sugar discovered immediately that he was in far better physical shape than his fellow soldiers. They would be exhausted after a quarter mile of jogging, while he was breezing along way out front, still breathing comfortably through his mouth. Excelling at basic training, however, didn't mask the ceaseless boredom of the camp. What was missing were his trainer Gainford, his cornermen Soldier Jones and Harry Wiley, and the sparring partners who kept the training camp abuzz with chatter and laughter.

After basic training, Sugar's orders were cut and he was assigned to the Army Air Corps at Mitchell Field in Hempstead, Long Island, about fifteen miles east of New York City, closer than Fort Dix, close enough for him to make quick trips to the city to see his beloved Edna Mae. When Edna Mae agreed to go to Chicago to dance at the Rhumboogie, a nightclub owned by Joe Louis, Sugar was plenty salty. Louis had bought the club, located on Garfield Boulevard, for forty thousand dollars and put Leonard Reed, a comedian and later his stage partner, in charge. Edna Mae, who had given up dancing at Sugar's request, missed performing and didn't think Sugar would mind since she was doing it as a favor to his friend. Plus, Sugar was off completing his basic training, and she was getting bored sitting around waiting for him to get a leave. This was an opportunity to jump-start her career, she thought, and might lead to her landing a dancing role in a Hollywood film. She was banking on Louis's contacts with film moguls and wealthy producers, since he had made a movie in Hollywood.

Sugar was furious. Some of his fury may have been the result of discovering that Edna Mae might have been one of Louis's many lovers, a roster of beauties that included the actress and dancer Acquanetta, vocalists Damita Jo and Lena Horne, and a bevy of blondes. A brief romance between Edna Mae and Louis was often rumored, but never confirmed. Neither Sugar nor Edna Mae ever mentioned it, nor did she address another persistent rumor of an earlier marriage to Willie Bryant, disc jockey and bandleader.

Sugar's objections notwithstanding, she packed her bags and left for the Windy City. The next day, practically on the train behind her, Sugar was in Chicago. Unable to secure a pass on such short notice, he left the barracks anyway and was absent without leave. He had called Edna Mae and told her he was on his way with intentions of marrying her and taking her back to New York. She thought he was bluffing, but Sugar was never one to bluff. They were married on May 29, 1943, at the home of one of Edna Mae's friends. One account asserts that Sugar was AWOL; another says he had secured a three-day pass. Dates were never Sugar's strong point, and he recorded the marriage year as 1944. Sugar was twenty-one and Edna Mae was twenty-seven. "There was gossip that Sugar's family, especially his mother, didn't want him to marry Edna Mae because she was so much older than he was," said Harlem chronicler Delilah Jackson.

They quickly returned to Harlem, where Edna Mae was sequestered at the Theresa Hotel. After a few days of celebration, Sugar went back to Mitchell Field and was restricted to quarters. She was soon able to obtain an apartment at 276 St. Nicholas Avenue and 124th Street, right across from Sydenham Hospital. "This would be our little love nest," Edna Mae noted.

But for the better part of July and August, Sugar was out of the nest, missing a most newsworthy event that summer: a riot that ripped Harlem apart. According to an article in the *New York Post* on August 2, 1943, "The trouble started at 7:30 . . . last night in the dingy lobby of the Hotel Braddock at 126th Street and Eighth Avenue. Sometime ago the police raided the hotel, and since then policemen have been stationed in the lobby twenty-four hours a day. Patrolman James Collins, of the 135th Street station, on duty last evening, tried to arrest a thirty-three-year-old woman for disorderly conduct. As he seized her a crowd began to collect, and Collins said that a Negro military policeman, Private Robert Bandy, of the 730th Regiment, stationed in Jersey City, attacked him. Bandy, the policeman said, wrested his night stick from him and hit him on the head with it, knocking him to the floor. As the soldier turned and ran Collins fired a shot after him, hitting him in the back. Collins got up and arrested the soldier, and in a few minutes other police arrived to help him."

But rumor outraced the facts, and soon there were people assembled in various sectors of Harlem, incensed by an erroneous report that a white cop had killed an unarmed black man. Pleading for calm, Mayor Fiorello La Guardia said, "This is not a race riot." By the time the melee was finally subdued hours later, six black men, shot by police officers, had been mortally wounded. Forty policemen and 155 civilians were listed by police as injured, and, according to one account, many more casualties of the wild and lawless night received minor injuries.

Edna Mae was perched high above the street disturbance, watching the chaos from the window of her suite. Meanwhile, Sugar was busy teaching boxing at the base or getting in shape for a series of exhibition fights to supplement his meager fifty-dollar-a-month allotment. The suite at the Theresa was costly. Mike Jacobs got him two fights in Boston in the spring, but then failed to pay him all the money he promised. Jacobs was notorious for shortchanging and underpaying his fighters. Sugar was about to wring his neck, but the quick-thinking Jacobs told him a sad story about one of Sugar's idols, Henry Armstrong. He convinced Sugar that a fight between them would be a lucrative payday for both of them, particularly for the destitute Armstrong. Always a sucker for a sob story, Sugar bit, and Jacobs went about staging the fight. Jacobs, known for his shrewdness, had no idea that Sugar was taking the fight with plans not to hurt his aging idol, but to hit him just enough to win the bout. When asked by sportswriters if his sentimental attachment to the warrior would affect him during the fight, Sugar said it wouldn't. There was no way he could reveal his plan, lest the New York State Athletic Commission strip him of his license to fight. This was his secret; not even Gainford would know.

Since it didn't appear it would be much of a fight, Sugar took it easy during training at Greenwood Lake, even taking time out to pose for pictures with members of his increasingly large fan base. In one photo, his long arms are embracing a bunch of kids who just happened to be passing near the camp, while their father looks on beaming. Sugar's pants are pulled way up on his torso, consistent with the zoot suit style of the period, his knit cap tight on his head. It's a relaxed and calm Sugar—an extremely confident Sugar. He was ready to rumble.

"When the bell rang in the Garden," Sugar remembered, "I tested Henry with a few left jabs that snapped his head back. Then I threw a couple of right hands to the body, and I could feel him sag. He really was an old man." [1] And a fading facsimile of the legendary "Homicide" or "Hammering Hank" who, in his prime, was considered one of the greatest fighters of all time.

Winning a ten-round decision, Sugar carried his idol, though he explained it otherwise to his cornermen, swearing he did all he could to take the old man out. Armstrong told reporters after the fight that even on his best night he never could have beaten Sugar. "He was too fast for me," Armstrong told Dan Burley of the *Amsterdam News.* (Apparently the arm and ankle weights invented by Langley Waller, which helped Armstrong in previous fights, were no longer effective.) This would be among Armstrong's last fights, but one of the best paydays of his long and glorious career. They drew 15,371 people, and the gross at the gate was $67,789. His boxing days over, Armstrong could only hope another stab at show business would provide some revenue, as it had for other pugs who'd hung up their gloves. In 1939, he had produced and starred in a film based on his life called *Keep Punching.* But other than a world premiere at the Apollo and a cast that included Canada Lee; Dooley Wilson, the piano player in *Casablanca;* Alvin Childress, who would later portray Amos on the television version of *Amos 'n' Andy;* and disc jockey/bandleader Willie Bryant, nothing distinguished this effort.

For his part, Sugar pocketed more than twenty thousand dollars, and gave Edna Mae five thousand of it. The take from the fight was a sizable addition to Sugar's meager military allotment, which was already a source of irritation to his wife, especially as he had to set aside a portion of it for his son from his first marriage. Edna Mae received fifty dollars a month; Ronnie, the child, a little less; and Sugar's mother an even smaller check.

To keep Edna Mae company while he was away, Sugar bought her a puppy, a pedigree boxer. Another entry into their lives at this time was a man named, according to Edna Mae's notes, Col. Hubert Julian Black, who shouldn't be confused with a man of the same name who, with John Roxborough, comanaged Joe Louis. "He was a commissioned colonel in the U.S. Army," she wrote, "and he was a good friend to us during Ray's Army stretch." That he was licensed to sell munitions, according to another note in Edna Mae's files, is a further clue that the "Black" had been tacked on and this was in reality the flamboyant Hubert Julian, who would have been about fifty years old then, but hardly a colonel, since he had been bounced from the Army in 1943 as a buck private. Still, Julian was as well known for his derring-do adventures as he was for masquerading and impersonating. He was called "The Black Eagle" for his aerial exploits in the 1920s, having twice parachuted from a plane to land on rooftops in the heart of Harlem. Such daredevil feats were standard practice for this soldier of fortune, who ran Haile Selassie's imperial air force in Ethiopia in the 1930s and later sold weapons and munitions to the highest bidders in the international market. [2]

Colonel Black, or Private Julian, or whoever, volunteered to look in on Edna Mae from time to time while her husband was in the service and entertaining troops as a member of the Special Services unit. But he wasn't there to check on her the day a Latin boxer talked his way into her apartment under the pretext that he was going to be meeting Sugar there. "He pulled a weapon on me and told me he was going to do terrible vulgar things to me to hurt my husband for not giving him proper respect," Edna Mae recalled. "I threw fruit juice in his face and ran out of the apartment to the super's apartment. We rushed back but he was gone. Sugar had a fight a few days away but I did not go. The Latin fighter was on the card. He was knocked out in his bout and died from the blow. Sugar was never told of the incident."

After the fight with Armstrong, Sugar was earning a monthly check touring with Joe Louis, during which they conducted boxing exhibitions at military camps. Having first met in Detroit when Joe was seventeen and Sugar ten, they had maintained a very close friendship, each attending the other's fights, leading the cheering section. They had much in common. Both were Taureans: Louis's birthday was May 13, Sugar's May 3. They were sons of the South, with little or no sustained relationship with their biological fathers, whose families migrated to Detroit and the city's Black Bottom. Neither fought under the name he was born with. Both became boxing immortals. And they would die on the same date, April 12, and at about the same age: Louis in 1981 when he was sixty-six, Sugar in 1989 when he was sixty-seven. So, it made sense that they would be in the Army together, exhibiting their manly skills in and out of the arenas. Virile and handsome, Sugar and Louis not only attracted the usual idol worshipers, but flocks of available women. Neither Sugar nor Louis ever demonstrated much self-control when it came to a beautiful woman—and in Louis's company, the temptations became even more unavoidable for Sugar. Not even his love of Edna Mae could stem his unfaithful ways.

On one occasion, Sugar invited Edna Mae to join him in Washington, D.C., but advised her not to come until that Saturday because he and Louis would be busy until then. To Sugar's misfortune, she showed up a day early and caught him in his room with another woman. Sugar was able to shift the blame to Louis, telling Edna Mae that the woman was really Louis's date. When he was caught a few weeks later with another woman, no excuse sufficed, and Edna Mae packed her bags and headed back to Harlem. It was the first of many separations.

Sugar's indiscretions while married to Edna Mae had begun—and they would multiply. Philandering was risky, but at least it wasn't as bad as some of the other trouble that dogged Sugar and Louis's tracks. In their day, when two black, Northern city slickers ventured to the land of Jim Crow, they usually observed the expected etiquette. Unless, of course, they were Sugar and the Brown Bomber.

Trouble tipped up on them at Camp Sibert, Alabama, on March 22, 1944. The camp, only two years old, was established as a basic training facility and for training in chemical weapons and decontamination procedures. Eleven days before Staff Sergeant Louis and Sergeant Robinson had arrived at the camp, there had been an incident in nearby Gasden in which a black soldier, Private Raymond McMurray of Chicago, was brutally murdered. Police alleged that he had raped a white woman. Later, a white man confessed to the crime.

Sugar and Louis went to the mainly white post depot to get transportation to nearby Birmingham. Because the bus for the colored soldiers was slow in arriving and there was a long line in front of them, the two boxers decided to call a cab. Louis headed to a phone booth where a group of white soldiers were waiting for a bus. When Louis came out of the booth he was accosted by an MP. Sugar later recalled the incident: " 'Say, soldier,' he said to Joe, 'get over in the other bus station.' From Joe's puzzled expression, I knew that he hadn't understood what the guard meant, so he asked, 'What you talkin' about?' 'Soldier,' the MP snapped, 'your color belongs in the other bus station.'

" 'What's my color got to do with it?' Joe said. 'I'm wearing a uniform like you.'

" 'Down here,' the guard said in his 'Bama drawl, 'you do as you're told.'

"I never saw Joe so angry. His big body looked as if it would explode at the MP. But knowing Joe, I realized that he was trying to control himself. Then the MP made a mistake. He flicked his billy club and poked Joe in the ribs.

" 'Don't touch me with that stick,' Joe growled.

" 'I'll do more than touch you,' the MP snapped.

"He drew back the billy club as if to swing it at Joe. When I saw that, I leaped on the MP. I was choking him, biting him, anything to keep him away from Joe. I wrestled him into the grass. But before Joe had a chance to get at him, a few more MPs ran up and separated us." [3]

At the jailhouse where they were taken, a ranking officer intervened, heard the story, and reprimanded the MPs. If the military police didn't know who they were, the colonel did, and to offset a possible riot at the camp, he had Sugar and Louis ride around in a jeep to show they had not been beaten up. A few years later, when Jackie Robinson would make a similar stand against Jim Crow injustices, he would attribute his boldness to what Sugar and Louis had done. [4]

Soon, Sugar was in deeper trouble. According to his account, he tripped and hit his head in the barracks and blacked out. A week later he was in a hospital bed at Halloran Hospital on Staten Island. The hospital report said he had suffered a bad case of amnesia, so bad that he didn't recognize Edna Mae or Gainford when they came to visit him. "He was transferred to this hospital on 4 April, 1944," the neuropsychiatric report read, "and on admission he was described by the nurse as 'very confused, repeating questions over and over.' " Sugar was given sodium amytal, or truth serum, in order to discover what had happened to him, but it proved ineffective, though there was some speculation that he might have faked it all to avoid going overseas. On June 3, 1944, Sugar was honorably discharged from the Army. Three days later, D-day, the invasion of Normandy, was launched.

CHAPTER 10

CHAMPION AT LAST!

Out of uniform and back in civilian life, Sugar had to redeem his standing both as a citizen and as a top contender for the welterweight title. He was being branded a deserter and less than patriotic in some newspaper columns because of his failure to stay with his unit when it was shipped abroad. It would take years before the jeers on this matter subsided, though he had been honorably discharged. The path was equally difficult in his pursuit of a title shot. Jacobs and other major promoters were not impressed by his six consecutive victories. Each time he requested a title fight he was told that he could make more money without the crown because he'd get more fights. But Sugar insisted that it was no longer about the money so much as it was about fame, glory, and international acclaim. He wanted to be known, like Louis, all over the world.

Promoters used a number of excuses as to why they

couldn't arrange a championship fight for Sugar, often citing how difficult he was at the bargaining table. They felt that he was hard enough to bargain with while a challenger. "Just think what he'd be like if he were the champ," they asserted. It was a proposition that few promoters, including Jacobs, were interested in encountering. Plead as he might, there was no title shot in the foreseeable future, Sugar was told repeatedly. Rather there were journeymen pugs such as the likable George Costner, whom Sugar kayoed in the first round February 14, 1945, in Chicago. "We attended a large celebration after the fight that was held in the cabaret room of one of the large hotels," Edna Mae recalled. "Costner and his handlers were invited guests also. Costner, whose nickname was also Sugar, came over to our table and congratulated Sugar on his victory and asked if Sugar would allow him to dance with me. Sugar then asked, 'Honey, will you dance with this fellow so that we both can teach him some lessons in the same night.'"

Althea Gibson was another apt student of their so-called lessons. She was a teenage string bean of a tennis player when she became associated with Edna Mae and Sugar just after World War II. Both strongly encouraged her to pursue her development on the court by studying with a reputable coach down South. They also helped Althea in her musical aspirations, which she would pursue professionally after vanquishing whatever opponent was unfortunate enough to be on the receiving end of one of her sizzling serves. "Edna Mae and Ray were kind to me in lots of ways. They seemed to understand that I needed a whole lot of help," Althea recounted in her memoir. "I used to love to be with them. They had such nice things. Sometimes they would even let me practice driving one of their fancy cars, even though I didn't have a license. I think it gave

Ray a kick to see how much fun I got out of it." Once, when Althea wanted to buy a saxophone, Sugar told her to seek the advice of a musician friend before she bought one. She found one at a pawnshop for a hundred and twenty-five dollars, and Sugar gave her the money to purchase it. "I've never forgotten it," she enthused. "I still have the sax, although I haven't tried to play it in a long time—which is a break for the neighbors. They're better off when I sing. I hope." [1]

Edna Mae recalls how Sugar became aware of Gibson's all-around athletic skills. There was a time in the early forties when Sugar used to take groups of children to the bowling lanes in the Bronx. "They swarmed all over Sugar when the word got out that he was on his way to the bowling alleys," she recorded in her notes. "Some of them were pretty good, and when they beat Sugar he had to pay for the game and refreshments. One of the young women that we met there was relentless in her efforts to beat Sugar, and he became fascinated by her skill and dedication. She really endeared herself to him and he became concerned about her being in the bowling alley at any hour that he'd show up and he finally asked her if she attended school. She told him that she'd lost interest in school. He worried her so much about continuing her education that she told him that she'd be willing to go back if he bought her a saxophone.

"Sugar shopped around the music stores with a musician friend of his and they selected a horn for her, and per their agreement, she was shipped off to school. She was a good student and kept Sugar and me abreast of her progress."

• • •

Looming before Sugar was another major hurdle—another certain, bloody showdown with the Bronx Bull, slated for

February 23, 1945, in New York City. But this "showdown," like their second one later that year on September 26 in Chicago, turned out to be more illusion than real, as Sugar easily beat LaMotta on both dates.

Meanwhile, Edna Mae and Sugar, who had by now changed his hairstyle from the high-peaked pompadour to the signature conk, had, at least temporarily, patched up their marriage and were breezing along with the postwar euphoria, settling comfortably once more into the fabric of Harlem. As per Bing Crosby's top song of the year, the two were "accentuating the positive" things between them, enjoying the good life with close friends and smooching at the Alhambra Theater on Seventh Avenue, especially when a Charles Boyer or Ray Milland film was featured. They were both hopeless romantics, and all of the dreams they shared were gradually coming true.

Things were also relatively smooth for Sugar's partner, Joe Louis, and his ex-wife, Marva. Louis owed her $25,000 in back alimony, but rather than settling outright, she agreed to a contractual arrangement that made her one of his comanagers. Given Louis's indebtedness, she believed the payoff would be far better that way. When the Brown Bomber knocked out Billy Conn at Yankee Stadium in June 1946, his purse was $625,000. After paying his obligations, he was able to bank $70,000. Of course, Marva got her percentage as well. Their amity was of such magnitude that they decided to remarry in July. "Marva rationalized her decision by explaining that during their divorce she had not met any man as interesting as her ex-husband. Unfortunately, their second marriage was destined to be an instant replay of their first." [2]

• • •

fall of 1946, Sugar was not in the best of moods. He was getting tired of the on-and-off-again discussions about a possible championship bout. Talking over the topsy-turvy developments with Edna Mae often cooled him down; otherwise, he was increasingly bitter and ready to take his disgust out on just about anyone.

Though Sugar had racked up an impressive number of victories against top contenders, one mishap after another prevented him from getting a chance to fight for the welterweight title, which by now was held by Marty Servo. After Servo lost to Rocky Graziano in a nontitle fight, Sugar was signed to fight Servo for the crown. Sugar was in training at Greenwood Lake one day when he was approached by two seedy-looking men who wanted a word with him. They offered him twenty-five thousand dollars if he wouldn't fight Servo. Sugar thought they were out of their minds. "Man, all I want to do in the world is fight Servo," he told them. [3] They persisted, asking him not to make the weight requirement. At last, Sugar told them to get out of his sight. Nothing was going to stop him from taking on Servo, he told them. But something did intervene. While in training, Servo's damaged nose was busted further by a sparring mate, and the fight was postponed. The injury was enough to force his retirement.

Fortunately for Sugar, the boxing commission insisted that another challenger be found to fight Sugar, with the victor claiming the vacant title. That eventful day finally came on December 20, 1946, when Tommy Bell arrived at the Garden to challenge Sugar. Physically, Sugar and Bell were almost mirror images of each other with their taut, slender bodies. And Bell, too, had been waiting for an opportunity to showcase his skills in a championship bout. Sugar was confident he could take him, since he had done so in an earlier fight in Cleveland in January 1945. Sugar appeared sluggish during the first seven rounds, as if he were sleepwalking.

But he was rudely awakened in the eighth when Bell's left hook found the mark and flattened him. "Twice Bell ripped Robinson with staggering shots, even dropping him to one knee once," Bob Roth reported in the *Youngstown Business-Journal.* The punches were coming so fast that even radio broadcaster Don Dunphy, with his quick tongue, was having trouble keeping up with the pace of the fight, and Bill Corum, who provided color, was unable to use his droll expression about "it not being a very interesting round."

"But Robinson wasn't recognized as the best-ever without reason," Roth continued. "As the fight got tougher, so did Robinson. From the 12th round on he was a combination machine. When the bell ended round fifteen, a Garden crowd of more than 18,000 stood saluting both fighters. A decision gave Robinson the championship he had long coveted." [4]

"I was at that fight," recalled Langley Waller, who often printed Sugar's posters and flyers. "And after Bell knocked him down, that's when Gainford, his trainer, began telling Sugar Ray to slow down, take it easy, and let the fight come to him. Sugar was good about listening to his cornermen, and with Bell he made no more mistakes."

Though it was a championship fight, Sugar didn't earn as much money as he would have against a top white contender, despite his singular, take-no-prisoners style of brinkmanship in negotiating a contract. David Remnick noted as much in his book on Ali, *King of the World.* "Sugar Ray Robinson fought one white after another—Bobo Olson, Paul Pender, Gene Fullmer, Jake LaMotta, Carmen Basilio; the promoters rarely offered remotely the same money for bouts against equally tough black challengers," he asserted, having made the same point in Ali's case.

For the first time, Sugar held a championship, the welterweight title, and it came at the same time Louis was heavyweight champ (an eventuality that seemed quite probable, since Louis held the belt for twelve years, from 1937 to 1949). Wearing the crown, however, didn't bring all the things Sugar desired.

A few months before the fight with Bell, Sugar had scouted Harlem for investment property, including several buildings on Seventh Avenue, next to the Hotel Theresa. One of the buildings was terribly dilapidated, and it was here he wanted his centerpiece, a café. The contractor had promised him that the work would be finished by the time he won the title, that his "throne room" would be ready to accommodate the champion. But there were delays in getting the wood and paneling that Sugar had specifically requested. He had hired Vertner Tandy, one of the best architects in the city and the designer of many of the luxury buildings in Harlem, but the work crew had fallen behind schedule. Even worse, he was told the work might not be finished until Christmas Eve. He had invested nearly a hundred thousand dollars in purchasing the site of the café and the two flats next to it, with an additional ten thousand for renovations.

"About two hours after I won the title, I drove up outside my café," Sugar recounted. "Inside, the workmen were installing the lights behind the bar. I had them working almost around the clock to finish it by Christmas Eve." One of the workmen told him the lights were working. "Hey, champ," the workman called to Sugar, "the sign's hooked up. Turn on the sign. It lights up like Coney Island." And it did. The neon glow from Sugar Ray's lit up the avenue. Unlike Jack Dempsey's Restaurant downtown and Joe Louis's ill-fated restaurant on 125th Street, Sugar had kept his café to a modest size. He wanted an intimate spot, with patrons elbowing each other for space. "The best advertising is to keep the place packed," he often explained.

Edna Mae was by his side when the neon lights bathed the street, and some of the glow fell on them as they embraced, then concocted a toast from a couple of Cokes and paper cups. For several hours they celebrated the new café, and Sugar admitted, "It was one of the nicest celebrations I've ever had." [5]

As the new champ, Sugar wasn't one to rest on his laurels. He eagerly followed Gainford's advice—keep busy, to keep sharp. Edna Mae was keeping busy too, overseeing their property and its development, now and then supervising the workers. Their new enterprise was the talk of the town. Unlike so many stars who had emerged from Harlem, Sugar was looking for ways to give back to the community, and at the same time make a little more money. "Eventually, Sugar ran a number of businesses," Edna Mae explained. "There was his café, a dry cleaners, and the Golden Glovers barbershop. All of them were right next to each other and took up the entire west side of Seventh Avenue between 124th and 123rd Streets. The last storefront was to be 'Edna Mae's Lingerie Shoppe' and was on the corner of 124th and Seventh Avenue. Sugar's ownership continued around the corner onto 124th Street for one more building. One of those tenants made a hair straightener and ran his business in his apartment, which he made into his laboratory and his office."

Edna Mae was made a full partner in the business, but Sugar kept her in the dark about most of his transactions. It would prove a mistake, given her eye for details and bookkeeping abilities. She kept copious notes and accurate records of each fight, the gate receipts, expenditures, and the percentages for each of Sugar's cornermen, handlers, and sparring partners. Her records showed, for example, that in February 1945, when Sugar fought LaMotta and won a unanimous decision, they earned $93,100. It was one of Sugar's largest paydays to date. (Later he would earn $250,000 from his two fights with Randy Turpin and a consolation payoff of $150,000 from his fight with Joey Maxim.) According to her records, their personal expenses for the LaMotta fight were $672.48, Gainford received $2,500, and for their work on fight night six handlers divvied up $750. An inveterate collector, Edna Mae saved everything: bills, ticket stubs, matches, programs, posters, photos, and nearly every item on which her husband's name or face appeared. In the end, she saved everything—but could she save their marriage, which, even as they celebrated their new businesses, was on shaky ground?

CHAPTER 11

A DREADFUL DREAM

In the spring of 1947, things were beginning to boom for Sugar and for Harlem. His businesses were gaining momentum in concert with the building boom in low-cost housing in the community. Eleven projects, both public and quasi-public and all enjoying tax exemptions, would give Harlem more than twelve thousand low- and moderate-rent apartments, and provide accommodations for some thirty thousand persons. Sugar and Harlem were blooming simultaneously, and this was good news for neighborhoods and residents who had seen their share of misery and hopelessness.

This optimism even reached major league baseball, with the Brooklyn Dodgers' signing of Jackie Robinson breaking the color barrier. Sugar kept one eye on the sports pages for the other Robinson's feats, but his main focus was on a list of opponents: Bernie Miller in Miami on March 27; Fred Wilson in Akron on April 3; Eddie Finazzo in Kansas City, Missouri, on April 8; and George Abrams at the Garden on May 16, almost two weeks after Sugar's twenty-sixth birthday. He pummeled them all into submission, knocking out the first three in fewer than five rounds.

These were nontitle bouts and Sugar easily forgot them all, except his scrap with Abrams, whose punches left Sugar with permanent scar tissue over both his eyes. The injury required him to postpone a scheduled title bout with Jimmy Doyle, a bulldog-like competitor out of Los Angeles. After several haggling sessions among the promoters, managers, and boxers, the date was set for June 24 in Cleveland.

Before Sugar got in the ring with any fighter, he and his trainers would do their homework on the boxer, mainly comparing common opponents. The most recent fighter Sugar and Doyle had in common was Brooklyn's Artie Levine, who possessed a wicked left hook, as both Sugar and Doyle discovered. Sugar managed to survive Levine's devastating punches; Doyle was not so lucky. He ended up with a concussion and had to be rushed to the hospital. Days later he had recovered, and resumed boxing within weeks, winning a decision over Ralph Zannelli, a fighter Sugar had edged in ten rounds in 1943.

Sugar arrived in Cleveland a few days before the contest and stayed at a friend's house. On the night before the fight, he dreamed he killed Doyle. To keep the dream from coming true, Sugar did all he could to postpone the fight. When he told the promoter, Larry Atkins, about it, Atkins laughed it off. "If dreams came true, I'd be a millionaire by now," he said, chuckling.

In the ring, "Doyle kept coming at me," Sugar wrote in his autobiography. "I was winning most of the rounds, but none of them were easy because he knew how to fight and he had guts. In the sixth round and in the seventh, his left hook had me backing up. In the eighth round, I saw the opening I had been waiting for, and I went for it. I threw a double right hand, first into his belly, then to his head. He sagged a little but he kept coming at me, and he'd started to throw a right hand when I beat him to the punch with a good left hook to the jaw." [1]

Doyle hit the canvas in three phases, his head thudding last against the ring apron. "I stood over him," Sugar continued, "transfixed, seeing my dream come true, horribly true." Doyle tried to get up but crumbled back to the canvas. His handlers jumped in the ring and told the referee it was all over. Immediately a hush fell over the Cleveland arena; the only voice heard was a call for an ambulance. Doyle was taken to the hospital and later Sugar, Edna Mae, and George Gainford went to see him. They arrived at St. Vincent Charity Hospital just as a priest concluded his last rites.

The next afternoon Doyle died, and Sugar's troubled and sleepless nights began. At the inquest following the fight and Doyle's demise, Sugar was asked if he had intended to get his opponent "in trouble." Sugar replied dejectedly, "It's my business to get him in trouble." Later, Sugar was far more contrite and compassionate. He wrote a note to Doyle's mother in Los Angeles. "I wanted to do something more for her." Out of the proceeds from a fight against Flashy Sebastian at the Garden, several weeks later—nearly $25,000—he sent her half. There was another benefit for Doyle, and Sugar donated $6,500 more, from which a trust fund was established to give Doyle's mother $50 a month. Sugar had yet another scare during the fight with Sebastian, when he failed to respond after being knocked out in the first round. But after some minutes he revived. Sugar said that if he had killed another boxer, he would have retired.

. . .

By the winter, the Doyle incident had begun to fade and Sugar was able to get back into a fighting mode without being troubled by what might happen. What happened, he had come to accept through the counseling of friends and Edna Mae, was not his doing, but was in God's hands. Whether in God's hands or Sugar's fists, Billy Nixon and Chuck Taylor crumbled to the canvas in December bouts.

While Sugar would not have a boxing match again until March 1948, his growing disputes with Edna Mae sometimes ended in physical abuse. By September, the Prince and Princess of Harlem were at war and living apart. Sugar had moved from their apartment and taken up residence with his mother in Riverdale. Since Leila never really got along that well with Edna Mae, she was pleased to have her Sugar back.

Sugar was now free for anything fancy, and when the word got out about the separation, young ladies showed up in droves at the café, waiting their turn to be noticed. One evening while Sugar was strolling through the café, he spied a pair of long legs that must have reminded him of Edna Mae's. A conversation was struck and a rendezvous planned, and the two took off on a whirlwind affair. Of course, Sugar and his new lover were careful about where they met; he was too well known and Harlem was too small for him to make a move without its appearing in somebody's gossip column. Still, word of the affair got back to Edna Mae, and she figured out where to find them. It wasn't difficult. Knowing Sugar, she knew she'd find them either at the lovers' lane overlooking the Harlem River, near the Polo Grounds, or outside the café.

When she approached them, Sugar was stunned. Edna Mae began begging him to come home. "We're separated," Sugar replied. Nothing she said changed Sugar's mind, and each new inquiry about who his date was only made a bad situation worse. Soon, Edna Mae was in tears as she hurried back to the waiting cab. Sugar's date was also in tears. Only a promise to take Edna Mae with him to the training camp at Greenwood Lake quieted her sniffling.

CHAPTER 12

A BROWN BABY AND
A PINK CADILLAC

Sugar doesn't report whether or not he was at the Garden the night Joe Louis successfully defended his title on June 25, 1948, against the ageless Jersey Joe Walcott, but it's a good bet that he was. And whether he was there or not, he must have been immensely pleased to see that his old friend, at thirty-four, still had some warrior left in him before intimating that this might be his last fight.

Three days after Louis beat Walcott, Sugar eked out a fifteen-round decision over Bernard Docusen in Chicago to retain his title. Docusen had presented more of a contest than Sugar anticipated, and he knew he had to be in better condition and have sharper punches against Kid Gavilan, whom he was set to tangle with on September 23, 1948. Back at Greenwood Lake, he began to prepare for a tougher engagement with the crowd-pleasing Cuban.

Gavilan, born Gerardo Gonzalez in Camagüey, Cuba, was, at twenty-two, five years younger than Sugar and an extremely flashy, versatile fighter. According to several experts on Cuban fighters, Gavilan, who was called "The Hawk," after the Spanish equivalent of his chosen name, was considered the latest edition of Kid Chocolate. Chocolate was Cuba's first world champion boxer, winning the junior lightweight title in 1931. He beat the best fighters of his era, including Tony Canzoneri. Like Henry Armstrong, Kid Chocolate was one of Sugar's favorite fighters, and many of his moves in the ring were patterned after Chocolate's repertoire. Sugar was also rumored to have adopted Chocolate's penchant for brightly colored, luxury sedans.

Until 1946, most of Gavilan's fights took place in Havana, but once he hit the mainland his reputation soared, and by 1948 he was taking on top contenders in the welterweight division. He fought Gene Burton, Sugar's stablemate, to a draw in January 1948, and it is very likely that Burton prepped Sugar on how to combat Gavilan's artful style, which bordered on the poetic. It would be poetry in motion versus the complexity of the sweet science reduced to fundamental coordinates of speed and power when he stepped into the ring with Sugar.

In their September thriller, Sugar was rocked several times by the gallant Gavilan, but when it counted, in the last few rounds, Sugar cut him down like the cane of his island nation; each time Gavilan tried to launch his menacing bolo punch, Sugar bobbed away and quickly countered it with rapid jabs and left hooks. The power of Sugar's punches snapped like a jackhammer, and each dazzling punch reconfigured Gavilan's face. They landed with such force that the Hawk's processed hair stood straight up as if electrified. The Hawk would have to wait until the following summer for revenge.

Energized by his victory over such an awesome challenger, Sugar stepped up his boxing routine, knocking Gene Buffalo unconscious in the first round in Wilkes-Barre, Pennsylvania, on February 10, 1949, and fighting Henry Brimm to a draw in Buffalo five days later. It was around this time that Sugar and Joe Louis, who would officially retire from the ring on March 1, were seeking to go into business together. Their first project was to secure a liquor distributing license. While they had been involved separately as entrepreneurs, they felt their combined celebrity and their connections would be enough to get them the license, which was by no means easy to come by. To this end, a meeting was arranged between Sugar and Louis and their company, World Champions, Inc., with the New York State Liquor Authority (SLA). They wanted the Authority to grant them a wholesale beer license in New York City. Raising the specter of racism, the treasurer of World Champions further complained that no license had been granted to any "Negro distributorship in New York City for any alcoholic trade, beer, wine or whisky. They've got a pattern in New York that doesn't look too good," he added. On the other hand, he continued, the Illinois Liquor Control Commission had fewer qualms with the application. [1] They were denied, the SLA basing its denial of application on the grounds that the Canadian Ace Brewing Company was one of the principal stockholders in World Champions, Inc., and that the brewing company was controlled by Harry Greenberg, a former associate of Al Capone.

They never got the license. However, there were companies such as Joe Louis Straight Bourbon Whiskey and Joe Louis Milk that capitalized on the Brown Bomber's name. Louis also owned a small interest in Joe Louis Punch, a soft drink that never quite found an audience.

Neither Sugar nor the Brown Bomber sulked very long over the setback; they each simply looked for other ways to make some money. And when they were together it was a matter of who came up with the scheme first. Both were avid golfers, so it could have been a mutual agreement to sponsor a golf tournament. Their maiden voyage in the summer of 1948 went very well, Edna Mae remembered, during a period when she and Sugar were trying to patch up things. "It all went well except for one thing," she recounted. "I was duped into thinking a young lady there was interested in Joe, but I learned later that she was my husband's guest." The tournaments would continue for a few years, with Sugar's friend Teddy Rhodes the resident pro.

• • •

Sugar had a string of six fights through the spring and early summer of '49, not one of them of any real significance. They were, to a large degree, paid sparring sessions in preparation for a return match with Kid Gavilan in July. This title scrap was slated for Municipal Stadium in Philadelphia, where both fighters were extremely popular. Sugar knew that the Kid was brimming with revenge, so he put in quality time at Greenwood Lake, and he even curbed his extracurricular activities.

Bettors at ringside in the jam-packed stadium—nearly twenty-eight thousand strong—were demanding more odds as they plunked their money down for Gavilan, many of them believing Sugar would be weakened after struggling to make the weight, the gaining of which was never easy for Sugar. During the middle rounds, the two fighters stood toe-to-toe, and in the eighth Sugar was staggered by a Gavilan combination. But he recovered before the round was over and completely dominated the second half of the fight. "It was anticipated that Sugar Ray would struggle, and trainer George Gainford had kidded about covering him with 'reducing salve.' Robinson was still a welterweight, and for that, every contender had to toast him—preferably with a high-calorie milkshake." [2]

What they didn't know was that Sugar had received an injection of glucose from Dr. Vincent Nardiello, the onetime state boxing commission's doctor. This provided him with extra pep after the struggle to make the weight, though the glucose was known to dehydrate and reduce salt content. When the sweat dripped into your mouth, as Soldier Jones had taught him, and tasted stale and not salty, it meant your sugar content had also dropped.

Gavilan was crestfallen and angry. "I didn't see too many rounds for Robinson," he said in his broken English, as reported by James Dawson for the *New York Times*. "The judge who gave him twelve rounds, he crazy. He hit me hard several times, but I was surprised at the decision and would like to make one more fight with heem." [3]

. . .

Sugar was training for his rematch with Gavilan, and trying to reconcile with Edna Mae. Whether intended or not, as a result of their reunions, Edna Mae was impregnated. In one way Sugar was excited to hear that he was going to be a father again, but he also worried that a child might affect his on-again-off-again relationship with Edna Mae negatively.

By now his oldest son, Ronnie, whom he saw only on special occasions, was almost ten years old. Sugar had no more of a father-son relationship with him than he had with his own father, Walker, Sr. Sugar promptly moved back in with his wife. There is no way to know how his mother felt about the new development, but intuitively Leila must have known that Sugar would probably never live with her again.

Having defeated Gavilan in a return match in July, Sugar prepared for a fight with Steve Belloise in August. The fight was really a makeup date for their cancellation of a fight the previous December. According to a story in the *Boston Post*, Sugar had postponed the fight because of an injury while sparring. The injury may have been the result of a punch from his sparring partner, the paper continued, but that punch was delivered on the street, not in the gym. When Tiger Wade, a hard-hitting light heavyweight whom Sugar was using to acclimate him to his fight with Belloise, demanded all of his money after being told he would have to take a cut in pay, Sugar resisted. Wade insisted on all of his money or else. Sugar was defiant. "Robinson started to tell his broken-down sparring partner that he would be lucky to get anything—but he didn't finish," wrote Gerry Hern. "Wade fired his Sunday punch that knocked Robinson to the sidewalk and then gave him a brisk going-over." An hour later the fight was postponed. In years to come, there would be other rumors of Sugar's stiffing his sparring partners, refusing to pay them what he'd promised.

• • •

When Sugar and Belloise finally squared off in August, "it wasn't too much of a fight," recalled political activist and jazz impresario Hilly Saunders, who was a spectator at this and many of Sugar's fights. "I think he knocked the guy out in the sixth or the seventh round."[4] He did it in the seventh. "Honest to God, I don't know what happened," a beaten Belloise told Bill Mardo of the *Daily Worker*. "I remember being in a flurry but I don't remember the punch that ended it. I don't remember the punch, the bell, nothing, except somebody picking me up and the next thing I know I'm sitting back in my corner and somebody is saying don't get up, Steve, it's all over." [5]

With fights scheduled for Chicago, Omaha, Houston, and Denver, Sugar was taking the long route to New Orleans to take on Vern Lester. He was in New Orleans on his way to the arena when Edna Mae called to tell him he had a son. Sugar was so excited that he knocked out Lester in the fifth round. "My son," Sugar said proudly. "My second son really, but somehow this was diffcrent. When my other boy was born, more than a decade earlier, I hadn't really known what it was all about. I was just a kid then myself. I wasn't able to appreciate the miracle of a birth. To be honest, that first child had created more problems than happiness for me, and for Marjie [his first wife]. But this time it was different. We had a name all picked out if it was a boy: Ray, Junior." [6]

Since he was already in the South, Sugar took on a couple of exhibition bouts with Gene Burton, his reliable sparring partner, in Shreveport, Louisiana, and in Dallas, defeating him in both places—as he would five years later in Hamilton, Ontario—before proceeding home to see his newborn son.

He was only back in New York City a week when he learned that the great dancer Bill "Bojangles" Robinson, the oldest of the three famous black Robinsons of New York City, had died. He always admired the dancer's nimble footwork, and Bojangles would loom even larger in his memory a few years later when he retired from the ring to pursue a stage career.

Seated on a pew toward the middle of the church during the funeral, his mind slipped back to Hell's Kitchen, where he'd first begun to imitate the dancer's intricate steps. "Heel and toe, heel and toe," he would repeat to himself as he performed outside the theaters not too far from where he lived. When the daydreaming ended, Sugar discovered he was surrounded by a cluster of celebrities who had jostled their way into the funeral at Abyssinian Baptist Church. Joe Louis, Jackie Robinson, Eddie "Rochester" Anderson, Duke Ellington, Brooklyn Dodger pitcher Don Newcombe, and W. C. Handy were among the more prominent African Americans who turned out to pay their last respects to a dancer who could run as fast backward as some could forward. The crowd at the funeral was nowhere near as large as the numbers who'd filed into the 369th Regiment Armory to view the dancer's body a few days earlier, but it certainly rivaled the massive assembly of folks at the funerals of two other prominent African Americans, actress Florence Mills's in 1929 and entrepreneur A'Lelia Walker's in 1931. For two days more than three thousand people visited the armory, many of them only vaguely aware of Robinson's prowess as a tap dancer, even if they knew him as the "Mayor of Harlem." [7]

From the funeral, Sugar headed directly home to help Edna Mae with the baby. This was his second chance at fatherhood, and he was doing his best, in his own way, to play the role. Still, there were some things he couldn't face. He was squeamish about changing his son's diaper and insisted Edna Mae have somebody available to perform this task when she wasn't around. After only a few weeks of domesticity, Sugar was eager to get back in the ring. It was far more appealing to be across the ring from an opponent, ready to go mano a mano, than it was to change a baby's diaper. On January 30, 1950, he knocked out George LaRover in the fourth round in New Haven, Connecticut. It was on the basis of such overwhelming victories that Nat Fleischer, then president and editor of *Ring*, deemed him the best all-around fighter of the year. Sugar, he wrote, pos-

sessed "fighting ability, hard hitting, clever boxing, ring general-
ship, masterful feinting and blocking and hitting . . ." [8]

• • •

As much as he despised the South, he accepted a bout in
Miami. He was partly motivated by the chilly February weather
in Harlem, and by an invitation to dine from noted columnist
and radio commentator Walter Winchell, whose broadcasts
with a clicking telegraph key in the background and the urgency
of his "Mr. and Mrs. North and South American and all ships
at sea . . . let's go to press" endeared him to millions of
Americans.

When Sugar arrived a few days before the scheduled event,
Winchell was determined to take him everywhere he went,
including to clubs and racetracks where blacks were forbidden.
One sign read: *No Negroes, Jews, or dogs.* Sugar nudged
Winchell, pointing to the sign. "Walter we're not supposed to—"

"Forget it, Sugar Ray," he barked. "You're with me, you
know."

"Yeah, but you're Jewish," Sugar said.

"I'm Winchell," the columnist snapped. [9] On another occasion, Rachel Robinson, Jackie's wife, was with Sugar and Edna
Mae in Winchell's company when he marched the couple into a
Miami Beach nightclub. "He [Winchell] literally led the way,
parted the waters, as Jack and I, Sugar Ray and his wife, followed like sheep to his table," she said. "It was more tense than
fun, but it was another barrier broken." [10]

Inadvertently, Sugar and Edna Mae, along with the other
Robinsons, were challenging discrimination in Miami and
thereabouts, though it is debatable what impact they had in
Miami. In Harlem, meanwhile, residents and activists were

screaming about the increase of discrimination in industry. There were concerted cries for more militancy. Speaking at the Theresa Hotel in September 1950, Milton Webster, vice president of the Sleeping Car Porters, a union founded by A. Philip Randolph in 1925, asserted, "Negroes are relegated to black men's jobs, where the work is hard, the hours are long, and the pay is poor." Webster scoffed at the notion that Joe Louis, Jackie Robinson, or Sugar Ray Robinson were "examples of Negro progress." To him they were but "isolated incidents." "They brought us here in chains," he blasted, "and we're still in chains, and we must break them ourselves." [11]

Fully involved in Harlem, to the extent that he even invested in it, he plunked down a few dollars at the pari-mutuel window at Miami's Hialeah racetrack. When he wasn't watching the galloping ponies circling the track, his eyes were fixed on the pink flamingos that waded in the track's infield pond. Pink also caught his attention later at a party, when he saw Willie Pep's manager wearing a pink tie. He begged the man to let him borrow it, because he was on his way to a car dealer in the Bronx and that was the color he wanted for his new Cadillac. There would be no more dark blue Buicks, which had hitherto been his trademark. After purchasing the car he drove it to a paint shop on 56th Street and 11th Avenue in Hell's Kitchen, not too far from where he lived as a kid. The paint job cost him three hundred dollars, but it was one-of-a-kind and exclusively his, Sugar boasted. There was only one Sugar Ray Robinson in the world, and now there was only one pink Cadillac, and always with a pair of gloves dangling from the rearview mirror.

Folks came from miles away to gaze upon the shiny new car, which in the sunlight radiated a special glow. For a moment it rivaled its owner in popularity, so much so that *Life* magazine sent a photographer to get pictures of it parked out front of the café. It stood as an emblem of possibility for a multitude of young black boys, who begged for an opportunity to polish it or to keep an eye on it for Sugar. When Sugar cruised through Harlem behind the wheel with the top down and his hair glistening, the sight was absolutely mesmerizing. "It was a spectacle you didn't want to miss, and once you saw it you never forgot," said boxing aficionado Clint Edwards. "No doubt about it, that was Sugar Ray."

Sugar drove his fancy car downtown on September 27, 1950, to attend the fight between his friend Joe Louis, fresh out of retirement, and Ezzard Charles. Louis wanted him there for moral support, but he could have used him in the ring as well. Charles punished him over the first half of the fight and then carried him to the end, winning an easy fifteen-round decision. The once potent Brown Bomber was but a shell of his former self, so badly beaten that Sugar had to lean down and help him put his shoes on. Louis promised then and there that he would call it quits. But he didn't, and bounced back in November with a victory over Cesar Brion.

Louis's star was fading as the Sugar was reaching the pinnacle of his glorious flight. As he ascended, many black Americans vicariously soared with him, celebrating his appearance on the cover of the June 25, 1951, issue of *Time* magazine. Pedestrians passing his cluster of businesses saw the cover taped to the window of each store. A poster-size version, probably mocked up by Langley Waller, the pioneering Harlem lithographer, leaned atop the jukebox inside the café. There hadn't been a black on the cover of the magazine since Louis "Satchmo" Armstrong made his appearance in February 1949, and there wouldn't be one after Sugar until Willie Mays arrived there in 1954. He was the second black boxer to receive this honor—Joe Louis was the cover boy in 1941. On his cover, Sugar is beaming proudly as two boxing gloves with legs climb up a globe, one glove bearing a 147-pound marker and the other a 160, indicating his conquest of the world welterweight and middleweight championships. Sugar was riding a gigantic wave of success; the world was truly his oyster. He was at the top of his game and, according to several accounts, worth more than a half-million dollars.

CHAPTER 13

"LE SUCRE MERVEILLEUX" IN PARIS

In 1951, A. J. Liebling, a highly respected writer on boxing, visited Sugar's café and offered this description in a lengthy article on Sugar for *The New Yorker*. It was "a narrow but deep saloon with walls of blue glass chips tastefully picked out with gold. The bar was as crowded as the street outside, but at the back of the place, where the bar ends, Sugar Ray's widens out enough to permit three parallel rows of tables, one row against each side wall and the third between them, and there were few empty seats. Since I could not find a place to stand up, I sat down at a table. The rear section . . . is decorated with four huge photomontages, two on each side wall. Two show him making a fool of Kid Gavilan, the Cuban fighter, who is a competitor of his for local fame . . . Another shows Robinson bringing an expression of intensely comic pain to the face of the French middleweight Robert Villemain, a muscle-bound, pyknic type with a square head. The fourth shows him standing above Georgie Abrams, a skillful pugilist who is so hairy that when knocked down he looks like a rug. Abrams got up after this knockdown, but from the picture it doesn't seem as if he ever would."[1]

On any given night, you might see Frank Sinatra, Jackie Gleason, Nat "King" Cole, Lena Horne, the Brown Bomber, and other celebrities strolling through the door. "It was really a high-class club," Langley Waller recalled, "and you had to check your hat and coat at the door, no matter how long you were going to be there."[2]

In the first half of 1950, Sugar was in perpetual motion, jumping from business to business and vacillating between the welterweight and middleweight divisions. This meant managing the seventeen-pound difference between the weight limits. Strangely, the weight fluctuation had no bearing on the outcomes in the ring. In June he defeated Robert Villemain in Philadelphia for the state's middleweight crown and in August successfully defended his welterweight crown against a veteran mauler, Charley Fusari. The fight with Fusari was memorable for a couple of reasons. Sugar learned at the weighing-in ceremony that he had to lose a quarter of a pound in one hour to meet the weight limitation—which he did. He was able to do this after several trips to the steam box and rubdowns. Later, when Sugar was asked what his toughest fight had been, he said it was the one with Fusari because "I had to fight my fight and his, too." This would be Sugar's last fight as a welterweight. Making the weight was getting to be too difficult.

The bout with Fusari was also memorable because Sugar took only one dollar from the purse. The rest he donated to the Damon Runyon Memorial Fund for Cancer Research, at the suggestion of Walter Winchell and in honor of his old Jewish teammate Spider Valentine, who had died of cancer. Sugar grew increasingly preoccupied with cancer and its causes and would support its elimination through various fund-raising campaigns throughout his life.

• • •

Having reached a pinnacle of success within the United States, Sugar began thinking about going overseas. Time and again he was being told of the rewards of exhibiting his talent abroad, of letting his European fans see him at his best. In November, Sugar gathered his entourage and booked passage on the SS *Liberté* for Paris. "On the pier with Edna Mae and me that day were my sister, Evelyn, George and Wiley, Honey Brewer, June Clark and Pee Wee Beale, and my barber-valet Roger Simon," Sugar recalled. They took with them more than fifty pieces of luggage. They were traveling like royalty, and Sugar was footing the bill, which would total more than fifty thousand dollars. It was an unforgettable moment for many in the group, Simon said in an interview years later. "We were all excited, and we knew that Sugar was ready to take on the best fighters in Europe." And Simon, a barber whose clients also included Duke Ellington, made sure Sugar was looking well groomed and properly attired for the captain's table on the ship.[3] They would be joined later by Jimmy Karoubi, a midget who served as a translator and mascot.

Traveling with a large number of friends and associates was not uncommon for Sugar. He seemed to relish having a crowd around him at all times. Hardly a moment passed in the day when he wasn't surrounded, like a monarch, by a knot of well-wishers, each seeking to get what was virtually impossible—his undivided attention. At the training camp, in his office, and even at his home, there was a constant flow of visitors. Among the hundreds of pictures of Sugar the family has, it is rare to find a photo of Sugar alone, unless it is one of those stock pictures with him posing. There are many with him amid an ensemble of men friends carousing in a nightclub, huddled in a gymnasium, playing cards, or settled behind a set of drums.

And if there were no drums, he was at the piano trying to pick out a tune. He was often complimented for his natural musical aptitude, which he had no idea where he came by. Many of his friends agreed that he had an innate feel for bebop's quick tempos, both with his hands and his feet, the coordination of which was particularly important for a drummer. There were many fights when Sugar was a virtuoso pianist with gloves on, a soloist in a pugilist recital, delivering a rapid arpeggio of stiff left jabs against an obbligato of right crosses, and then standing in awe of his combination of chromatic punches as he looked down on another fallen opponent. To watch him skipping rope or shadow-boxing or perfecting his balance and movement with a sparring partner was to see an athlete in complete control of his body and the laws of rhythm, no matter how complex and demanding. And what a body. When he had completely filled out his six feet and weighed between 150 and 160, he had a model's physique. With long slender legs and a well-developed upper body, Sugar was the perfect fighting machine, swift afoot and with power in his punches. He possessed all the tools of the ultimate warrior, in the opinion of most boxing experts. By the late fifties he'd come to exemplify the modern age, with his flair, lifestyle, world traveling, and glamorous associates, giving him a popularity that extended well beyond the ring. And he had practically mastered all the elements of the sweet science as no other boxer ever had; he had squared the ring better and faster than Pythagoras, the great Greek mathematician, who was reputed to be somewhat of a boxer himself.

There were also pictures of him playing pool, which was another one of his hobbies. "He was very good around the pool table," said Johnny Barnes, who portrayed Sugar in the film *Raging Bull* and who has emulated his idol by developing his own prowess with a cue stick.

In most of these settings, Sugar could be seen amid a gaggle of his male friends. How this extensive male bonding, in which machismo was usually the expected behavior, may have abetted Sugar's tendencies toward violence, domestic and otherwise, we can only speculate.

Edna Mae often commented on Sugar's violent temper and how for the least little annoyance he would slap her or anyone else who disobeyed an order or made the mistake of crossing him. The abuse, which started as a slap here and there and escalated to violent punches, would continue—along with his infidelities—throughout their marriage. When he hauled off and slapped her a few hours before the SS *Liberté* launched from New York to France, it made headline news. "Sugar Ray Kayos His Wife," the *Amsterdam News* reported on its January 1, 1951, front page. For its using the word "kayo," Sugar sued the paper for fifty thousand dollars. Dr. C. B. Powell, the paper's owner, contested the libel claim, arguing that the word "kayo" meant "emphasis." After a two-day trial, a jury upheld the charge, but reduced Sugar's demand to twenty-five thousand dollars. [4]

In Edna Mae's notes, but not in her memoir, she said the blow came as a result of her discovery that Sugar was fooling around with a young Frenchwoman, and that it was she who brought the lawsuit against the weekly. "I tried to leave, but Sugar wouldn't let me," she said. "The lawsuit was a gamble to get some money, since his first wife had just won a settlement and we were short on funds following the tour of Europe. I declared under oath that I had not been beaten." Because of the lawsuit, there was never any mention of this suit in the pages of the *Amsterdam News*. That's one story that they wanted to forget. Sugar, in short, was used to resolving conflicts and disputes with punches. Fortunately, but not always, he reserved most of his aggressive behavior for his foes in the ring, and he would need a good supply of it as he headed for Europe.

• • •

The first fight on the European tour was against Jean Stock, a tough middleweight, at the Palais des Sports on November 27, 1950. More than seventeen thousand spectators attended, many of them in typical European style, with bottles of wine and bags full of cheese and bread, as though they were going to a picnic. They had hardly taken a swig of wine and a bite of cheese before Stock was out for the count in the second round. Sugar had been informed that Stock couldn't take a hit to the belly, so to spare the fighter and prolong the bout he aimed his punches at the head, connecting with devastating results to the Frenchman's chin. Apparently, Sugar had been given the wrong information. Stock's chin was his weak spot, not his belly.

No matter—the spectators erupted in cheers for Sugar and he graciously accepted their warm regards. Some of the fans began yelling *"Le sucre merveilleux"*—"Marvelous Sugar." Others screamed to him that he was an *artiste*. Not even at Madison Square Garden had he been greeted with such unbridled enthusiasm. Parisians were as enthralled by Sugar as a previous generation of boxing fans had been dazzled by Panama Al Brown.

Brown, who was black, was in France in 1926 after living in Harlem, and it didn't take him or his extravagant lifestyle long to be all the rave on the streets of Paris and in commodious ateliers. For, much like Sugar, he was far more than just another American curiosity. Not only was he able to amaze Parisians with his fists, but he also stood with them at the gaming tables, nightclubs, and wherever else raconteurs and boulevardiers gathered for the good life. Brown attached himself to other luminaries in the City of Light, including Jean Cocteau and Maurice Chevalier, and from Pigalle to the bistros of Montmartre he was the center of attention, the ebony bon vivant. "He dressed elegantly, frequenting the best tailors in London and at times changing clothes six times a day," Tyler Stovall observed in his engrossing *Paris Noir: African Americans in the City of Light*. Brown, according to Stovall, once proclaimed that all he needed to live was "20,000 bottles of champagne." [5] As Sugar would find later, Brown reveled in a milieu seemingly devoid of racism, moving comfortably amid a sea of admirers. A year of fighting in France kept him in money for champagne, and as a bantamweight he even fought the European welterweight champion, Henri Scillie of Belgium, to a draw.

Sugar wasn't there for even a year, but he was there long enough to encounter Robert Villemain, whom he'd decisioned in June in Philadelphia. The promoter of Sugar's European tour, Charlie Michaelis, took advantage of the fortuitous meeting and quickly arranged a December 22 bout in Paris between them. Sugar shook hands in agreement. With Michaelis, he would never need a contract: His word was his bond, and he

never violated his trust with Sugar. But before a return engagement with Villemain could be realized, there were two other
contracts he had to fulfill on the Continent. In Brussels, he
stopped Luc Van Dam in the fourth round; a week later in
Geneva, it took a little longer to earn a ten-round decision over
Jean Walzack. These would be minor events compared with the
buildup for the showdown with Villemain.

On the day before the fight, the owner of a clothing shop
came to Michaelis requesting half the tickets. He did not blink
when told it would cost him fifteen million francs to buy up the
nine thousand tickets, which he planned to make available at his
store as part of a publicity campaign. The idea backfired, however, when the next day thousands of people descended on his
shop and practically ripped it apart in their rush to buy the tickets. To salvage his shop, the owner called Michaelis and
pleaded with him to take the tickets back. Michaelis obliged,
and the man and his shop were spared any further damage.

To Michaelis's delight, the Palais des Sports was completely
sold out. It was a record sales event, grossing thirty million
francs, or eighty-five thousand dollars. When Villemain came in
over the weight limit at 164 pounds, it disqualified the fight
from being a championship bout. Thus, Sugar's title was not at
stake.

In their previous match, Villemain had managed to stay on
his feet for fifteen rounds; he didn't make it nearly that far the
second time, and was sprawled across the ropes taking a pounding when the referee mercifully stopped Sugar's onslaught in
the ninth round. Once more Sugar heard his name attached to a
variety of pleasant-sounding French adjectives: *magnifique;
brillant; l'artiste ultime!* The adoration of the French was still
ringing in Sugar's ears when he departed for Frankfurt,

Germany, to meet Hans Stretz, who lived up to his name as he lay stretched across the canvas in the fifth round. It was Christmas night, and poor Stretz had received a most unwanted present.

As Sugar related in his autobiography, he had earned fifty thousand dollars within a month, and given the bills run up by his retinue, he needed every penny and more. Edna Mae alone had done considerable damage during her forays at the designer ateliers, including Schiaparelli's and Jacques Fath's. The spree embellished her already fabulous collection of fur coats, which included a full-length ranch mink coat, a Russian lynx coat, a Persian lamb broadtail coat, a platinum mink jacket, mink stole, and a silver-blue mink stole.

Before their departure from France, Sugar learned that he had been granted a title match against Jake LaMotta, who had won the middleweight belt from Marcel Cerdan, the Frenchman who died in a plane crash before he could have a return match with LaMotta. The other good news was that the Boxing Writers' Association (BWA) had voted him the Edward J. Neil Memorial Plaque, named for the former Associated Press boxing writer who was killed in 1937 while serving as a war correspondent in Spain. The plaque was awarded to the boxer who had done the most for the sport that year.

Hearing these announcements as the entourage boarded the *Liberté* for home only added to Sugar's celebrity and made the voyage all the more pleasurable. Sugar had conquered France, Belgium, and Germany with the same panache that had made him such a star attraction in Harlem.

His exultation was clouded by only one thing: Reporters kept baiting him to talk about any racism he might have encountered in Europe. They wanted him to refute the charges made by Paul Robeson regarding rampant discrimination in America. "Mr. Robeson speaks for himself and not for Americans," Sugar commented to the press, doing his best to dodge an issue that had ensnared Jackie Robinson, and which had compelled the baseball star to denounce Robeson before the House Un-American Activities Committee the year before. Sugar refused to accept the bait, adroitly avoiding the sucker punch, and thus any controversy.[6]

CHAPTER 14

THE ST. VALENTINE'S DAY MASSACRE

Another person licking his chops for Sugar to return was Jake LaMotta. Now that the way was cleared for them to face each other for the sixth time, the Bull was practically pawing the turf, eager to charge across the ring and punish the man who had beaten him four out of five times.

Sugar was looking forward to the match as well, but there were a few things he had to do before the February 14 date. First of all, there was the BWA award ceremony to attend. The event took place at the Waldorf-Astoria, and Sugar was resplendent in his tuxedo. Of all the accolades and praise he received that evening, one thing stuck out in his memory. It was a telegram from LaMotta, reminding him of their bout. Sugar smiled when he heard the message read by the master of ceremonies. He was stunned that the Bull knew about the event and knew exactly where to send the telegram. Later, while training at

Pompton Lakes, New Jersey, a change from his regular site, he realized that the telegram was less LaMotta's doing than his manager's or someone close to him, since the gesture was not characteristic of the Bull.

That person, he assumed, was Frankie Carbo, who was not only close to the Bull, but also very close to the mob and to the International Boxing Club, a major organizer of fights. The suspicion was verified a few days later when Carbo, using an alias, phoned Sugar at camp and requested a meeting. Because of his experience with Blinky Palermo, the mobster who had tried previously to entice him into a fix, Sugar knew what Carbo was up to. When they met near the camp's entrance, Carbo made Sugar an offer: Sugar was to win the February 14 match with LaMotta, then lose the return bout; the third and final fight would be left for the best man to win. "You got the wrong guy," Sugar told him, rejecting the fix. Unlike LaMotta, who had thrown a fight for the mob in order to get a title shot, Sugar was not about to capitulate, no matter how much money was involved, no matter how dangerous it was to refuse these notorious underworld figures. Sure, he'd carried a few fighters and pulled his punches on occasion, but he had never taken a dive or cut a deal by betting on his opponent. If the mob hadn't gotten to him when he was younger, it was too late now, as he reached the apex of his career.

"Throughout the fifties, to read Dan Parker in the *New York Daily Mirror* or Jimmy Cannon in the *Post* was to scan a bill of particulars against a dirty fight game run entirely by mobsters—mainly Italian and Jewish mobsters," David Remnick observed. "After the war there was not a single champion who was not, in some way, touched by the Mafia, if not wholly owned and operated by it. [Senator Estes] Kefauver (with substantial help from his chief counsel, John Gurnee Bonomi) intended to prove the case and instigate a reform of boxing." [1]

Sugar was neither squeaky clean nor a Goody Two-shoes, but if there was any evidence of his being in bed with the mob, it escaped detection by a gaggle of nosy sleuths and inquiring reporters. Moreover, if the reporters of the day didn't have the wherewithal to ferret out the dirt, the Senate investigating committee did, and it could sling the mud too.

With varying degrees of sympathy for Sugar, Dan Parker, Jimmy Cannon, Hype Igoe, Arthur Daley, James Dawson, Lester Bromberg, Bill Gallo, and Bert Sugar infused sports journalism with a dash of analysis and literary flair, though, in general, it was a far cry from the singing, zinging prose of the writers of the previous generation—Heywood Hale Broun, Damon Runyon, Grantland Rice, Paul Gallico, and Ring Lardner.

Bromberg was a particular favorite of the Robinsons, and he made sure they received all his clippings and photos from the *New York World Telegram* and *Sun*. Perhaps Bromberg was eternally bothered by his testimony in 1947 before the New York State Athletic Commission, in which he divulged that Sugar had in fact been approached by the mob and offered a deal not to fight Marty Servo. For not disclosing the information, Sugar was fined five hundred dollars and suspended for thirty days. [2] Bromberg died in 1989, a few months before Sugar.

• • •

Reaching the top of his craft had not been easy, and Sugar had used all sorts of tactics and strategies to keep his opponents off balance. Sometimes he psyched them out—as he may have with

LaMotta at a luncheon a few days before their fight. Sitting near the Bull, Sugar asked the waiter if he could have a large glass of beef blood. Both the waiter and LaMotta were puzzled by the request. Sugar stressed his order, clarifying that he did not want gravy, but actual beef blood, extracted "before the meat is cooked," he said. The waiter obeyed and returned with a glassful of blood. Sugar downed it in one long gulp. Wiping his mouth, he explained to a bug-eyed LaMotta that he had been drinking it for years on the advice of Chappie Blackburn, Louis's trainer. It was the equivalent of a stare-down at the weigh-in. He told the Bull that it was his secret weapon and gave him the strength to overcome bigger and stronger opponents. LaMotta told Sugar that he was out of his mind.

Sugar would have likewise questioned LaMotta's sanity when he drank two or three shots of brandy before their fight. LaMotta said he did this to give him a sense of false courage to hide his real fear. He knew he wasn't in good enough shape to fight Sugar. One fighter was half drunk on brandy and the other was juiced up on beef blood. If the bettors had known, there would be no guessing where their money would have gone.

At the sound of the bell, the din in Chicago Stadium increased, and the Bull, as was his style, leaped from his stool and rushed headlong across the ring, his gloves locked to his side like padded horns. Sugar was faster than ever in sidestepping the charges, delivering stinging jabs and swift counterpunches to the Bull's awkward flails. And this would be the pattern for the first several rounds, with Sugar slicing and dicing LaMotta with such rapid, laserlike precision that the Bull became more frustrated with each blow.

There was very little toe-to-toe punching during the first seven rounds, though there was plenty of superb boxing by

Sugar "the matador" and headfirst assaults by the Bull. However, over the next three rounds Sugar battered LaMotta unmercifully. But the Bull was as stubborn as ever, refusing to fall. When it was over, LaMotta lay sprawled across the top ropes, his face bloodier than a slab of beef. He had only the strength to mutter, "You couldn't put me down, you black bastard. You can't put me on the deck." These were the words Sugar heard, but in his autobiography LaMotta remembered the slaughter this way: "Robinson had me but I wouldn't give the son of a bitch the satisfaction of knocking me down, so I told the referee I'd murder him if he tried to stop the fight. I got my arm wedged around one of the ring ropes and stayed there, defying Robinson to knock me down. He couldn't, but I got about as bad a beating as I've ever had." [3]

The referee, Frankie Sikora, stepped in and halted the match in the thirteenth round. Under Illinois regulations, Sugar was awarded a technical knockout, and indeed, the Bull was virtually out on his feet. Because of the beating LaMotta took on this day, February 14, 1951, the fight was called "the St. Valentine's Day Massacre," recalling the mob-related execution on the same day in 1929 in the Windy City. In LaMotta's own words: "Well, Robinson didn't have a machine gun and there was only one victim, but it was still a massacre. . . . If the fight had gone another twenty seconds, Sugar would have collapsed from hitting me so much."

But it was the self-deprecating LaMotta who was on the verge of collapsing, causing the doctor to order an oxygen tank to relieve the gasping fighter. "LaMotta collapsed in my arms," said Al Silvani, who worked in the Bull's corner that night. [4] For a half hour he was on the tank, and was not allowed to leave the stadium for two hours. All agreed: LaMotta had been the recipient of a thorough shellacking. "Sugar and I fought so much that I should have died from sugar diabetes," LaMotta quipped during an interview after the fight. This was their last bout, and it was the worst one for the Bull, who had taken a severe beating and lost his title. But then, he should have known how much of a challenge it was going to be to whip somebody revved up on beef blood.

Boxing authority Dr. Ferdie Pacheco ranked the thirteenth round of this fight as one of the greatest rounds in fight history.

CHAPTER 15

IT'S TURPIN TIME

By spring, Sugar was once more in Europe, and once again back with Edna Mae. On this trip he had an even larger troupe than before. Sugar, the middleweight champ (he had to relinquish his welterweight title because it became too difficult to make the weight), was shopping for fresh adversaries. His favorite promoter, Charlie Michaelis, had scheduled fights that would take him across the Continent, including a bout in England.

While the Toast of Harlem was in Paris, the Toast of Paris was in Harlem. May 20, 1951, was Josephine Baker Day in Harlem, and the chanteuse/dancer rode at the front of a long motorcade throwing kisses to a crowd of cheering fans—estimated at one hundred thousand—who lined the streets, braving a gloomy wet Sunday. The police convoy had a hard time keeping a gaggle of admiring kids from leaping onto her car. When the caravan completed its run, the festivities continued at the Golden Gate Ballroom, where diplomat Ralph Bunche, a recent Nobel Prize winner, presented Baker with an award for her work against prejudice in the theater. The daylong celebration concluded that evening at the newly reopened Savoy Ballroom. Throughout the day, former dancer and later to be the first New York state assemblywoman, Bessie Buchanan—who was also the wife of the owner of the club, Charlie Buchanan—was Baker's personal escort (and rumored to be her ex-lover), making sure everything went off as planned. [1]

Comedian Timmie Rogers, songstress Thelma Carpenter, Duke Ellington, Billy Daniels, Juanita Hall, and the Whites—Walter and Poppy—were among the famous entertainers and political leaders who dropped what they were doing to come and honor "La Baker." The eighteen-hour-long celebration was sponsored by the New York branch of the NAACP, and Baker went nonstop "from the moment she left the Statler Hotel in Boston until she went to bed in her suite at the Theresa that night." [2]

. . .

On May 21, Sugar arrived in Paris to fight Kid Marcel, the French welterweight champion, who had put on extra weight for the match. Sugar was welcomed by a massive turnout. The French cheered him lustily, many of them thanking him for beating LaMotta, who had beaten their champion, Marcel Cerdan. Later, with the Kid Marcel fight behind him, Sugar caused quite a stir at a reception when he kissed the wife of the president of France, twice on each cheek. At first, the action stunned the upper crust who'd witnessed Sugar's goodwill gesture. But they, like the first lady, Madame Vincent Auriol, quickly warmed to the occasion, and applauded, particularly after the champion placed a check for ten thousand dollars from the Damon Runyon Memorial Fund for Cancer Research in her hands. Some of the dignitaries at the reception, which was held in a gilded salon near the Arc de Triomphe, were a bit put off because of Sugar's late arrival. "I got lost in traffic," Sugar apologized after stepping from his pink Cadillac wearing, according to him, a pink tie, a neat gray suit, and a gleaming white handkerchief in his breast pocket. Michaelis had imposed only one condition on Sugar's sojourn—that he bring his Cadillac this time. After Sugar's speech, a crush of grave old men and women with diamonds glittering from every part of their personages pushed to meet him. [3]

A few weeks after Sugar's glorious reception and his knockout of Marcel in the fifth round, things took a turn for the worse: He was asked to leave Paris's luxurious St. Cloud Country Club at the request of members. Sugar felt the request to bar him from the links and a few rounds of golf had been made by American members of the exclusive club. "I was told we could only play in the mornings, when not many golfers are on the course," Sugar told the press. "Finally, they asked both myself and two friends to leave." The club's manager said the exclusion was a result of Sugar's violation of a rule that permitted nonmembers to play only three times every six months, and only on a member's invitation. Apparently some members became disgruntled when they noticed that Sugar was bringing along his friends with him. If the specter of racism entered Sugar's mind, he never expressed it. [4]

Extremely hurt by his treatment at the club, Sugar packed his golf clubs and headed for Italy for a scheduled warm-up bout with Cyrille Delannoit in Turin, Italy, before meeting

Randy Turpin in England for the biggest match of the tour. Sugar easily bested Delannoit, knocking him to the canvas to stay in the third round. This provided some solace for Sugar and his wife, who two days earlier had reported to the police that her watch and diamond ring, together valued at seventy-five hundred dollars, were missing. They could not say if the items had been stolen or lost. [5] A greater loss was awaiting them in London.

• • •

In Randy Turpin, the black Englishman and former bricklayer, Sugar found more than he bargained for. He was hoping it wouldn't be a repeat of the fiasco that had occurred in Germany two weeks earlier against Gerhard Hecht, when he had been disqualified for landing a blow to Hecht's kidney area. (Later the commission reversed its ruling and called it a "no-decision.") The West Berlin fans were so upset by the outcome that they began hurling bottles into the ring, one narrowly missing Sugar's head. Sugar and his crew had to scramble for their lives.

There were no bottles raining down on them in London, just Randy Turpin's unorthodox style, his way of yanking his head back to avoid a punch. One would have thought that Sugar would have little trouble with Turpin, since Turpin had lost to Jean Stock and Sugar had bopped Stock in two rounds. But that logic doesn't always apply in boxing. One fighter may have less difficulty with a puncher than with a skilled boxer. Other factors, such as one's psychological disposition or physical preparation, or one's tactics, might be the right ingredient against one fighter and absolutely wrong against another. In Sugar's case, it was mainly a lack of preparation; Turpin's awkward style did baffle Sugar.

Photographer Gordon Parks, sent to cover the highly publicized fight for *Life* magazine, recalled that Sugar was not mentally or physically ready for such a grueling slugfest. "There were no workouts," Parks said. "Sugar Ray played at golf through the days, and at card tables late into the nights." Meanwhile, Turpin, "a dockside brawler," trained like a man possessed. He certainly was possessed with a determination to take the title, while Sugar took long snoozes, worked the links, and upped the ante at frequent poker sessions that went on to the wee small hours of the morning. Moreover, his popularity, the constant badgering from fans, had made it impossible for him to find quiet lodging in the heart of London. Gainford found him and Edna Mae a room over a pub in the suburbs, where it was a bedlam of unbroken noise after midnight. Consequently, when Sugar wanted to get some rest the mayhem below kept him awake. He was irritable, rest-broken, and unprepared to fight even a lesser talent than Turpin.

The fight took place on July 10, 1951, and it was going Sugar's way until the sixth round, when Turpin miraculously recovered from a sound pounding to deliver some of his own punishment. By the last rounds—it would go fifteen—Sugar was in trouble; Parks saw it, and when he looked across the arena and saw Edna Mae's face, he knew she saw it too. At last, when Turpin's hand was raised declaring him the winner, the roar shook the stadium. Sugar's eye was so badly damaged that Dr. Vincent Nardiello, who had come over for the fight, decided to stitch it right in the dressing room rather than back at the hotel. It took eight stitches to close the gash, and according to Edna Mae, it was done without any painkillers, other than a couple of aspirins. "Sugar didn't return to his hotel that night," Parks recounted in his memoir, *Voices in the Mirror*. "He didn't want to see the reporters, the crowds, Edna Mae, or anyone else. The two of us slipped out a side door and I found a cheap obscure hotel near the stadium. Early the next morning the two of us took the boat train to Paris. The pink Cadillac, Sugar Ray's wife, and the fifteen-man entourage would come later. Thankfully no one on the train recognized him in the dark glasses and the slouched hat lowered over his forehead. 'I'll kill him the next time. So help me I'll kill him,' Sugar said over and over again."

Parks wrote nothing about their time in Paris or France, particularly on the Riviera. Dr. Nardiello had advised Sugar to soak up as much sun as possible to help the healing of the tear above his eye—and to avoid the casinos. Telling Sugar to stay away from the gambling tables was akin to throwing a rabbit into a cabbage patch and expecting him not to eat until he bloats. "Jack Warner and Darryl Zanuck, the movie producers, were vacationing there then [in Cannes]," Sugar related in an article he wrote for London's *Sunday Express*. "The three of us were regulars in the baccarat game. We'd put up about a thousand dollars apiece every night and we were the bankers. We lost so much that they reserved our seats. They wouldn't let anyone play until we got there." [6]

• • •

Despite his surprising loss to Turpin, the son of a British Guiana soldier and an Englishwoman, Sugar and his horde were loudly cheered upon their return to the States on the French liner *Liberté*. Hundreds turned out for ceremonies at City Hall and in Harlem to give him a hero's welcome. "I promise you that on September twelfth I'll do my sincere utmost to again bring the middleweight championship back to America," Sugar told a throng of well-wishers after Mayor Vincent

Impellitteri's introduction. He made no excuses for his defeat, brushing aside an insinuation that his diet might have been to blame. "Turpin was eating the same kind of food," he said, promising not to take it easy in the early rounds of the rematch as he had done in London. "It'll be a different story next time." Incredibly, in his eleven years of professional boxing, this was only the second loss Sugar had ever suffered, and the first to a black man.

Sugar's speech was followed by remarks from newscaster and columnist Walter Winchell, who praised him for his numerous contributions to the Runyon cancer campaign, to which he had donated nearly forty-seven thousand dollars in proceeds from various bouts. At City Hall, the mayor presented him with a scroll citing him as one "whose interest in the welfare of his fellow human beings, as manifested in his varied activities as ambassador at large for the Damon Runyon Memorial Fund for Cancer Research, had secured the heartfelt appreciation of the people of the City of New York." Sugar stood next to his mother, while Edna Mae stood next to the mayor as they listened to music provided by the Police Department Band and a serenade by the Police Athletic League Glee Club. [7]

A similar outpouring of love and affection greeted Sugar and his group when they reached Harlem, accompanied by an eighteen-car motorcade. Following the usual speeches and accolades, Sugar was asked about rumors that he was going to be making movies. Those rumors were almost five years old by now. Ever since his first fight with LaMotta, there had been overtures from producers seeking to get the photogenic Sugar in films. In fact, both he and Edna Mae were courted to star in a love story that would be a black version of *Body and Soul*, made famous by John Garfield. But Sugar had been doing so well in the ring, with such lucrative contracts, that the thought of being in movies was brushed aside. However, now that his popularity had increased and there was the promise of more money than before, Sugar apparently changed his mind. Gainford responded that his fighter had agreed to make a couple of films, but only after he had regained the crown. When that was accomplished, he continued, Sugar would appear in Jean-Paul Sartre's *The Respectful Prostitute,* to be filmed in Paris, with another project planned for Rome. Gainford added that Edna Mae had also been offered roles. If Sartre's play was ever made into a film, it did not include Sugar, although the combination of Sugar and Sartre might have had some special appeal. But make-believe was one thing Sugar didn't have too much time for; he had to focus on the dangerous threat Turpin represented.

• • •

The rematch was held two months later, on September 12 at the Polo Grounds in Harlem. Two hours before the fight, the tickets were sold out. More than sixty-one thousand spectators crammed into the stadium, including such luminaries at ringside as Toots Schor, Joe DiMaggio, Walter Winchell, and even General Douglas MacArthur, who had just been relieved of his command in Korea.

Over the first nine rounds of the fight, Sugar was slightly ahead on points, but not in command, as he usually was. In the tenth, a head butt from Turpin opened a deep gash over Sugar's left eye. This riled Sugar; there is nothing like the sight, smell, and taste of blood to motivate a top fighter. "It was either do or die," he said after the fight. He went after Turpin savagely, pelting him with a series of combinations that left him bewildered. Then came a perfectly timed right cross, and Turpin went down, but he was up at the count of nine. The crowd unleashed a bedlam of cheers and squeals that carried all the way to Lido Pool, where Sugar had met Edna Mae. The roar alone was enough to quell Turpin, who was unable to protect himself anymore. In twenty-five seconds, Sugar hit Turpin with thirty-one punches. At the 2:52 mark, referee Ruby Goldstein stopped the fight and Sugar was once more at the top of the heap, the cream of the crop.

His mother had been a prophetess—she had told Sugar he would win it in the tenth round. "There has seldom been a more thrilling round than the tenth in that Turpin fight," Jimmy Cannon, the great sportswriter, reflected several years later. "There was a gash over Robinson's eye. The blood ran in a rill down his face. Most fighters would have stalled until the round closed, so that the crude surgeons in the corner could attempt to close the cut. But Robinson proved his greatness by turning it on and he punched until the referee ended the fight." [8]

Turpin felt he had been robbed—that Goldstein had stopped the fight too soon. "I felt that Sugar was losing on points," he told a reporter. "Everything was going just as I planned it. I knew that I was outboxing him, especially when I cut his left eye wide open. He looked hurt and worried." [9] Turpin said that when the referee halted the match, he was just "clearing the fog out my head" and waiting for the end of the round, just eight seconds away.

There would never be a third bout for Turpin to attempt to prove his superiority.

• • •

On September 13, 1951, a day after Sugar had regained his middleweight crown from Randy Turpin, thousands of

Harlemites jammed the streets in and around the Theresa Hotel, waiting for their hero to appear on the second-floor balcony. Not since Joe Louis knocked out Max Schmeling in the first round in June 1938 had there been such a massive demonstration by boxing fans on the streets of Harlem. Boxing historians often talk about the eruptions of joy in the black community when heavyweight champion Jack Johnson celebrated Independence Day by manhandling Jim Jeffries, "The Great White Hope," in Reno, Nevada, in 1910, or how jubilant the Senegalese immigrants in Paris were the evening the colorful, flamboyant Battling Siki blitzed Georges Carpentier for the light heavyweight championship in 1923, but those celebrations couldn't have been any more jubilant, than the one up and down 125th Street, where traffic came to a standstill. The police estimated the Harlem crowd at more than ten thousand frantic residents, all of them dancing and singing, and screaming for Sugar to appear.

"Down at my café," Sugar said, "about thirty blocks from the Polo Grounds, most of the rounds were on me that night. By the time I got there, there wasn't anyplace to park for blocks, except for the spot reserved in front for my flamingo Cadillac. That was Cadillac Night on Seventh Avenue. It looked like an assembly line." [10] Bop singer Babs Gonzales, then living in a kitchenette at Hamilton Terrace, said of the Cadillacs, "There were hogs everywhere."

"After Sugar had regained his title from Randy Turpin," Edna Mae said of her and Sugar, "we were proud and happy." The first thing they did was to take a break from the city and venture south to Miami. This was an opportunity to give Sugar's torn and battered eye a chance to heal, and for him to rest uninterrupted by friends and acquaintances. It also put

him in the tender love and care of Lucia, Edna Mae's grandmother, who applied effective home remedies to Sugar's
swollen eye. "We could afford to take a vacation because our
enterprises were doing more business, on a consistent basis,
than any other spot in our area . . . We were enjoying life in our
apartment in Harlem . . . Ray had hired Mr. Wilfred Springer
(the real estate agent who had sold him his mother's first home)
as a business associate in whom he placed great trust and
greater responsibility. Mike Headley, a former musician, was
made manager of the bar, and an old friend of mine was also
hired, Mr. Herman Du Bois, as an alternate manager and
chargé d'affaires. They all seemed to be doing credible jobs.
Harlem was also growing, and black property owners; propri-
etors of good, thriving business ventures; and leaders in civic
and community projects were universally prospering." Little
did they know that someone among those they counted as
friends would betray them.

Though the sojourn in Miami lasted only a couple of
weeks—Edna Mae had to get back in order to prepare for a fashion show-cum-cabaret in Washington, D.C., at the Lincoln
Colonnade on October 14—the good times continued for the
couple and "baby Ray." Christmas, 1951 was almost ideal, the
only disappointment being Joe Louis's loss to Rocky Marciano
in October. It was then that Sugar promised himself he would
never end up like his friend. Louis had squandered a fortune
and was forced to box even after he had lost his great skills in
order to pay debts he owed Uncle Sam. Sugar vowed that once
he retired that would be it; there'd be no coming back like
Louis, to be beaten and embarrassed.

· · ·

The new year dawned with good news for Sugar: *Sport* magazine had named him its Man of the Year. Along with the plethora of plaques, citations, and trophies that preceded and followed this honor, he enjoyed the pride of seeing his businesses booming. There was cash enough now for him to buy his mother a new house in Riverdale near where she used to live; he and Edna Mae moved in on 248th Street when she moved out. For the next several months, Sugar broke in his new home, supervised his operations, and tried to be a good husband and father.

Sugar and Edna Mae's dream house commanded the cover story of the September 1953 issue of *Ebony* magazine. The house was an imposing ten-room, four-story structure with a two-car garage built into the ground level. Though lavishly decorated and plush, the home was by no means ostentatious, the article reported. "Equipped with a keen business sense, Ray kept his expenditures well in hand so that the estimates of his total costs did not exceed fifty thousand dollars—and the bulk of this was spent for remodeling, decorating, and furnishings." Dominating the huge living room was a sectional sofa designed by Edna Mae, complemented by a marble-topped circular coffee table imported from Italy. Sprawled here and there were ten thousand dollars' worth of fine rugs and carpets.

There were four toilets, four television sets, and an intercom system so they could talk to each other in the vast house. A solarium was furnished with tropical furniture made of bamboo, and matchstick blinds shaded the expansive windows. Spread over the baby grand Steinway piano, which had been in the house since 1948, was a shawl that had been in Edna Mae's family for four generations.

It was a commodious love nest Edna Mae had obviously

conceived to curb Sugar's wanderlust, his need to rove away from home and find comfort in someone else's arms.

"Moving to Riverdale was great for us, and I was so happy to have so much beauty surrounding us and the direction of our lives taking on such positive dimensions," Edna Mae enthused in her memoir. "We met so many fine residents of the area who involved themselves into all phases of decent life and humanitarian pursuits. Andrea Simon of Simon & Schuster [one neighbor] was my introduction into the most satisfying relationship." Indeed, the Simons would play a decisive role in breaking down some of the racial barriers that normally kept blacks from living in the vicinity.

The house's showpiece, a seven-foot-diameter circular bed with a mirror above, occupied the master bedroom. Once it was over between them, this bed (minus the mirror) would be one of several things Edna Mae retained until her death in 2002.

CHAPTER 16

BUMPY, BOBO, AND ROCKY

In the early spring of 1952, Sugar was in camp again at Pompton Lakes, getting ready to defend his title in San Francisco against Carl "Bobo" Olson in March. He hadn't fought in six months. Each time he peppered the heavy bag, it was an attempt to erase the memory of his buddy, Joe Louis, being vanquished by Rocky Marciano. The image of his idol and friend sprawled between the ropes had moved him so much that he'd leaped onto the ring apron and begun consoling the fallen warrior. "You'll be all right, Joe, you'll be all right," Sugar almost chanted after Louis was counted out. Louis's head on the ring apron haunted him almost as badly as the ghost of Jimmy Doyle, the boxer his punches had killed in 1947. "Some people were belittling Joe," Sugar wrote, "saying how maybe he hadn't been that good after all. And, someday, I realized, they would be saying the same thing about me if I overextended my career." It was a prophetic insight, but one given only a passing thought by Sugar.

Beyond the Brown Bomber and Olson, Sugar had another thing on his mind when he arrived in San Francisco: He wanted to visit Alcatraz, the island prison in the bay. Two inmates—the notorious Bumpy Johnson and Skeets Cabella—were lifelong friends who had attended all of Sugar's fights and were often big-time spenders at his various establishments. Johnson, a native of Charleston, South Carolina, arrived in Harlem in 1919 when he was thirteen, and within a decade had manipulated and strong-armed his way into the fledgling numbers racket. His quick success as a kingpin in this illegal operation was facilitated by Madame Stephanie St. Clair, who was considered the Queen of Numbers. (The numbers then were like the lottery of today, only now the state controls the game and the winning numbers are determined by various forms of random selection, not from horse races, as in the past.) Together they staved off attempts by such infamous underworld mobsters as Dutch Schultz to take over their "business" in Harlem.

Johnson had been incarcerated at Alcatraz a year when Sugar went to see him. They had a lot in common: Just as Sugar was virtually unstoppable with his gloves on, Johnson was unrivaled with a knife or a machine gun in his hands. Harlemites respected Johnson and saw him as a modern-day Robin Hood. Like his predecessor, Casper Holstein, Johnson shared his accumulated wealth in a variety of ways. Many students were provided scholarships by Johnson, who was well read and somewhat of an intellectual. He was often in the company of Madame St. Clair, who was twice his age. "She and Bumpy both loved music, especially opera, and regularly attended concerts at Carnegie Hall," said Abiola Sinclair, who wrote extensively on Johnson's life before her death in 2001. "She enjoyed walks through Central Park on the arm of her young confidant, and the two shared a love of poetry, music, art, and money." Helen Lawrenson, a former editor at *Vanity Fair,* spoke of her affair with Johnson in her memoir, *Stranger at the Party,* noting that he had other white lovers as well.

Johnson was sent to prison for drug dealing after appealing his case all the way to the Supreme Court, Sinclair wrote. He maintained that he had been framed. No drugs were actually found on him or in his home, the case being made against him by several "informants" who claimed they ran drugs for him. He was released from prison in 1963, and died five years later while dining in a Harlem restaurant.

"We had been skeptical about whether permission would be granted," Edna Mae wrote about their first visit to Alcatraz, "because [Johnson] was the acknowledged and accepted head of all alleged illegal or questionable activity above 110th Street. Skeets was also a well-known sportsman, who spent money lavishly and wined and dined the most beautiful women, a real Beau Brummell." But they had no problem getting permission; Sugar's visit was a joy to all of the prisoners, Edna Mae noted, and most of the papers raved about Sugar's compassion and loyalty to his friends.

• • •

After the visit to Alcatraz, Sugar prepared to meet Bobo Olson, a native of Hawaii. It was to be a rather lackluster bout. This was Sugar's first defense of his second title reign, and he donated all but one dollar of his purse to the Damon Runyon Memorial Fund for Cancer Research. Sugar's magnanimous gestures to the Cancer Fund were universally praised, though there were some who felt that he could have given equal contributions to the NAACP and the National Urban League. [1]

Sugar won a unanimous decision, but it was not the Sugar of old, not the refined boxer who many were beginning to call one of the greatest fighters of all time. Maybe Sugar, at thirty, was past his prime. Or perhaps it was the long layoff—he hadn't been in the ring since his victory over Turpin in September. A five-month layoff for a fighter who had been averaging two fights a month might have upset his rhythm.

Down the road, a match was slated that would clear up this issue. Like Louis, Sugar had a formidable Rocky to deal with.

• • •

Sugar versus Rocky Graziano: This was the fight everybody was demanding. Even Hollywood couldn't top this for excitement. Once more, as when Sugar faced the Bull, it would be a simple case of the boxer against the slugger. Fortunately, the bout was slated for Chicago Stadium, Sugar's lucky venue, on April 16, 1952. It promised to be a thriller between two thirty-year-old boxers, each of them wondering if he had been around too long or wouldn't be around much longer, to paraphrase a quip popularized by comedienne Moms Mabley.

"Fight night was a stellar evening," Edna Mae enthused. "Sugar and Rocky faced each other in the ring. You could see the mutual respect. They waded into each other and Rocky landed a hell of a blow on Sugar's head that hurt me more than Sugar." Sugar recalled the same punch: "When the bell rang, Rocky was scowling instead of smiling. He came out of his corner with curly black hair flopping on his forehead, and with his right hand cocked like a revolver. While I watched that right hand, he caught me with a good left hook in the first round."

Edna Mae resumed, "It was all I could do to stay in my seat. The round was rough and I was so relieved when the bell rang. Round two was equally rough. It was apparent that Rocky was hoping for a knockout. Sugar was able to outsmart his sudden lunges and stay balanced." Still, according to Sugar: "He whacked me on the side of the neck and I went down. Some of the sportswriters claimed that one of my legs had merely brushed the canvas, that it wasn't an official knockdown. None of them had been swatted by that right hand. I was down, and Rocky put me there. When he saw me down, his instinct was to move in for the kill. That was a mistake . . . I've met many tough fighters in my long career, but no one ever stung me more than Rocky did."

Edna Mae added: "Sugar was up quicker than I, but . . . seconds later, Ray had Rocky on his back on the ring canvas. He attempted to rise but was in big trouble! He fell down again and his body lay there jerking with the worst twitch I've ever seen. The full count ended, and his corner rushed in to get him." Sugar had hit Rocky so hard that his mouthpiece flew out of the ring and landed in someone's lap. The punch also almost literally knocked Graziano into retirement—he would have only one more fight. When Graziano got up just as he was counted out, he leaned against the ropes and kicked his legs as if to get some feeling back into them, to get the blood circulating again. He had been bashed so hard, and so repeatedly, that the blows apparently had affected his nerve endings below the belt.

"Graziano and his aggressive style, leading with his chin, was perfect for a fighter like Sugar Ray," said boxing enthusiast Clint Edwards. "After the fight his face looked like it had gone through a meat grinder . . . he was chopped liver." Scholar Gerald Early cast the fight in a deeper, metaphorical gloss:

"The fight was symbolically the war machine, the white natural man against another type of natural man, the noble savage made American slick. Fictive psychopathic rage against fictive animal cunning." [2] Like LaMotta, who called Sugar a "black bastard" while taking his blows, Graziano admitted he too had cursed Sugar and called him out of his name.

In Graziano's final fight before he stepped out of the ring for the last time, he lost a decision to a soft-hitting southpaw, Chuck Daley, out of Michigan in December 1952. He became a comedian and actor, later writing a successful autobiography, *Somebody Up There Likes Me.* The quick-witted Graziano offered a sample of his humor during a television interview in recalling the time he floored Sugar: "After he knocked me down," he said, "Sugar Ray tripped over my body."

For a moment, after Graziano had walloped Sugar, fans of Ralph Ellison, whose *Invisible Man* had just been published to great acclaim, might have wondered if he was the lucky yokel of Ellison's imagination. "Once I saw a prizefighter boxing a yokel. The fighter was swift and amazingly scientific. His body was one violent flow of rapid rhythmic action. He hit the yokel a hundred times while the yokel held up his arms in stunned surprise. But suddenly the yokel, rolling about in the gale of boxing gloves, struck one blow and knocked science, speed and footwork as cold as a well-digger's posterior. The smart money hit the canvas. The long shot got the nod. The yokel had simply stepped inside of his opponent's sense of time."

CHAPTER 17

TAKE IT TO
THE MAXIM

To overcome the weight advantage of his next opponent, light heavyweight champion Joey Maxim, Sugar would have to step inside Maxim's "sense of time," solve the rhythm of his attack without losing his deft, scientific boxing skills. "Rhythm is everything in boxing," Sugar had once said. "Every move you make starts with your heart, and that's in rhythm or you're in trouble."

Nelson Mandela, who admits he was never an outstanding boxer, eschewing its violence, offered a similar analysis. "I did not enjoy the violence of boxing so much as the science of it," he wrote in his autobiography, *A Long Walk to Freedom*. "I was intrigued by how one moved one's body to protect oneself, how one used a strategy both to attack and retreat, how one paced oneself over a match. Boxing is egalitarian. In the ring, rank, age, color, and wealth are irrelevant." While one may not concur with the South African leader's conclusions about age, Sugar would probably have agreed with him on the subject of pacing, especially when he went up against the bigger and stronger Maxim. Maxim, however, would have another ally on that fateful evening at Yankee Stadium—the humidity. At ringside, the temperature would approach a torrid 105 degrees.

On the night of the fight, June 25, 1952, the rain was the first bad omen; then came the humidity. Perhaps most ominous of all was the fact that on the day before the fight, Sugar dreamed that he—not his opponent—was going to die. The stadium in which Sugar and Maxim were to fight was packed and, according to Edna Mae, "felt like a Turkish bath." Moreover, Sugar was not in the best frame of mind going into a fight with a man who outweighed him by more than fifteen pounds.

The early rounds belonged entirely to Sugar, as he danced around the slower Maxim, beating him to the punch, working his strategy to perfection. He was also expending an enormous amount of energy in the process. The sweltering heat was so overpowering that referee Ruby Goldstein had to quit during the fight and Ray Miller was brought in to replace him. Even the spectators were drenched in sweat. "The pants of some of the men were soaking, as if they had wet on themselves," recalled Carl Jefferson, a longtime Harlemite who was at the fight and sat in the right-field bleachers. "No matter where you sat, it was scorching hot." [1]

"Fighting out of a crouch, ignoring the weight handicap, Robinson blazed through eleven," *New York Times* sportswriter James Dawson reported. "He punched Maxim almost at will, with left jabs, lefts to the head and body. In the third, seventh, and eighth rounds, Robinson jolted Maxim's head and he kept up a two-fisted fire to the midsection."

By the eleventh round, with Sugar well ahead on points, the heat was taking its toll on the smaller, more mobile fighter. Maxim barely moved from the center of the ring, wisely conserving his energy. In the twelfth round Sugar jolted Maxim with a right to the jaw but could not take advantage of it, as the bell sounded. It would be his last significant punch. Sugar was on the verge of heat exhaustion by the thirteenth round, his limp body almost pushed through the ropes by one of Maxim's lesser attacks.

At one point Sugar fell to the floor after missing a sweeping right. He was too tired to be embarrassed. Clinging to the ropes at the end of the round, Sugar had to be dragged to his corner by his handlers. Ice packs and smelling salts failed to revive the exhausted fighter, and when Dr. Alexander Schiff leaped into the ring and asked him if he could go on, Sugar shook his head and said no. This was the first and only time Sugar would ever be stopped. And it took a day for him to recover from the heat, which had left him barely able to function, his eyes glazed over. Gainford thought a cold shower would help Sugar's condition, and with the assistance of the other handlers dragged Sugar to the shower. "One of the main reasons Maxim won that fight is because he used his weight advantage at every opportunity and he leaned on Sugar Ray," said Clint Edwards.

"Having a killing lead," the legendary Grantland Rice reported in the *Sunday Mirror,* "Sugar could have afforded to take things easier after the tenth round. But there is still the chance that the collapse hit suddenly. The heat wasn't all of it. Punching a much bigger man is a heavy burden. I recall at Toledo that many critics wondered why Jack Dempsey got so arm weary just before Jess Willard surrendered." [2]

The bout resembled the 1909 match between middleweight

champion Stanley Ketchel, "The Michigan Assassin," and heavyweight champion Jack Johnson. On that occasion, Ketchel was the smaller fighter, giving away more than thirty pounds to his opponent. For eleven rounds it was a rather polite fight, as they had agreed it would be. But in the twelfth round, Ketchel let loose a wallop that stunned Johnson, and he tumbled to the canvas. He picked himself up, glared at Ketchel, and within seconds landed a withering uppercut that dislodged five of Ketchel's teeth. It took an hour to revive him. As with Sugar and Maxim, a good big man had triumphed over a good little man.

"He didn't knock me out, did he?" was the first question a still dazed, half-conscious Sugar asked before the flood of cold water chilled his feverish body. "No," came a chorus of responses from his handlers and admirers. "It was the heat." But Sugar thought otherwise: "The heat didn't beat me, God did." [3] Political activist Ron Daniels, who boxed a bit himself before joining the civil rights movement, watched the fight at the New Granada Theater in Pittsburgh. "That was the first time I'd seen Sugar Ray fight, and he was sharp with precision punches, a pretty stylist that I tried to emulate later in my brief career in the ring. He had the fight won until he ran out of gas."

Sugar was totally dehydrated after the fight, his son recalled. "People don't know how near dying Dad was," he said. "His body was covered with blisters. He could not retain anything in his stomach for two days; and he was delirious and was not well for six months after the fight."

Given Sugar's state of mind and limp condition, the rules forbidding women in the dressing room were suspended and Edna Mae was allowed to enter. She immediately began to massage her husband and console him with soothing kisses. "Sugar was still groggy and was fighting anyone who came near him,"

Edna Mae said of the people milling about, wanting to get close to their hero. "Ray demanded that he not be taken to the hospital and I told him that we were taking him home to Riverdale. He was so thirsty and begged for more juice, but the doctor advised me not to give him more than a spoonful at a time. Sugar took two spoonfuls, then quickly took the large glass out of my hands and emptied it before he put it down. He immediately threw it up all over the bed. While the housekeeper hurriedly changed the bed, I took off my wet outfit. Sugar yelled, 'Honey, I forgot to tell you how beautiful your outfit was!'"

Sugar had a restless night, and Edna Mae's was not much better. The next morning she was alarmed to discover that Sugar's body was covered with fever blisters, which were the result of his boiling blood. Despite reports to the contrary in his autobiography, for several days Sugar was ill, unable to go anywhere, Edna Mae insisted. "The fight had been a sobering experience for Sugar," she wrote. "He later announced his retirement and was now ready to listen to some of the wonderful offers that were being waved in front of his face to try a career in show business. I thought with the right teachers Sugar could do anything."

Sugar announced to the press that he was going into show business because he had always loved to dance; he stopped short of saying he was retiring from the ring. Film footage of Sugar twisting and spinning attests to his nimble footwork, though he would be the first to admit he wasn't Fred Astaire or Bojangles, who had taught him a few nifty moves. An opportunity to strut his stuff before a national audience occurred on November 2, when he was invited to appear on *Toast of the Town*, which by 1955 would be renamed *The Ed Sullivan Show*. Sugar did his tap-dancing routine, applying some steps taught to him by Ray Bolger and Hal LeRoy, and this was perhaps a wise move, given that his singing was only mediocre. Singing would have been out of the question during this appearance, since he was sandwiched between the powerful voices of Frankie Laine, with his rendition of "Jezebel," and pianist/vocalist Alec Templeton, presenting arias from *Samson and Delilah*. Sugar's version of "Mr. Success" during one of his television appearances revealed his ability to at least carry a tune, although his high-pitched voice was rather ordinary and unappealing. The rousing applause at the end of the performance sounded as if it had been canned.

• • •

Later that year, on December 5, Sugar was hanging out with Roy Campanella and other celebrities, including popular cowboy movie actor Gabby Hayes, at the grand opening of Jackie Robinson's men's apparel store at 111 West 125th Street. During a confidential moment, Sugar warned Jackie about the challenge he faced selling men's apparel in Harlem. He particularly stressed how terrible Edna Mae's lingerie shop was doing, though his ever-popular café seemed to be doing reasonably well. [4]

CHAPTER 18

TOP HAT AND TAILS

$\mathcal{A}$ week before Christmas in 1952, following his loss to Joey Maxim, Sugar announced his retirement from the ring. But soon he got restless sitting around his Riverdale mansion with little to do but manage his various businesses, including real estate property and a number of demanding tenants. Finally, he conceded to the badgering of Joe Glaser, who sought to be his agent and to convince Sugar to put on dancing shoes, grab a jump rope, and skip across a stage in time to "Sweet Georgia Brown."

It was around this time, duded up in a tux, that Sugar made his debut at the French Casino, located inside the Hotel Paramount on 46th Street, just west of Broadway. "He's on and off, throughout the show," writes Robert Dana. "He dances, sings, and kids with customers such as Milton Berle." Sugar had put on a good act for the audience; in fact, he was feeling rather depressed following yet another blowout with Edna Mae. "But the audience, seeing Sugar in this new role, was ecstatic over him and overly generous in their cheers and applause," Edna Mae remembered. "We soon knew that the dancing (there was a chorus line of long-limbed lovelies imported from France) was exciting and good, but the dialogue was poor. It was as if it had been resurrected from a bad show in the days of burlesque. Not risqué, but not funny. I frankly was embarrassed."

Gradually, the show improved, though Sugar was adamantly opposed to any suggestion from Edna Mae or Joe Glaser, his agent, that his dance partner, Scotty, be removed. Meanwhile, Edna Mae began rehearsals for her part in an off-off-Broadway production of *Born Yesterday*. She had a starring role in this popular three-act comedy by Garson Kanin. The premiere was on December 30, 1953, at the President Theater on 48th Street and Broadway. Edna Mae portrayed Billie Dawn, who seems a stereotypical airhead but whose intelligence shines through in the end. Three years earlier, Judy Holliday had deservedly won an Oscar in the role, beating out Bette Davis in *All About Eve* and Gloria Swanson in *Sunset Boulevard*. Edna Mae was also featured in several national ad campaigns in which she endorsed all sorts of products, including In the Mood, a Mary King perfume created by the J. R. Watkins Company, whose goods were distributed in the black community and were akin to the Fuller Brush items in the white community.

Soon, Sugar and Edna Mae were moving along quite successfully with their shows, which minimized their contact. "Mine picked up interested backers, to the great joy of our company, but when Sugar was asked to allow me to continue with the show the answer was a final no," she related. "We had an excellent show and one young man with only nonspeaking roles later became the very fine actor Raymond St. Jacques. When the backers learned that I would not stay with the company, they withdrew their offers and the company was disbanded."

There was more trouble brewing. When Edna Mae returned home from the abbreviated theatrical run, she discovered a passel of expense sheets left by Sugar's valet. "I saw all the Mr. and Mrs. Ray Robinson suite statements," she lamented, realizing that while she had been busy trying to revive her career, her husband had been checking into hotels with other women posing as his wife.

These bills were clear evidence of his extramarital sexual encounters, which, to some extent, matched his general cachet with young African Americans. After demolishing Rocky Graziano, Sugar must have known how much his image and persona were affecting thousands of young black men. They were copying his style of dress, getting their hair processed, and hustling to own a Cadillac. Sugar's image would have been even more widely disseminated had plans to make a film of his life gone beyond the talking stage. Independent film producer Abner J. Greshler, taking his impetus from filmmaker Stirling Silliphant's announcement to make a movie of Joe Louis's life, contacted Sugar with an offer for a biopic, with Sugar playing himself. (Later, comedian Eddie Murphy would option Sugar's life, with the promise of a film that has yet to be done.) Silliphant was able to complete his project on Louis (though his greatest success was yet to come—his scripting of television shows such as *The Naked City* and *Route 66*), while Greshler's project fell by the wayside. [1]

Movie or not, at least one renowned musician had already appropriated some of Sugar's mannerisms—trumpeter Miles Davis, who in 1952 was deeply ensnared in a heroin habit. To get the monkey off his back, Davis turned to boxing, but with no intention to fight anything but his drug habit. Watching Sugar work out on 116th Street, Davis felt that the rigor of the training might help him both mentally and physically to overcome the demon. "I had already met Bobby McQuillen, who was a trainer at Gleason's Gym in midtown Manhattan," Davis recounted in his autobiography, written with Quincy Troupe. "When I'd go there he and I would sit around and talk about boxing. He'd been a top welterweight fighter until he killed a guy in the ring and then he quit and started coaching and training fighters . . . I asked him if he would train me. He said he would think about it."

When they next met McQuillen read the riot act to Davis, telling him he wanted nothing to do with anybody strung out on dope. The words hit Davis harder than a left hook from Sugar, and he made up his mind then and there to take McQuillen's advice and go back home to East St. Louis and kick the habit. It would take several months before Davis completely banished the junkie plague. When it was finally over he met Sugar and told him that he was responsible for his getting clean. "He just smiled and laughed," Davis said of the conversation.

Sugar's meeting with Davis would have been a perfect opportunity for him to discuss his love of jazz and his prowess on the drums. Since he was a teenager, Sugar had been playing the drums, often practicing on others' sets before purchasing his own. But he may have been intimidated by Davis's stature and renown, preferring to restrict his musical aspirations to local jam sessions among lesser musicians, or merely practicing alone, working on his timing and rhythm.

And musicians such as percussionist Max Roach understood, as Sugar did, the relationship between drumming and boxing. "I know quite a few boxers who make a point of having something to do with a percussion instrument," Roach told drummer Art Taylor. "Sugar Ray Robinson and Johnny Bratton both played the drums. Quite a few fighters got involved with music so they could develop the kind of coordination that was required. Dancing has a lot to do with good boxing, too, because it's very rhythmic." Many ring experts contend that if Sugar and Bratton had ever fought, it would have been as though they were fighting their reflections, so similar were their styles. [2]

Miles Davis and Sugar must have made a striking pair, each aware of his popularity and the singular position he held in American culture. Both were stylish dressers, and had a den of fine ladies they often abused. Each demanded the latest and finest in everything, including beautiful cars, though Sugar preferred colorful Cadillacs and Lincolns, while Davis leaned toward the luxurious foreign models. They were the personification of slick and sleek black urbanity in the 1950s and 1960s. Possessed of suave masculinity, with more than a dollop of hedonism, and endowed with ample supplies of magnetism, the two icons, a couple of American originals, were ever the target of the media. That both were able to rebound from setbacks—Davis got off heroin, and Sugar got off the canvas—may have enhanced their popularity. Yes, they were human after all, with weaknesses and foibles; even so, they were able to transcend these failings and return to the top of their respective craft. But it was the mastery of their chosen professions, the radiant hipness and a defiant cool they exuded that was probably the main source of the countless imitators dogging their every move.

Miles and Sugar never took to the stage as a duo, but Sugar's idol, Joe Louis, was attracting crowds to his comedy routine with Leonard Reed. While Sugar was mulling over the

idea of becoming an entertainer without a mouthpiece and boxing gloves, Louis and Reed were playing to standing-room-only
audiences at the Apollo in the spring of 1953. A highlight of
their routine was a mock boxing skit. Reed recalled: "He'd
knock me down two or three times, and the last time he
knocked me down, I just fell flat out. He said, 'Come on, get up.'
I said, 'Shit, you didn't get up when Marciano knocked *you*
down!' The people would just scream."

• • •

Sugar's foray into the realm of tux and tap was a bit more tenu-
ous, as was his financial security. "Sugar was plagued with business problems," Edna Mae observed. "The superintendent of
his buildings owned a dog that had bitten the man who was
delivering the oil to us one day and the man sued Sugar. The
dog had bitten him on Sugar's property. The oil man got a hefty
settlement. That hurt Sugar, but not as much as learning someone in his employ had assisted the plaintiff to help him win the
case. I found that very difficult to believe, but so many things
began to happen involving his employees against him that I
could no longer cope with the frustration of why his trusted
friends were forsaking him and I began to stay away from his
businesses as often as I could."

Edna Mae may have stepped back from the businesses, but
she got more involved in helping her beleaguered husband with
his theatrical pursuits. She volunteered to show Sugar a few
fancy steps and how to strut and spin across the stage.
Eventually she enlisted dancer Henry Le Tang as a tutor, and
the instructor had Sugar doing simple rhythmic steps on his
first visit to the studio. As Le Tang, whose instruction was
sometimes augmented by Pete Nugent, put Sugar through the

hoops, working on his movement and tempo, smoothing out the rough edges, Joe Glaser, his agent, was contacting clubs and talking to movers and shakers on the entertainment circuit.

"In the weeks before my debut . . . I trained harder than I ever had as a boxer," Sugar recalled. Le Tang repeatedly reminded Sugar that his legs must be as strong as they were in the ring. "I had to do roadwork every morning, five miles a day. In the afternoon, I was dancing, five hours a day. I'd do my routines over and over. Whenever I made a mistake, the piano would stop and Henry would glare at me. 'You must understand,' he liked to say, 'that you are telling a story with your feet.' " But it wasn't only his feet that had to do the talking— Sugar had to provide patter, tell a few jokes, and generally be a kind of a song-and-dance man: "I kept telling myself that it wouldn't be any different than the time I was a kid dancing for two dollars a night at the Alvin Theater." Le Tang worked him as hard as his boxing trainers had; he wanted to be sure Sugar had sufficient stamina to dance through the night if necessary. Of course, Sugar couldn't dedicate all his time to perfecting his routines; there were still businesses to run, as well as a wife and child with emotional needs.

"Our relationship had been lacking in the kind of close warm giving of ourselves, because of the demands of his new show business career," Edna Mae mildly complained. "It was all I could do to satisfy his ardor. I often looked up into the mirror on our ceiling at his beautiful long limbs and the motions of his strong sinewy muscles as they responded to his efforts to relieve himself of all his pent-up emotion. I slid my hands over the smooth surface of skin, feeling the moisture forming on his back, then closed my eyes and felt our souls take flight before our bodies calmed and relaxed. We lay there until the chill air caused him to reach for some cover to pull over us. He drew close to me, put his mouth against my ear, and attempted to talk. I pressed my fingers against his lips and refused to allow him to speak. I just kept him quiet until he dozed off. I did not want that tender exchange of our caring spoiled by his usual vows of fidelity. I knew the man was different from the champion. That night I'd been loved by the man."

Their relationship would reach a plateau on May 23, 1953, when they celebrated their tenth wedding anniversary. Among the hundreds of photos in Edna Mae's collection, none captures their bliss like those snapped by noted Harlem photographer Marvin Smith at their home and later at the café. Edna Mae is radiant as she plays the perfect hostess in a colorful dress, filling platters of food, pouring drinks, and attending to her son and husband without missing a beat. Sugar's silk shirt is almost iridescent, with a sheen to match his freshly processed, silky hair. He is the only one wearing dark sunglasses. Ray II is outfitted in short pants and a jacket, looking for all the world like the most well behaved of children, a veritable Little Lord Fauntleroy. Later, at the café, the party intensifies, and Edna Mae continues to make sure everybody is comfortable, their glasses brimming with drink. She is perpetually smiling and just as content as she was when Edward R. Murrow visited their home to televise one of his famous interviews, or as she appears in the life-size photo of her suspended above Sugar's desk in his office at the Enterprises. Sugar told Murrow that he never enjoyed fighting, that "it was just a business with me."

• • •

In the winter of 1954, Sugar, the Dominoes, and Count Basie were booked for a second appearance in Chicago. By

Christmas, Basie's band would be featuring vocalist Joe Williams and his glorious baritone, while the Dominoes answered request after request for their popular "Rags to Riches," with dynamic lead singer Jackie Wilson have replaced Clyde McPhatter. (Though this Jackie Wilson also boxed, he should not be confused with Sugar's old adversary and sparring partner.) This touring package was indicative of the musical mélange of the day, during which it wasn't unusual to find various styles coexisting. Amidst their run at the Chicago Theater, they agreed to do a one-night stand at the DuSable High School auditorium. "A total of not more than five hundred people saw the two shows that night," an article in the April issue of *Ebony* magazine reported, "and those who had come to the second show, scheduled for 10:30 P.M., had to wait until almost midnight before Sugar would go on. He zipped through a mediocre performance, insulted an influential Negro disc jockey, ignored a talented nine-year-old dancer who had appeared in the first show and stayed costumed until after 1 A.M. with the understanding that he was to appear on Sugar's second show. The handful of stalwarts who stayed until the end left Sugar's show firmly resolved never to see him again."

Sugar's being so peripatetic didn't stop Edna Mae from having her share of joy, and her sense of fulfillment continued right on into the new year. Meanwhile, Sugar took his act overseas. He played a few clubs on the Riviera in preparation for a more critical performance in Paris. Jazz pianist/singer Bob Dorough was Sugar's musical director for the tour. They had met in Henry Le Tang's Times Square tap dance studio, where Dorough was making three dollars a class as an accompanist. One day, Le Tang said, "I've got a five-dollar gig for you," Dorough recalled. He welcomed the opportunity. Le Tang introduced him to Sugar, who was just beginning to put his act together. When Le Tang said "play 'Green Eyes' for Sugar Ray," Dorough said he knew exactly what to do. Afterward, wiping his brow, Robinson said: "You're going on the road with us." To Dorough it was a command.

The revue was billed as "The Champ." They sailed over in first class, doing their act en route (singing for their supper, as it were) on the *Ile de France*. "We bombed in Paris . . . Larry Adler (the harmonica player) stole the show," Dorough said. Film clips of Sugar in Paris show him wearing a vest emblazoned with "Le Tang Dancers," and he demonstrates his tapping ability to what may be Dorough's piano accompaniment while a chorus line of cancan dancers, their skirts raised, look on adoringly. (When Sugar and his retinue sailed back, second class, Dorough stayed in Paris to work at the Mars Club for the French franc equivalent of $11.65 a night. It went a long way in Paris in the 1950s. He recalled: "I was in pig heaven." Dorough would later work with Miles Davis and comedian Lenny Bruce.) Only when Sugar relented and put his rope-skipping routine back in his act did he connect with his audience. Arrayed in his boxing trunks, to an up-tempo musical beat, Sugar skipped effortlessly underneath the turning rope. It reminded him of his training days—it reminded him too much.

Soon, there were discussions with Edna Mae about returning to the ring. The gushing articles that had tapped him as a bright new star on the entertainment circuit were no longer in the daily newspapers. The laudatory columns had vanished almost as fast as the one hundred thousand dollars he'd made during his first year as a song-and-dance man. Though the money was earned with less risk to his health, it didn't compare with the same amount he could once make for a mere hour or less in the ring. Like so many ex-athletes who try to parlay their popularity from sports to entertainment, Sugar did well at first, but audiences began to demand more and there was very little more to deliver after a few jokes and a dance routine. Also, and more damaging, Sugar's short temper and sometimes demanding negotiating practices turned off many promoters and producers. Apparently he never gave more than a passing thought to the idea of teaming up with Edna Mae or with his sister, Evelyn, with whom he had won several lindy-hopping contests at the Savoy Ballroom.

With the need for money becoming increasingly acute, he decided that the ring was the only sure bet of a big payday. Edna Mae strenuously objected, believing he would risk serious injury. But it was either risk getting your head bashed in or getting knocked for a further loop in his business investments, which were steadily declining. Both Sugar and spouse agreed there was only one option—back to the ring of resources where he was lord.

When the money was plenty, Sugar had, as Billie Holiday sang, "lots of friends," and a lot of desperate Harlemites in need of a helping hand, lest they fall victim to hunger, eviction, or something worse. Sugar was always a soft touch, ready to open the safe and give whatever was needed to get the landlord off the back of an elderly lady or to rescue a mother with a brood of kids on their way to the poorhouse. Doling out sizable sums was no sweat for him at a time when Dun & Bradstreet had valued his businesses at three hundred thousand dollars. Before the excursion to Europe he was under the impression he was pretty solvent, but the urgent message he received there to return home told a different story. He checked his books to discover that two hundred and fifty thousand dollars had disappeared.

"I was threatened with foreclosures on my mortgages," he told sportswriter Dave Anderson. "My taxes were unpaid. My stock portfolio was virtually worthless." The man who had done so much to relieve others was now perilously close to needing help himself. "You see, Sugar Ray was not the most astute businessman," said Langley Waller, who processed posters and placards for Sugar Ray Enterprises, "but he was nobody's fool either. It was the people around him who made a mess of things. They got him in trouble. He told me one time that it was hard for a young person with a lot of money to manage it well. He was doing all right, but he had a lot of scumbags around him who were eager to rip him off, and they did."

Glaser had provided Sugar with some lucrative dates as a dancer and promised more, but it was not enough to defray the accumulated debts. He told Edna Mae that he could make more money in one fight than what he earned in a whole year of dancing on stage. "After bragging about how I was going to end up differently than Joe Louis . . . ," he said, "I couldn't swallow my pride and admit it"—that, unfortunately, he hadn't.

CHAPTER 19

RETURN TO
THE RING

Without too much fanfare, Sugar eased out of retirement and back into the ring with a six-round exhibition fight against Gene Burton, his stablemate, one bone-chilling night in Hamilton, Ontario, on November 29, 1954. Burton was no match for Sugar. Nor would Joe Rindone present any real opposition as a new year dawned. Sugar called Rindone the "ugliest guy I ever fought," and he dispatched him in the sixth round with a booming left-right combination, thereby avoiding any further clinching with the mauling, flat-nosed, hairy-chested ex-Marine from Roxbury, Massachusetts. So overwhelmingly loud was the crowd of nearly twelve thousand at Detroit's Olympia Stadium that Sugar never heard the count.

It had been a while since Sugar had performed in Detroit, where the boxing cognoscenti included Emanuel Steward, a promising bantamweight and future trainer; vocalist Jackie

Wilson, once a Golden Gloves champion in the city and at that time lead singer with the Dominoes; and Berry Gordy, who'd boxed on the undercard of a Joe Louis bout as a featherweight in 1950 but was now dreaming of owning his own record company. "Friends drove us over to Canada, where Sugar had been invited to be a guest at the ice hockey match," Edna Mae remembered. "He was introduced and cheered enthusiastically by the crowd . . . he was given a hockey stick and a puck by the team's captain. This was what Sugar missed—being loved by the crowd."

Still, Sugar was not exactly pleased with his performances against Burton and Rindone. There was evident rust that needed to be brushed away, and not until Joe Glaser told him everything was going to be all right, that he was making progress, was Sugar reasonably assured. "He had been in retirement for a couple of years, and in boxing it takes a while to get your timing back," said the Reverend Dino Woodard, who had joined Sugar's stable of sparring partners during the early days of his comeback. "I was brought into Sugar Ray's camp by Harry Wiley, his trainer, who was also my manager. I was there to help Sugar prepare for his fights against Gene Fullmer, Carmen Basilio, and others. I never feared him while I was sparring with him and getting him ready, but I was aware that I was in the ring with one of the greatest fighters of all time. My job was to get him ready, make him miss, make him learn from his mistakes . . . Sugar hired other sparring partners from time to time, but during the last years of his career I was the main one."

Woodard's main objective was to imitate Fullmer, Basilio, or whomever, to mimic their style. "I like to think I helped him in his victory over Fullmer, when he delivered that left hook that put Fullmer to sleep. There were times when we were sparring when we would really tear into each other, when Sugar wouldn't pull his punches and I would try to stay right with him. These moments only made him better, more confident when the real deal went down."

Toward the end of 1954, however, rather than approximating the styles of Fullmer and Basilio, Woodard should have been giving Sugar a better facsimile of Ralph "Tiger" Jones. On January 19, 1955, in Chicago, two weeks after Sugar came out of retirement with the victory over Rindone, Jones was every bit his nickname as he ripped into Sugar with a savage attack. Almost from the opening bell, Sugar knew he was in over his head, and he barely remained on his feet. (A premonition of the defeat to Jones had come in a remark made by Sugar's six-year-old son, Ray II. "We were dining one day in Chicago," Edna Mae recalled, "when a sportswriter asked Ray, Jr., who would win the fight between his dad and Tiger Jones. Our son answered 'Tiger Jones' as seriously as he could. We were stunned, and equally happy that Sugar was out of earshot. What a prophecy!")

Respected sports columnists Arthur Daley and Jimmy Cannon wrote blistering commentaries on Sugar's performance. He was not the Robinson of old, but an *old* Robinson, Daley summarized. Cannon said that Sugar could not face the truth of his new situation. "He was marvelous, but he isn't anymore," he wrote. "That's no disgrace, either. The years did it to him, and not Tiger Jones, but the records don't include such information." Even his cornermen were disappointed in Sugar's performance against Jones, and both Gainford and Wiley walked out on him, telling him he should retire. But Sugar got the last word: "Gainford and Wiley weren't walking out on me," Sugar asserted. "They were walking out on my money. All these years, they had lived off me, lived high, lived like millionaires, but now they thought that there wasn't going to be any more money. They were deserting the sinking ship. And right there, I vowed that the ship wasn't going to sink. I vowed to prove that I wasn't through, to pursue my comeback, to show Gainford and Wiley, to show everybody."

It took weeks before Sugar was able to fan away the funk over his defeat by Tiger Jones and the "desertions" of Gainford and Wiley. But through Edna Mae's ministrations and counseling, he finally agreed to allow them to return as he prepared for a March 29 bout against Johnny Lombardo in Cincinnati. Once again Sugar's performance was lackluster, as he narrowly edged Lombardo in a split decision. He possessed neither his normal quickness nor the crisp punches that had once overwhelmed opponents. And once again his handlers and manager were dismayed, and all the more determined to convince Sugar to call off his comeback. But Sugar was already slated for another match, with Ted Olla on April 14 in Milwaukee.

A short walk and talk with Edna Mae around this time proved to be a revelation. "You don't look like you used to, Edna Mae told me," Sugar recalled. "You look like you're trying to knock out everybody. You're so anxious to fight again, you just want to show everybody how great you once were by knocking out all of your opponents. But that's not how you were great. You're not using the bag of tricks that made you great. That was your gift, the tricks were what God blessed you with—the tricks, the science. You don't use that anymore. You don't look like *the* Ray Robinson anymore." Edna Mae also provided spiritual nourishment to her troubled husband, praying with him and reading him passages from the Bible.

Reading from Proverbs and Psalms had their healing

effects, but Edna Mae didn't rely on them exclusively. "He could not sleep without pills to induce it, and I dreaded any kind of artificial assistance to gain normal emotions or activity. I'd seen other athletes go under because of such dosage. I'd try sexy or funny 'show time' routines for him in our bedroom. That always would break the spell of gloom. He loved to see me dance and loved looking at me unclothed," she wrote.

It was about this time that Sugar pledged his undying, everlasting love for Edna Mae. "We have been married eleven years now, and believe me, this is one marriage that is going to stick," he told a writer for *Tan* magazine. "It is so easy for persons in the sports or entertainment world to drift apart for one reason or another, but that is not going to be the case with us. We are married to each other for *life* and nothing is going to pull us apart." [1] Indeed, *nothing* didn't pull them apart; it was *something*.

• • •

Soon another source of solace and inspiration entered their lives. On the train trip to Milwaukee, Sugar and Edna Mae had met a Franciscan priest who was sharing a breakfast table with them. The priest was such a warm and endearing person that Sugar invited him to come by the hotel before the fight, if he had a chance. Father Lang accepted the invitation and showed up hours before the fight, and prayed with Sugar and Edna Mae. Sugar's lightning-fast jabs, his renewed focus on using his "tricks," and Father Lang's good wishes were too deadly a combination for the overmatched Olla, who crumbled under a barrage of blows in the third round. At ringside was Joe Louis, who was the first to hug and congratulate Sugar.

It appeared as if the Sugar of old, newly refined, had

returned. In Detroit, Garth Panter, living up to his surname, could hardly catch his breath toward the end of the fight, as Sugar bested him in ten rounds. This was quite a birthday present—Sugar had turned thirty-four on May 3, a day before the fight. To toast the victory and his birthday in a city he was fond of, he held a celebration, to which he invited his father, who was the life of the impromptu party. "You know where Junior got his punch?" his father told Gainford, who had returned to the fold. "From me. When I was working my farm in Georgia before I came to Detroit, I had a big ole mule I used to ride around. One day we were out in the fields and that mule didn't want to go back to the barn. Didn't want to budge. I balled up my fist and hit him between the eyes, and that mule went to his knees. When he got up, he knew who was the boss. He trotted right back to the barn. And that's where Junior got his punch."

Partying with his friends and his father was great fun, but there was more ground to cover in his march toward the championship, and none of it rougher and tougher than the upcoming bout against Rocky Castellani. San Francisco was the site of the fight, and the city was enduring an unseasonably cold spell, so much so that at the end of July a pregnant Edna Mae called home and had a fur piece flown to her. It was a particularly difficult pregnancy, and one day she experienced severe pain and had to be rushed to the hospital. Sugar insisted on remaining at his wife's bedside, even if it meant canceling the fight. Eventually, however, she convinced him to leave and go on with the bout. Sugar did, and won in a unanimous ten-round decision.

He salvaged the victory, but Edna Mae's pregnancy could not be saved. "When Sugar did not want to leave me to go to fight Castellani," she wrote in her memoir, "I assured him that I

felt great, but we did not let him know until after the fight . . .
that we'd lost the baby."

It wasn't the first baby she had lost, nor would it be the last.
"I think one of the reasons my mother had so many miscarriages was because of the abuse she suffered from my father,"
Ray II said. "I can recall him hitting her on several occasions,
often for no reason at all."

• • •

Sugar was soon skipping rope and wearing out punching bags
at Greenwood Lake, getting ready for Bobo Olson, the current
middleweight titleholder. He had his own camp at the lake now
and didn't have to depend on working out at Joe Louis's; he
also had his own special visitors, including Langston Hughes,
who admired Sugar. (Although the writer's stays would be limited nowadays, since he was virtually secluded in his 127th
Street residence, revising a memoir and collaborating with
Milton Meltzer on a pictorial history of black Americans.
"Nicest thing about going away," Hughes said in a letter to his
alter ego, Arna Bontemps, "is to get back to Harlem again.")[2]

Meanwhile Edna Mae had recovered from the miscarriage
and was back to her normal routine of taking care of Sugar's
demands. Her disciplined approach to things rubbed off on him
just when he needed it. She was as unflinching and steadfast as
ever, not only whispering words of encouragement and cooking
the steaks that Sugar craved days before a fight, but also, once he
finished up at Greenwood Lake, taking over the duties of two
parents in raising their son. "I had to teach our son sports,
because Sugar had no time for this sort of parenting," she
explained, "and though Sugar loved his son passionately, he had
never enjoyed a close relationship with his own father, who just

could not share himself with his son. He thought sincerely it was the mother's duty. Hadn't his mother done it? So after I taught Ray II how to run track, I tackled baseball, until he broke two large bay windows in our home. But he was superb doing it."

When asked if she would want her son to follow in his father's footsteps as a boxer, Edna Mae wrote a lengthy reply for publication: "I certainly would not. The champion seems to lead such a glamorous and beautiful life, with so much financial security, but the anxiety and heartaches which beset his wife are difficult to describe. Half of everything that is beautiful is missed by the fighter. Once he reaches the top, he meets too much temptation. Since he has the necessary money for pleasure, he seeks it in a driving, eager manner to compensate for the years of work and punishment he has received in the ring. It really isn't fun. I wouldn't want to inflict the cruel things that go with professional fighting on my son." [3]

On the same topic, Sugar, too, told a reporter in London that he would not like to see his son follow in his footsteps. "I would try to dissuade him. There are too many risks in the game, unless you've really got what it takes to take them." [4]

• • •

With his training in place, Sugar could envision being seen as a top-notch contender against Bobo Olson, even if he was not as sharp as he wanted to be. When he and his entourage arrived in Chicago, it was a crisp, windy December 9, 1955. There was even a slight chill in the arena as Sugar and Olson paced nervously about the ring, waiting to be announced.

The peal of the bell starting the fight was still resonating above the crowd's roar when an unusually aggressive Sugar stunned Olson. Having such an early opportunity to finish off an opponent almost caught Sugar by surprise, but the opening was too good to ignore. "I planned to box him and take potshots at him at every opportunity," he told a reporter from *Ring* right after the fight. "I knew I could hurt him, because he had difficulty making weight, but he made it easy for me by altering his style." A right uppercut set Olson up for a finishing left hook. He tried to stand at the count of eight, but it was to no avail. Sugar had regained the middleweight championship, holding it for the third time. And as he watched Gainford, Wiley, and the others leap around in joy, he felt a special jolt of satisfaction, and wished he could have screamed out loud to them, "I told you so."

As ever, except for the disastrous thumping he'd taken from Tiger Jones, Sugar had conquered the Windy City. "Emotionally, I collapsed," Sugar said after the fight. "I was sobbing so much that my body shook. I felt the tears rolling down my face. They were tears of happiness but also tears of anger. They were tears of pride but also tears of revenge. Wrapping a towel around my face, George led me out of the ring. I let him do it, even though I had really wanted to walk out of that ring alone, the same way I had made my comeback."

Even the grim shadow of the Internal Revenue Service could not dampen the extreme exhilaration he derived from the moment. With his businesses in a steady decline and employees embezzling money from his various operations, Sugar had trouble paying his taxes. As a result, the IRS put a lien on his earnings for eighty-one thousand dollars. Still, as he had proven in his fight against Olson, he was back on top, and the IRS was not going to rob him of the pleasure of being the champ again. He missed and needed the adoration of fans, many of whom crowded around him, wanting his autograph, wanting to touch their idol, wanting to smother him with affection. He was back in the spotlight he adored and that adored him. So brilliant was his iconic glow that it radiated all up and down the train that carried him back to New York City. So powerful and engaging was his celebrity that rather than speeding into Grand Central Station, the train made an unscheduled stop at 125th Street to allow Harlem's hero to be closer to his office.

A victorious Sugar was swamped with requests—for personal appearances, award ceremonies, luncheons, photo sessions, interviews—and a desk overflowing with business matters begging for his attention. Among the television appearances that brought him national exposure was his appearance for the second time as a mystery guest on CBS's *What's My Line.* Dressed nattily in formal wear, Sugar signed his name to the blackboard with his usual flair and answered the questions put to him in a fairly fluent French as a way to avoid detection. But it didn't take comedian Jack E. Leonard long to identify him, after his colleagues had chipped away at the disguise with their queries; plus, Sugar's high-pitched voice gave Leonard a tonal clue. (But the national exposure didn't always work in Sugar's favor. During the mid-fifties, Sugar was also a frequent guest on *The Ed Sullivan Show,* or he would sit in the audience, where on one occasion he was introduced and asked by Sullivan to stand with his wife; Sullivan was informed later that the woman with Sugar had not been Edna Mae.)

Still, a few hundred dollars from guest spots on television variety shows was a long way from the bundle of money he needed to square things with the IRS; moreover, electrical, plumbing, and personnel expenses had accumulated in his multiple businesses. Then there were Edna Mae and his son. Suddenly, there was not enough money to sustain his household and businesses, nor enough hours in the day or night for him to relax. Even his habits of carousing and gambling had to be put on hold while he tried to bring order to the chaos of his life.

But a fighter is a fighter, and so Sugar entrusted others with handling the mundane affairs—he had to get ready for a return match with Olson in May. He thought his record, especially his conquest of Olson and the regaining of his middleweight belt, warranted the Fighter of the Year Award for 1955, but it went to Carmen Basilio. Basilio? Sugar made a mental note of this emerging contender as he wore out the bags, the road, and sparring partners at the lake. Maybe in the future.

In the meantime he had to prepare for his rematch with Olson. "It was to be fought in Los Angeles," Edna Mae wrote of the planned encounter, slated for Friday, May 18, 1956. In Los Angeles Sugar had engaged Gilman's Training Camp in San Jacinto, on the edge of the California desert. Edna Mae stayed in Los Angeles until two weeks before the fight, when her presence was requested by Gainford to release some of the Sugar's tension. Specifically, she was to have a conjugal visit with her husband. "One of the big sacrifices in being a champion is sex," Sugar related. "If you're a fighter you need your energy. You can't leave it with a woman, even if she's your wife." Ordinarily, Sugar would abstain from sex six weeks before a fight, and if he hit his peak early, a "break" would be necessary; then, a few days before the fight, the peak would be reached again. Sugar welcomed the opportunity, and so did Edna Mae. [5]

Sexual abstention was the boxer's first commandment, and it wasn't until three years later, in 1959, that enforced chastity was soundly banished. Author Roger Kahn said that he heard this rule spouted for years in boxing camps, where women were considered taboo. Then, in 1959, Ingemar Johansson of

Sweden arrived to challenge Floyd Patterson for the heavy-weight title, accompanied by a lissome blonde, Birgit Lundgren. "After taking steady body punches and losing the first two rounds, Johansson suddenly threw what he called 'Toonder,' his overhand right. The wallop landed squarely between Patterson's eyes. Six knockdowns later Johansson had become champion." [6] Johansson's "Toonder" dispatched Patterson and put sexual abstention forever on ice.

Harry Wiley, Sugar's trainer, when asked about sex and the boxer told this story about Sonny Liston's sex drive and what he did to curb it: "Liston used to take his sex drive out on opponents. I heard they told Liston that Lena Horne would see him if he whipped (Floyd) Patterson . . . He slaughtered Patterson in the first round in both fights . . . They used to tease Liston, telling him that a beautiful woman was out there waiting for him, but if he wouldn't knock his opponent out by the third round she wouldn't see him. Then they'd set a woman at ringside, and at the end of the second round she'd get up and walk down the aisle and they'd whisper to Liston, 'Well, there you go. You lost your chance.' Liston would hurry to get the fight over."

As for Sugar, Wiley said he never had any trouble with him on this matter. "At his peak, Sugar Ray was the best-disciplined fighter in the trade. He valued his looks too much to take a chance getting hurt in the ring. When it came time for him to stop, his willpower was like iron. He could sleep next to Venus without touching her." [7]

There's an incident in Ali's autobiography related by Bundini Brown, who was a trainer with Sugar before he joined Ali's team. He writes about his sleeping with "a champ" who is the best fighter in the world, "pound for pound." "I was green," Bundini said. "First time I'd been with a champ. No woman ever told me to get in bed with her husband before, and I didn't know what to make of it. 'Just lie in bed with him,' she says . . . He's lying there in the bed and I get in and lie next to him, and he cuddles up with my arms around him and goes to sleep. And the wife peeks in the door and sees me with my arms around her husband and says, 'That's good.'" By all indications, the man Bundini is cuddling is Sugar. [8]

· · ·

As smooth as things were progressing with his comeback, Sugar was not happy with the business side of things. A dispute had arisen over the allotment of ringside seats Sugar had been promised for the Olson fight. Sugar had requested five hundred seats but received only two hundred fifty, with just ten ringside seats in the package. This snub came on top of a previous disagreement Sugar had had with the promoters of the fight—the IBC (International Boxing Club)—and the Hollywood Legion Stadium group. Sugar was furious with Truman Gibson, the IBC secretary, and with his friend, Joe Louis, who was acting as a functionary for Jim Norris, the IBC's honcho, for attempting to pressure him into fighting Olson in Miami. Ernie Braca, one of Sugar's managers, said that the Robinson team would not cooperate in any future fights with the IBC. "I suppose the IBC would like to see us lose the title," Braca told reporters. "If they think we're hard to get along with now, wait until after we win this fight. Then, we'll really be hard to get along with." He said: "We owe the IBC the return match with Olson. But we'll take command when this obligation is paid. We'll have no tie with the IBC, and we'll fight where, when, and for whom we please."

Sugar's gripe with the IBC can be traced back to 1949, just two years after the organization was established. Ironically, Joe

Louis, Sugar's lifetime friend, was a key player in the formation of the IBC, receiving $150,000 in cash for facilitating exclusive promotion rights to such prominent heavyweight fighters as Ezzard Charles, Jersey Joe Walcott, and Lee Savold. Thus empowered, the IBC bought exclusive leases to Yankee Stadium, and St. Nicholas Arena, as well as Sugar's contract, which until then was held by Mike Jacobs. "This virtually assured IBC control of nearly half of all championship boxing in the United States," noted Jeffrey Sammons, a boxing historian. "For example, from 1937 to 1949, 45 percent of all championship bouts were held in Yankee Stadium, the Polo Grounds, or St. Nicholas Arena. No wonder the IBC became known as the 'Octopus.'" [9]

And a tentacle of this "octopus" choked Sugar's chances at a middleweight championship bout in the mid-1940s, after he had held the welterweight title for three years and wanted to move up to the next weight division. Because he refused to cooperate with the IBC and its mobster connections, Sugar was often bypassed; and none of the snubs was more hurtful than when the IBC offered LaMotta a championship shot, even though Sugar had beaten him four out of five matches. Not until their sixth and final fight in 1951 was Sugar given an opportunity to beat LaMotta for the belt. Now, with the IBC denying Sugar the seats he had been promised, his ire was refueled.

"The bout was held in broad daylight (to make up for the three-hour time difference on the East Coast) in Los Angeles at Wrigley Field," Edna Mae wrote, "and the crowd was loud and enormous. Both boxers were very cautious at the beginning. Olson constantly clinched with Ray, more like a wrestler than a fighter. We wondered why the referee, Mushy Callahan, didn't break them apart and caution them to move and fight. Sugar had said that he'd observed previously that Olson would drop his right arm when he delivered a good punch with his right hand. In two minutes and fifty-one seconds of the fourth round Olson did just that, and faster than lightning, Sugar delivered a punch with his left hand to Olson's right jaw that must have made him see stars as he sagged to the canvas like a bag of cement. The roar of the crowd was music to my ears." And the roar of twenty thousand fans was in sharp contrast to the boos that had greeted the fighters for the first three rounds. It was the fourth and final time Olson lost to Sugar.

There was also the sound of cash registers, as the two fighters raked in more than six figures apiece, including what they racked up in television rights for a fight beamed across the nation. The IRS stepped in immediately and snatched the bulk of Sugar's $150,000 purse—nearly $90,000—while Olson's estranged wife, Helen, got most of his. The lien against Sugar stemmed from an accumulation of taxes and penalties dating from the years 1944 through 1949, plus 1953. [10] But Sugar wasn't thinking about the money yet—he was still too busy savoring the victory and criticizing his performance. "I didn't get a chance to test my legs, because the fight didn't go long enough," Sugar told reporters outside his dressing room. "I was hit well in the body in the third round, and that punch was Bobo's ruination. Why? Because I then encouraged him to open up. After he hit me in the body, I lagged my left, and that gave him confidence. He got brave and came on in the fourth, and when he started to punch the body again, I hit him flush on the jaw with the left. It was hard, but I wasn't sure I had him until the count reached ten." [11]

"I guess he's just got a jinx on me," a battered Olson told reporters, slumping on his bench the same way he did the summer before after Archie Moore knocked him senseless. It had been another boo-boo by Bobo.

According to an article by the famed columnist Louella Parsons, motion picture editor for the International News Service, there was a phone call from Frank Sinatra, then in Madrid making *The Pride and the Passion,* to Sugar that in her estimation "clinched the deal for Frank to make the prize-fighter's life story." Sugar, who had always yearned to be an actor, would play himself in the film, Parsons continued. "Frank will produce it as one of his independent pictures," she wrote. She said the picture would be made that winter "while Sugar is between fights and Frank has some free time." The two never got around to making the biopic, but they did share the screen in a couple of other productions, including *The Detective,* in which Sugar had a small part as a police officer. Sinatra often said that Sugar was the best fighter he had ever seen.

CHAPTER 20

THE PERFECT PUNCH

Sugar and Edna Mae returned to Harlem, and the fans smothered them with praise and adoration, as ever. The café was jammed each night with well-wishers, all of them looking for a chance to toast and touch the champ. But behind Sugar's radiant smile was the memory of the purse-snatching by the IRS; he needed another title bout—or something that would bring in money. That "something" came within a few days, when the dancer/actor Gene Kelly called him to appear on his TV show. "I was delighted, and asked Ray to please accept it," Edna Mae related. "He went down to his office in Harlem to talk privately with Mr. Kelly. Sugar asked for so much money that Mr. Kelly decided he could manage without him."

Edna Mae was furious that Sugar had priced himself out of an opportunity to show his versatility and to appear with one of the greatest dancers in the country. She sprang to action to see what could be done to repair the situation. After she talked to both Kelly and Sugar, a lower price was agreed on. "I rehearsed him at home, showed him some great stage tricks that charm and delight audiences. Sugar remembered them all and nearly stole the show; he was sensational. Mr. Kelly called me and thanked me for helping him. I truly was helping my champion. We needed Mr. Kelly, not vice versa."

• • •

Another Gene was on Sugar's agenda for January 2, 1957, at the Garden: Gene Fullmer. Fullmer, a stocky Mormon from Utah, was a thick-necked battler who didn't know the meaning of retreat. The fight had originally been scheduled for sometime in December, but Sugar had developed a virus. The Fullmer camp saw it as just another instance of Sugar's delaying tactics.

When the match finally got under way, Edna Mae, as usual, had a ringside seat. "Ray appeared to lose stamina in the later rounds as Fullmer never stopped holding on so closely that it was impossible for Sugar to deliver effective blows. He'd hug and then punch Ray all over his head and shoulders. Fans were screaming and shouting at the referee (Ruby Goldstein) to break them apart, but he never did. In the last round Sugar came out looking so calm and in control that we began to hope that Sugar had won. We were wrong."

Roscoe Bennett, a sportswriter for the *Grand Rapids Press*, captured the feelings of those who believed that Goldstein had mishandled the bout by allowing Fullmer to get away with so many illegal punches. "They point to the rabbit punches, the wild flailings to the back of the head and the neck, and the persistent clinching that the brawl was one of the most disappointing of the season. Boxing rules decree that only punches to the front and side of the body are legitimate blows. Fullmer landed more punches to Sugar Ray's back than he did to the front and side of the body, two to one." [1]

"That night I was in the ring but *Ray Robinson* wasn't," Sugar lamented after losing his middleweight belt to Fullmer. He said that he was thrown off his game by Fullmer's bullying style, which bore all the trademarks of that of a barroom brawler. "I even let him get me against the ropes, something I seldom did . . . One of the ropes even broke, and I almost fell out of the ring. It wasn't my night." Though Sugar lost the fifteen-round decision, the IRS at least let him hang on to the $140,000 purse, $50,000 of which was personally his. After expenses, it would be more than enough to set aside for a few weeks of fun with his new lover from California, a woman whose presence would threaten his marriage.

Edna Mae was wise to Sugar's new affair. "I don't know if she knew that she wasn't the only one that I shared him with," she asserted, "but somehow those women seldom rocked the boat." This woman, however, seemed to be different.

Even Ray II witnessed his father's indiscretions. "My father would take me with him to various places where he hung out," he remembered. "When he wasn't in training he spent a lot of time with other civic leaders and businessmen such as Joseph Wells; Ed Smalls, who owned Smalls' Paradise; Red Randolph, owner of the Shalimar, just across the street from Dad's businesses; and underworld types like Bumpy Johnson. Sometimes he would drop me off with Bundini (Brown) at the Apollo or leave me in the lobby of the Theresa Hotel when Charlie Rangel was the desk clerk, while he went out and checked his 'traps,' his various female partners."

There had been so many dalliances, Edna Mae confessed, that after a while she became inured, feeling that they came with the territory, were simply a hazard of his celebrity. "There were so many of them and just one me," she said. "He always changed them. Of course, they had fun and enjoyed the good times and none of the bad, but somehow Sugar always tired of them and came home. I now changed my tactics. I really gave him lots of space."

And Sugar would need all the space he could get as he prepared for a title rematch with the bull-like Fullmer, scheduled for that spring in Chicago, several months after their first encounter at the Garden in January. The oddsmakers had Fullmer at three to one to retain his championship over the aging Sugar, who would turn thirty-six two days after the May 1 bout. The majority of sportswriters agreed that Sugar was five years past his prime and on his way to a slaughter.

Edna Mae was of a similar mind, and perhaps that is why she doubled her prayer sessions with Father Lang, with whom she had stayed in touch, and even added another minister to the fold to ensure that her prayers were answered. When she wasn't praying she was attending to Ray II, who had come down with chicken pox, which meant he had to be quarantined and kept away from his father. This had to be accomplished along with her usual duties, particularly her task of preparing Sugar's meals. On the night of the fight, Edna Mae showed up at the arena with her hair dyed freshly blonde, and assumed her ringside seat in plain view of her husband's corner. If Sugar noticed her new hairstyle, he never registered it—Fullmer had his full attention, and he knew it would take the full arsenal of his skills and concentration to defeat the mauler.

• • •

Fullmer took the first three rounds, but Sugar rallied in the fourth. In the fifth round, Fullmer advanced across the ring with his right hand to his chest, like Boris Karloff as The Mummy. Sugar sensed the opening he had been looking for. Without hesitation he set his feet, stepped a bit to the side, and aimed a left hook to Fullmer's exposed jaw. It was a perfect punch from a nearly flawless fighter, and Fullmer never knew what hit him. "I don't know anything about that punch," Fullmer told reporters later, "except I watched it on movies a couple of times."

Edna Mae remembered much better: "He astonished that crowd of fourteen thousand, seven hundred and fifty-seven spectators by knocking out Fullmer in one minute and twenty-seven seconds of the fifth round . . . After the referee had completed the count, Fullmer struggled to rise but needed the referee's help. He said later that he did not remember hearing the count. Also he said that he could not remember ever being hit harder." Seated near Edna Mae was Joe Louis, and the two of them rejoiced in the victory.

Sugar was so elated that he effusively thanked everybody who had ever believed in him, thanking them for their prayers and for keeping their faith in him. Special kudos were expressed for Father Lang and Edna Mae, and he rewarded his platinum blonde wife with a beautiful white mink stole, which she added to a collection of expensive fur coats that was constantly growing larger, despite their problems with the IRS and the decline in the profitability of their businesses. The Fullmer victory only whetted the appetite of boxing fans, who now hungered for a match between Sugar and the former onion farmer Carmen Basilio, then a leading contender.

Sugar, his face unmarked, was given a passel of telegrams from his fans after stopping Fullmer, but the most significant papers in his hands were the two checks he received—one for $37,479 from the gate receipts, one for $30,000 for the television rights. Fullmer received equal payments. If it's true that money breeds more money, Sugar's stash proved it, because soon offers were pouring in for him to make even more on future bouts. Despite their differences, Jim Norris, president of the IBC, was already talking to Sugar about a title fight against Basilio, the welterweight champion. "That fight could do at least three-quarters of a million in Yankee Stadium," Norris surmised. "I'm going to try to make it as soon as I can." On the same day, Sugar got a call from promoter Jimmy Dundee in San Francisco, who offered Sugar one hundred thousand dollars to defend his title against the winner of the Chico Vejar–Joey Giambra fight on May 14. Then, of course, there was a possible return match with Fullmer. But even before he could mull over the good fortune awaiting him, the federal government stepped into the mix. [2]

A day after the fight, Sugar got an early birthday present from the IRS—the Feds had placed a $23,000 lien on Robinson's purse after his victory over Fullmer. This amount, the government charged, was the claim against Sugar for back income taxes. Edna Mae's aunt Blanche told the press that Sugar was not to blame for the mismanagement of his personal and business financial affairs. He "was very young when he started these businesses in Harlem in 1945," she told a reporter at the *New York Times*. "He had confidence in his hired help and managers, but they just lacked the qualities to run the businesses properly." She explained that things got out of hand during his tour of Europe in 1954, and that shortly thereafter members of the family, including Edna Mae, took over those responsibilities. There was nothing exactly dishonest about the employees, she continued, putting a press agent's spin on the matter, and added that Sugar Ray Robinson's Harlem Enterprises was once again "stable."[3]

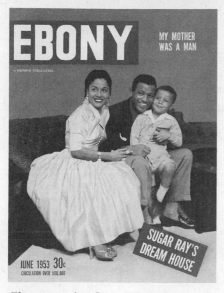

Ebony magazine, June 1953

Sugar Ray Robinson arriving in
Chicago with family

Sugar Ray Robinson fighting Jake LaMotta

(All illustrations courtesy of the Sugar Ray Robinson Estate, unless otherwise noted)

Edna Robinson posing alongside their Cadillac

Sugar Ray Robinson, Evelyn *(left)*, and Edna Mae Robinson *(right)* arriving in Paris, 1950

Sugar in various scenes

Edna Mae Robinson dancing atop
a huge drum

Bill "Bojangles" Robinson and
Edna Mae Robinson

Sugar Ray Robinson
and Ray Robinson II

Potrait of Sugar Ray Robinson, 1952
(COPYRIGHT © JOE GLASER)

Edna Mae as a young girl preparing for
a dance recital

Sugar Ray Robinson with Frank Sinatra

Sugar and Edna Mae,
late 1950s

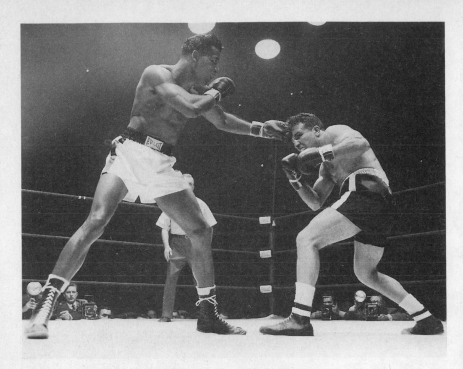

Sugar and Jake LaMotta, 1951, Chicago

Sugar Ray Robinson's
sister and wife watching
a middleweight fight

Sugar Ray Robinson and
Edna Mae at home, 1953

Sugar Ray Robinson,
Ray Robinson II,
and Edna Mae, 1953

Joe Louis and Sugar Ray
Robinson, late 1940s

Sugar Ray Robinson shaking
Curt Horrmann's hand
(COPYRIGHT © MARVIN SMITH)

Group photo of Sugar
Ray Robinson,
handlers, and friends
(COPYRIGHT © WAUGH
ILLUSTRATED)

Sugar Ray Robinson
and Edna Mae arriving
in Paris (COPYRIGHT ©
INTERNATIONAL NEWS)

CHAPTER 21

BROKE!

With his financial situation becoming more uncertain with each raid by the IRS, Sugar had to sit down with the IBC and work out a deal. Pride goeth before a fall, he had decided, and there were few alternatives to paying the mounting bills. It was Norris and Basilio, or the poorhouse. He knew that to bargain with Norris was like cutting a deal with the devil; since there was no way he was going to come out ahead, he chose to let the devil take the hindmost. A date was set with Carmen Basilio, an ex-Marine whose battered, craggy face was like a road map of his struggle to reach the pinnacle of the fight game.

Sugar had scheduled a couple of tune-up fights to get ready for Basilio, who had an extreme dislike for Sugar (which may have stemmed from Sugar's arrogance) and who was known to wade right in, taking all the punishment his opponent could dish out. He was the kind of fighter who would gladly take ten punches to land one of his own powerful hooks to the jaw. In boxing circles, Basilio had a reputation as a phenomenally strong fighter, a banger who scorned defense to wear opponents out with a punishing two-fisted attack. He had an iron chin and lots of heart, which made him a perennial crowd pleaser. If Basilio was on the card, the promise of seeing a toe-to-toe donnybrook was guaranteed. "When people buy a fight ticket, they're paying to see blood and knockdowns," Basilio told a reporter. "Every time I go into the ring, I expect to be busted up; it's as much a part of the business as the boxing gloves."

Sugar knew he had to be at the top of his game, ready to pump pistonlike jab after pistonlike jab, in an effort to wear down a fighter who had taken all Johnny Saxton and Kid Gavilan could muster, absorbing blows like a human punching bag. The match would be a classic encounter between a superb boxer and a relentless stalker. Ultimately, it would be Basilio's iron chin versus Sugar's devastating arsenal of combinations.

One element of Sugar's arsenal, according to his most vehement detractors, was his threat to cancel or postpone a fight. And sure enough, he stunned the promoter of this fight, Jim Norris, when he said he was pulling out of the fight if he didn't get his way with the disposition of television rights. Norris had signed with Theatre Network Television, but Sugar insisted that he jettison that deal and sign with another closed-circuit concern, TelePrompTer. Long before Don King stormed onto the scene, Sugar had already deployed the tactics of guerrilla negotiations. "Hauled on the carpet by Julius Helfand, the chairman of the State Athletic Boxing Commission, the middleweight ruler got into a shouting match with Helfand and defied him, too," wrote Arthur Daley in the *New York Times*. "It was a disgraceful exhibition." Sugar's hysterics were for naught, but it once again put the commission and Norris on notice that they were not going to breeze in with their plans without any opposition. Sugar conceded this time. But it was merely to await a better time to drop his bombshell at the bargaining table.

"Advance ticket sales were very good," Edna Mae remembered. It was a chilly September fight night in New York, and Edna Mae admired all the rich and famous assembled at or near ringside. "Ray's mother sat with me and the opera diva, Charlotte Holloman, the wife of the then-president of New York's Health and Hospital Corporation, and Marguerite Mays, then the wife of Willie Mays. Sugar had just given me a chinchilla wrap. I wore it that evening."

The fight was fifteen rounds of hell, and Sugar gave as much as he took, but in the end the split decision went to Basilio. The ex–onion picker matched blow for blow with Sugar. The scar tissue over Basilio's half-closed eyes made it difficult for him to make out the often swirling image in front of him, but his punches found the mark with unerring ferocity. It was all Edna Mae could do not to turn away from the carnage, and she was hoarse from screaming, particularly at the reporters and fans after the fight who insisted her husband was through. "Sugar is finished" was practically chanted by a vocal knot of Basilio supporters. With Sugar struggling to catch his breath, Edna Mae was furious, refuting any contention that her man was over the hill. "He was always champion," she wrote. "Our personal differences had nothing to do with how great he was in the ring and I hated the way many columnists vacillated. Even when he'd have my heart in pieces and, yes, maybe my eyes and body badly bruised!" she lamented.

. . .

Sugar wasn't too beaten to voice his opinion about the rampant incidents of police brutality in Harlem. In one filmed interview, according to Ray II, "He said that the police would have to start treating people the same way they treated him, Joe Louis, and Jackie Robinson or there was going to be continuing trouble." Such a bold statement in 1957 on police affairs was quite a leap for a man who had said on various occasions that he didn't get involved in politics.

The police attack on Hinton Johnson in December was just the kind of atrocity that had prompted Sugar to speak out. Johnson was a Black Muslim and a member of Temple Seven, where Malcolm X was the minister. When Johnson and another Muslim failed to move as fast as the police wanted them to, they were viciously assaulted. As Malcolm related: "Brother Hinton was attacked with nightsticks. His scalp was split open, and a police car came and he was taken to a nearby precinct." Alerted to the attack, members of the Nation of Islam quickly assembled in tight formations outside the police station. Behind this phalanx of men in bow ties were rows and rows of onlookers, each one waiting to see who would win the Mexican standoff between the Fruit of Islam and the men in blue. At first Malcolm was told that Johnson wasn't there; then the police said he was but that no one was allowed to see him. "I said that until he was seen," Malcolm wrote, "and we were sure he had received proper medical attention, the Muslims would remain where they were." When the assembled learned that Johnson was out of serious condition, Malcolm gave a signal and the Muslims dispersed. "No black should have that kind of power," a white police officer reportedly muttered.

What Sugar had to say about the police in Harlem was consistent with his remarks about the racist policies and bigotry of Governor Orval Faubus of Arkansas. "I never interfere in politics, no kind of way, but I'd give that Faubus my whole purse and take him on after Basilio," he told a *Time* magazine reporter. Sugar had a few barbs for President Eisenhower, too. "There he is playing golf and his country is darn near revolution."

Such comments were fodder for the tabloids, each of them eager to pump up controversy, particularly when it came from high-profile celebrities. Sugar was getting additional attention beyond the local media in New York City, but it wasn't the sort he welcomed. Not only had he suffered the indignity of a loss in the ring, now the IRS was on his tail again. Unbeknownst to Sugar, another lien had been placed on his earnings once the bell sounded in his fight against Basilio. A notice was served by an IRS agent ordering the IBC to hold all of Sugar's money, both from the live gate and the ancillary rights. "I owed the government about eighty thousand dollars in taxes from the previous year, in disallowed expenses," Sugar explained. "The government wanted to get square." Sugar garnered almost a half-million dollars from the fight, and he wanted to pay the IRS in increments, but the agency rejected his plan as illegal. The situation called for a tax lawyer.

With Howard Rumpf handling the case for him, Sugar was soon granted $100,000 of the earnings from the fight to pay his immediate employees. After several more sessions at the IRS, there was no final verdict on the situation and Sugar and his lawyers had no recourse but to wait. Sugar was also in the middle of another financial tiff, with his former manager, Ernie Braca. Braca brought his suit against Sugar and one of his trainers, Harold "Killer" Johnson, charging that he was entitled to a

share of Sugar's earnings over the last three years, earnings estimated at close to $200,000. Bronx Supreme Court justice
Sidney Fine decided in Braca's favor, awarding him an $18,000
settlement of a suit filed for $150,000. Neither Braca nor Sugar
appeared in court. [1]

Even more distressing, there was a rumor that his purse
from the return match with Basilio, scheduled for March 28,
1958, was also going to be confiscated by the IRS. Anticipating
this situation, Sugar finally hired Edward Bennett Williams, the
famous Washington, D.C., lawyer who would later represent
Adam Clayton Powell in his tax evasion trial. Sugar's case was
so helpless that even a lawyer of Williams's stature could provide only momentary relief. He had dug a hole so deep that it
was impossible to extricate himself and ultimately he had to pay
the debt or shift it to Edna Mae, which he did.

Sugar took his frustration out on Edna Mae. Around this
time, his sister was given only a short time to live, and Sugar sent
for his father in Detroit to come and see her. "I was very pleased
to have him stay with us," Edna Mae noted. "He was asleep in
our guest room one morning when Sugar became abusive to me
and then began slapping me viciously. His dad heard us and ran
into our room and tried to stop Ray and begged him not to hit
me again. While he tried to hold him, I ran downstairs and called
the police precinct, which was only blocks away, and in minutes
they were at our front door. I ran and opened it. They were
shocked to find out it was 'Sugar Ray the champ.' Ray told them
that he barely touched me, despite the fact that my face had the
full imprint of his hand across it. He offered them drinks, which
they accepted, showed them around the house, and gave them
autographed photos of himself. They, and Ray's dad, asked me
not to press any charges, and with big smiles and handshakes to

Sugar and his dad, they left our home to return to the precinct. So much for our protectors in uniform."

This incident caught even Ray II off guard. "It was about this time that I first witnessed my father hitting my mother," Ray II said. "Until then I had no idea their relationship was so abusive—so abusive that it was the cause of five miscarriages."

Behind closed doors Edna Mae was at the mercy of Sugar's rage; in public, her bruises covered with makeup, she was the dutiful companion who was escorted to various functions. Whenever they appeared in the audience at Ed Sullivan's television show, the host would introduce them and the couple would stand and wave to the audience, a seemingly happy twosome. They put on happy faces for Edward R. Murrow as well, when he invaded their Riverdale home to feature them on his *Person to Person* show. You would have thought they were Ozzie and Harriet the way they cuddled and gushed in response to Murrow's questions about their home life. The ruptures, some of which led to separations, between the Robinsons rarely made the press, and when they did they were usually deeply embedded in gossip columns that few took as credible.

CHAPTER 22

SUGAR'S DILEMMAS

No matter how often Sugar abused her, Edna Mae was almost always at her husband's side during a major prizefight, expressing an uncommon loyalty or hoping that he would someday end his abusive ways. And Sugar would need her companionship and loyalty more than ever as he prepared for the second showdown with Basilio, which was to take place in Chicago, Sugar's lucky town, on March 25, 1958. During this period, Sugar came down with a virus, and everybody around him begged him to postpone the fight. Even Frank Sinatra, in Las Vegas, had heard about the rumored virus. When he visited Sugar he told him the smart money was going with Basilio. "You're my friend," Sugar told Sinatra, "and I'd like to see you win your bet, and maybe you ought to bet with the smart money."

"But the smart money isn't going to be in the ring," he said. "*You* are."

"Let me tell you something, Frank," Sugar replied honestly. "I'm going in there to get that title, and I don't care what anybody says, or what the smart money thinks."

"That's all I wanted to hear, Ray," Sinatra said.

In preparation for the fight, Sugar was given two injections. One shot was penicillin for the virus; the other shot was B-12 for strength. Maybe he consumed a couple of glasses of beef blood, too. In any event, he was plenty fortified. By the fourth round the scar tissue above Basilio's vulnerable left eye was open and bleeding. Two rounds later, Sugar's blows had closed it completely, and it puffed up like an onion bulb. Soon, Basilio was practically blind and was groping around the ring trying to find his swift, crisp-punching adversary. "It was a fight between a mole and a hawk," Bob Considine wrote in the *New York Journal-American*. Edna Mae was equally colorful in her description of Basilio's eye: "That eye swelled like baking powder was in it. It was the size of a golf ball."

Despite being as sightless as Samson, Basilio plodded on, using one hand like radar and pounding away with the other. "He hit me right in the eyebrow," Basilio offered, "and broke the blood vessels . . . and blew my eyelid up. My eye shut. This was about the middle of the sixth round. And I fought the next nine rounds with one eye. It was a grueling fight."

Both fighters were on the verge of collapse, but they continued to slug it out. Neither would back off; neither would go down. They went the full fifteen rounds, and in the end, Sugar, though he had taken his lumps, triumphed. He was so exhausted that he could barely stand and wave to the crowd. For the fifth time, he had won the title, an unprecedented feat. Two hours later, in his dressing room, he felt faint and had to be carried up to his hotel room. He was, as he said, "beat but not beaten," with every bone in his body sore. It was as if he had been "fighting ten men." But it was all worth it, because now he was a celebrity again. The first one to his door was Walter Winchell; then came Redd Foxx, his head shaved, with only a large letter "R" of hair adorning the top. Sugar had no way of knowing it, but this would be his last great victory in the ring, and his only fight that year.

. . .

When he was younger, especially at the start of his career, Sugar didn't wait too long between fights. He didn't need time to wallow in victory or to lick his wounds after a defeat, which was rare on his remarkable résumé. But as he got older, it took increasingly longer for him to recuperate, to get his juices boiling again. After the Basilio bout, he took it easy, pondering business options, spending time with his family, taking out his aggression on a worn drum set. But beating a drum only reminded him of pounding the bags, of working over a torso, of drubbing an opponent into total submission, like Carmen Basilio. Some of Sugar's fans said he was insane to be pursuing another fight with Basilio. These sentiments were shared by Edna Mae, and she quietly hoped it wouldn't happen.

Several things interfered with the possibility of a return match between the two fighters, none more exasperating than the money demands they both made. The promoter, IBC, was in trouble. And there were all kinds of business finaglings surrounding Madison Square Garden. When Teddy Brenner was named the new matchmaker by Harry Markson, who gained control of the famed arena, he was just one of many promoters eager to get Sugar back in the ring with Basilio. Some of them even threatened to strip Sugar of his title if he didn't comply. But until Sugar got what he wanted in terms of money, he had no intentions of complying.

Meanwhile, Sugar was trying to cut a deal with light heavyweight champ Archie Moore for a bout. "Sugar invited Mr. and Mrs. Moore to our home for dinner so that he could talk to Archie about a plan for them to fight," Edna Mae recalled. Milton Gross, in his column in the *New York Post,* reported on their meeting, recounting how Sugar sent his car to the Hotel Warwick in midtown Manhattan to fetch the Moores. Gross said Sugar told him, "Archie and I were never on a social basis, but we're both businessmen and certainly there was nothing wrong in our planning to fight each other for a million-dollar purse that we'd share equally." [1] Nothing wrong with it at all, even though Moore had scored more knockouts than any other fighter in history.

However, Sugar's plan to fight "The Ol' Mongoose," as Moore was called because of his sly ring tactics, fell through. Instead, the ageless Moore (he said he was forty-four but many believed he was older) met a crude, rugged Canadian, Yvon Durelle, in December 1958 and punished him severely before decking him for good in the eleventh round. The same fate might have awaited Sugar.

On May 4, 1959, the National Boxing Association vacated the middleweight championship after Sugar refused to meet Basilio in a return match, which left Sugar holding the title in only two states—New York and Massachusetts. This setback had followed even more distressing news two weeks earlier, when his sister, Marie Brewer, succumbed to cancer. Brewer, the wife of one of Sugar's trainers, Clyde Brewer, was forty-one when she died at Francis Delafield Hospital in New York City on April 19. With his marriage as rocky as ever, his sister dead, and his title up for grabs, Sugar desperately needed to find some comfort and cheer. It seemed there was still a possibility of luring Moore into the ring, but once again the deal faded and the Mongoose fought Durelle a second time, this time knocking him out in the third round. Sugar's disgust intensified when he learned that Fullmer and Basilio had signed for a bout to determine a new middleweight champion. Now, virtually broke, he regretted not having had a third fight with Basilio right after their crowd-pleasing second romp. "I made a big mistake," Sugar would say in a later interview. He had been offered a guaranteed half-million dollars, but he'd declined, insisting on more money.

Fullmer stopped Basilio in the fourteenth round. Now Sugar pursued Fullmer, but the new champ was not interested; nor was Basilio. For Sugar the year 1959 was much like the preceding year—he managed only one fight.

Sugar was strangely invisible, but by the fall and winter of 1959 his oldest son, Ronnie, to whom Sugar had never been much of a father, was grabbing sports headlines as a member of the New York Chiefs roller derby team. Ronnie, twenty-one, said he became interested in roller derby after watching it on television. "I never cared for fighting," he told a reporter. Perhaps his distaste for the sport stemmed from the distant relationship he had with his father. "My dad was Dad to lots of children, except his own," he said. He also recalled how his father had once knocked him down. "I looked up at him and said does that make you feel like a champion now?"[2]

Meanwhile, Sugar continued to lie low when it came to boxing, though he was diligently pursuing other interests. He was studying for the role of Jim in Sam Goldwyn's version of Mark Twain's *Huckleberry Finn*. Jackie Robinson discussed this involvement, which had been going on for several weeks, in his column in the *New York Post*. "I think Ray wants very much to get out of the ring, once and for all, and apparently he feels very strongly that this may be his big chance," Robinson wrote. "He admitted to me that he would really like to do this role, and revealed he has been working very hard in coaching sessions for it. Of course, this is not the first time that he has sought his fortune outside the ring. But Robinson is not as young as he once was, either, and he knows that label 'old-timer' is bound to catch up with him, too, sooner or later. But if this new career does come to pass for Ray, then boxing will have lost its most colorful performer to the Hollywood screen."[3]

He may have also been in hiding from the prying eyes of a ravenous press corps and their inquiries about a paternity suit that had been filed against him. A beautiful, olive-skinned Barbara Trevigne, a nightclub hostess, charged that Sugar was the father of her six-year-old son. Sugar denied paternity of the child, claiming it was a "shakedown." He did, however, admit that he knew the woman and had once given her money when she was in financial distress. "I met Barbara Trevigne in show business, and she appeared to me to be a nice girl," Sugar said. "She visited my bar a number of times." Mrs. Trevigne had no comment to the press, directing all questions to her lawyer. She promised to tell her version of the affair in court. A "No comment" was also Edna Mae's response when asked if she was going to stand by her husband through the ordeal.

An affidavit filed by Mrs. Trevigne's lawyer, Thomas Roberts, charges that Sugar had in effect admitted paternity by having contributed to the child's support. Furthermore, the lawyer said that Sugar had been lax in his payments and had not made any recently. Mrs. Trevigne, according to a story in the *Amsterdam News,* a onetime nightclub singer, was married and the mother of three children, one born before Paul, the child in question, and one after. [4]

By January 1961, Sugar had admitted having been intimate with Mrs. Trevigne over a number of years, but continued to deny that he'd fathered the child. He told the court he couldn't have been the child's father because at the time she said the child was conceived he was in training at his Pompton Lakes camp, getting ready for his fight against Joey Maxim in 1952. His statements were later supported by Gainford and Charles Austin, his office assistant. The testimony brought a loud gasp in the courtroom from an astonished Mrs. Trevigne. [5]

A panel of special sessions judges ruled two to one in favor of acquitting Sugar of the paternity charge, despite his admitted intimacies. It appeared the judges decided on the basis of the child's having been born between two other children by her husband. In October, the Appellate Division of the Supreme Court dismissed an appeal by Mrs. Trevigne. Sugar had slipped the yoke again. None of this had been decided on December 14, 1959, when Sugar—in his only fight that year—was in Boston, knocking out Bob Young in the second round.

. . .

As each promised match with a leading contender faded, the Robinsons' debts mounted. To get away from her often ill tempered, disgruntled husband, Edna Mae began doing volunteer work for various charitable and political organizations. Her work with an African research and medical organization that raised money to build medical mobile units and to transport patients over rough terrain in Africa was very fulfilling, she said, despite an incident involving jazz musicians Miles Davis and Max Roach. Davis, through Edna Mae's influence, had been contracted to perform for the foundation. According to Edna Mae, this date at Carnegie Hall was Davis's first concert engagement in New York City as a leader. "In the middle of Miles's classic solo on 'Someday My Prince Will Come,' Max Roach walked onto the stage and sat down in the middle of the floor. Miles stopped playing and walked off the stage." Roach, whose black nationalism was widely known, was there to protest an event in which money was being raised to assist the apartheid government of South Africa. After Roach was bodily removed, Davis returned to the stage as though nothing had happened and resumed playing. [6]

When she wasn't lending a helping hand to institutions and organizations, Edna Mae was doting over her child. Ray, now ten, was ready to be confirmed, and Edna Mae made sure it was a memorable occasion. Sugar was there, and beamed as his son received the blessings from the priest. If he was not entirely absorbed in the ritual it was because he was thinking about a conversation he'd had with Langston Hughes about taking a role in his play *Tambourines to Glory*. "Looks like Sugar Ray might play Buddy in my show," Hughes wrote in a letter to his close friend and associate, Arna Bontemps, in November 1959. "He phoned yesterday for the book to read. And seemed interested and excited." Bontemps, in his reply, opined that Sugar would be just right for the role. "And he's bound to be a draw in his first play." It took until 1963 for Hughes to find funding for the gospel play, by which time Sugar was struggling to add a few more years onto his boxing career. The role went to Louis Gossett.[7]

Make-believe was an enticing possibility for Sugar, who never saw a stage he didn't like, but the reality of a looming fight date in Boston on January 22, 1960, with a fairly unknown fighter named Paul Pender called for real, and serious, preparation. "Paul who?" Sugar had asked his manager when given the name of his next opponent. Gainford told him that Pender was the New England middleweight champ and that Sugar had been guaranteed seventy thousand dollars for the bout. "For that money, I'd fight Paul Revere in Boston," Sugar said, laughing.

Pender was a skinny, seasoned veteran with ten consecutive victories over equally unknown fighters, and Sugar may not have taken the match that seriously. He should have. Pender, using his speed to elude Sugar's advances, took a surprising split decision and added the world championship belt to his collection. Sugar's manager was beside himself with anger, charging that it was "highway robbery." A rematch was set for June. To Sugar and his management's dismay, Pender won another fifteen-round split decision.

"These defeats had more to do with the promoters' desire to bolster the career of an up-and-coming local favorite than it had to do with rendering a fair judgment," suggested Dino Woodard, one of Sugar's most dedicated and loyal sparring partners. "Sugar lost many of his remaining fights to unknown fighters whose careers would be enhanced if they could add a victory over Sugar to their record. Either he had to knock them out or beat them decisively. The close calls, at this stage of his career, went against him. This is something we all came to understand as part of the territory for the ex-champ."

• • •

Sugar had been so consumed with winning the second encounter with Pender that he'd had little time for the usual throng of admirers who sought his attention, even if they were upcoming heavyweights such as Cassius Clay. Clay, whose amateur record was almost as unblemished as Sugar's, came to Harlem to meet his idol, but when he arrived at Sugar's café, accompanied by another boxer and sportswriter Dick Schaap, Sugar was not in. They decided to walk around Harlem and kill some time in hopes that Sugar would soon be back.

According to Schaap, Clay was fascinated by the street corner speakers who held forth near the Theresa Hotel and Lewis Michaux's National Memorial Bookstore on Seventh Avenue and 125th Street. Like the speakers in London's Hyde Park, the Harlem radicals often addressed controversial issues, including scathing indictments of "racist America," and many of them called for a return to Africa. Carlos Cooks, Pork Chop Davis, Dr. Yosef ben Jochannan (Dr. Ben), James Thornhill, Bessie Philips, Charles Kenyatta, and Malcolm X were among the more celebrated and commanding speakers who were guaranteed to arouse spectators. It is not clear who Clay heard during his walk, but he was amazed that they could get away with what they said without being hauled off to jail. And given the flamboyance with which he himself spoke, he was probably fascinated by their elocution, seeking ways to garnish his own spiels and limericks. After circling the central district, they headed back to Sugar's place just in time to see him pull up in a purple Caddy, which by 1960 had replaced the pink one.

Schaap was a bit apprehensive about this meeting of the two flamboyant boxers. Would Sugar acknowledge Clay? Would Clay open his big mouth and upset the legend? But "Clay was humble, even hesitant," David Remnick summarized in his book *King of the World.* "Robinson gave him just a few moments. With a bored and superior air, Sugar Ray said hello and then strode on past them into his bar. Clay was goggle-eyed. 'Someday I'm gonna own two Cadillacs—and a Ford for just getting around in.'" Years later Clay would recall being sloughed off by his hero, and promised he would never behave like that to any of his fans.

In his autobiography, Sugar offers another take on this meeting. In fact, he devoted a whole chapter to Clay, discussing how they first met and what they talked about. They had quite a long exchange, he said, with Clay asking him to be his manager. "But that's impossible," Sugar told him. "I'm still a fighter myself. That's a full-time thing. I couldn't possibly be fighting myself and managing you at the same time." Clay, in his customary garrulity, was not about to take no for an answer. "Maybe after you retire, you'll be my manager," he continued. Sugar wished him luck in Rome in his quest for an Olympic medal and ducked into his café. As he stood at the bar with a customer, he looked through the window, and Clay was still standing there with Schaap. "If that kid can fight like he can talk," Sugar said, "he'll be something."

• • •

Sugar suffered a third consecutive defeat when he and Edna Mae separated. They had agreed to disagree, Sugar wrote. "We had enjoyed some beautiful times, but we had battled through some bad times," he said. "She never liked the idea that *I* was the celebrity in our marriage, not her. I never got used to her show-biz habit of letting guys kiss her, guys I didn't know." Agreeing to go their separate ways for a while was all the room Sugar needed to rekindle an off-and-on affair with Millie Bruce, who resided in California. It had been the one fling that Edna Mae had instinctually felt threatened by.

Now, in the summer of 1960, Millie visited New York City as a member of the Rinky Dinks, a social and civic organization that did charity work; like Edna Mae, she spent time working with charitable organizations. Millie told Sugar she was staying at the Park Sheraton, at about the same time that Edna Mae was returning to the city with Ray II from Florida, where they had gone for a short visit. They were riding in a taxi when they passed the hotel and Ray saw his father's car in the parking lot. "He wanted to stop and to go find his dad," Edna Mae said. "I knew better and asked him to escort me home first and then we'd call his dad. When we called the hotel, the switchboard operator said, 'Mr. Robinson is not in, but Mrs. Robinson is. Would you like to speak to her?' I said, 'But of course.' The next voice was that of the California lady. I asked is this Mrs. Robinson and she said, 'Well, no. But who is this?' I answered I'm Mrs. Robinson also. Will you tell my husband that we're home from Florida and his son wants to see him? Later, Sugar went and picked up his son, took him for ice cream, and then brought him home." Sugar didn't, however, leave, but rather cuddled up in the bed with Edna Mae.

Things continued as up and down as they'd ever been with the couple, but by Thanksgiving their relationship hit a more disturbing bump on the marital road: Sugar told Edna Mae and his son that he would be having dinner with his "other" family, and not with them. It was then that she decided to file for legal separation. Within a few weeks, though, Sugar had charmed his way back into her life—though they remained separated—and resumed stopping by occasionally to see Ray. These were also times when he would badger his wife into preparing him a meal, which she obediently did, until the day she discovered a pair of ladies' shoes in his car. What really miffed her was that he had come by and asked her to prepare him a lunch. "I realized I had prepared *their* lunch," she said. "The man was incredible."

CHAPTER 23

MILLIE AND
THE MORMON

*Sugar wasn't the only notabl*e Harlemite with his marriage on the rocks. Adam Clayton Powell, Jr., was also experiencing marital woes. His marriage to pianist/vocalist Hazel Scott ended in a Mexican divorce, and Powell wasted no time tying the knot again in Puerto Rico with Yvette Diago, his twenty-nine-year-old Puerto Rican secretary. Now Harlemites had some juicy gossip to replace all the fading hoopla over the visit Fidel Castro had made in September.

Still, for many residents, such as Maya Angelou, it would take years to erase that memory. In her book *The Heart of a Woman,* the famed poet captured the moment when Castro embraced Russian leader Nikita Khrushchev on the corner of 125th Street and Seventh Avenue, his metal, made-in-Moscow teeth bared for all to see. "It was an ole and hallelujah time for the people of Harlem," she wrote. A celebration for Harlem was a propaganda defeat for the U.S. State Department. Another witness to Castro's stay in Harlem at the Theresa Hotel was attorney Conrad Lynn. He recalled that "crowds of black people stood outside the Theresa night and day, and when members of the delegation walked the streets of the ghetto they were followed by admiring throngs. Blacks on the street absorbed more political education on these occasions than they had from any lesson since the Great Depression."[1]

All the hullabaloo about Castro, who had outlawed professional boxing in Cuba, and his visit to Harlem were of little consequence to boxing fans. They were eager to see if the Sugar man could whip Fullmer again. At stake was Fullmer's National Boxing Association crown—Pender held the world title at that weight. Sugar was promised 20 percent of everything. The deal was sweetened considerably when Sugar was told the fight would take place on December 3, 1960, in the new Sports Arena in Los Angeles. This venue would put him near Millie, and a long way from Edna Mae. The two women had met in a supermarket during one of Millie's visits to New York. Millie was with Sugar's mother when Edna Mae ran into them. "I thought she was certainly as lovely as so many others that had preceded her were," she said of Millie. "I felt no malice. I knew I was over whatever battered esteem that had prompted my incredible martyrdom . . . I felt free."

And Sugar was free to carouse as much as he desired now; his separation from Edna Mae had become official. While training for the fight, he stayed in the desert near San Jacinto. He invited Millie and one of her girlfriends from San Francisco to spend the weekend at the camp with him and his team of handlers and trainers. Millie and her girlfriend slept in the room with Sugar, but as he related: "With me in training, they were safer than they would have been in a monastery." Apparently, a little sexual exercise to relieve the tension was not ordered by his manager, as he had several times before.

Sugar wasn't aware until late the following morning that one night that weekend, in the early hours before dawn, a prowler had been outside his cabin. It was Millie's ex-boyfriend, spying on them. He had come in the cabin and asked Millie to return with him, but she'd refused. Sugar asked her why she didn't wake him, and she explained that to have done so might have caused more trouble. Infuriated by the incident, Sugar fumed several minutes before his manager stepped in and told him to save the anger for Fullmer.

Finally, the day of the fight arrived—somewhat anticlimactically. For after fifteen rounds of exchanging punishing blows, Sugar and Fullmer saw the bout end in a draw. Sugar's thirty-nine-year-old body was stretched to the limit, and his quest for a sixth championship had gone for naught. Throughout the contest, Fullmer was wary of the left hook that had flattened him in Chicago. He kept his right forearm high to protect his jaw from a left hook or any other "secret" weapon Sugar might deliver. But there was to be no secret punch. Sugar's disgust with himself was mitigated somewhat by a fifty-thousand-dollar payday, part of which he spent while he and Millie celebrated.

Celebrate they did, but Sugar's temper put a damper on the fun. Not long into their relationship, Sugar had begun to slap Millie around. According to Edna Mae, it happened with enough frequency that Sugar's mother had to step in on at least one occasion to help contain his rage. Edna Mae recounted several other instances in which Millie was apparently assaulted by Sugar, so badly that she was seen in a photo wearing a cast on her arm necessitated by a blow from Sugar, Edna Mae said. The beatings occurred with such regularity that Millie begged Sugar to see a counselor. She even volunteered to stay in the hospital with him if he would seek treatment. Still the battering continued, and there were snide remarks from a few close associates that Millie was simply his latest punching bag and sparring partner as he prepared for yet another tangle with Fullmer.

. . .

In his autobiography, Sugar has a long chapter called "The Woman in White." Separated from Edna Mae and with Millie in California, he was free for anything fancy, and that fancy came in the form of a beautiful white woman he called Beverly, but who several informants believe was a French actress, either Denise Darcel or Martine Carol. [2] Darcel's bio lists only two films of any note—*Vera Cruz,* starring Burt Lancaster, and *Dangerous When Wet,* featuring swimmer Esther Williams. Her roles were as brief as Sugar's would be when he performed in a series of B flicks. Like Sugar, she would also be a mystery guest on the popular television game show *What's My Line.*

At a time when his boxing career was in great jeopardy, when his debt was mounting and his personal life in disarray, Sugar began a torrid affair with this lover, who toward the end of their affair was insisting on matrimony. But Sugar lectured her on what that would mean to his current quest for the championship, and do to them as a couple. "Everybody would beat you down, and beat me down too," he pleaded. She quickly countered his fears of an interracial marriage. "But other prominent Negro men have married white women—Sammy Davis, Harry Belafonte." His reply was: "They're not Sugar Ray Robinson." After exhausting her stock of feminine charms, "Beverly" finally gave up, and literally drove off into the sunset.

It could have been Martine Carol. Carol was born Maryse Mourer, the name she used early in her stage career. After some experience on the French stage she debuted on screen in 1943, working her way up to starring roles by 1948. It was reported that she attempted suicide in 1947 by jumping into the Seine River. A voluptuous blonde, she was France's biggest box-office attraction in the early fifties, occasionally appearing seminude. With the rise of Brigitte Bardot, she was overshadowed as a sex symbol, and her career declined in the late '50s. Carol attempted without success to revive her popularity in international films, but died of a heart attack in 1967 at forty-five.

Sugar's affair with Beverly was over by early 1961, at a time when there was an increase in black pride and awareness, and when he might have been ridiculed for being associated with a white woman.

. . .

The date for the rematch with Fullmer also meant dates with Millie, since the fight would take place in the West—this time in Las Vegas. One week before the fight, Sugar checked into the Dunes Hotel on the neon-lit strip. He wanted Millie to see his new Lincoln Continental, which was being driven to the Coast by one of his friends, Kelly Howard. Howard also said that he often was a "beard," or front, for Sugar's trysts when they stayed at a hotel. "I would get a room under my name and Sugar would use it to meet his ladies."[3]

Though, for the most part, he was impervious to the lure of the casinos, he was a sucker for the nightclubs, especially when the likes of New Orleans trumpeter Al Hirt, Nat "King" Cole, and Sammy Davis, Jr., were among the headliners. He was extremely excited to learn that his close friend King Cole had an engagement at the Sands. At that time he was an honorary member of Sinatra's Rat Pack, who were in Vegas celebrating JFK's election. Each night Sugar was there in the audience for Cole, and the singer returned the favor by showing up each afternoon to witness Sugar in the final stages of his training in a makeshift ring set up in the lobby of the Dunes.

Things were moving along quite smoothly for Sugar and his coterie until Dr. Joseph C. Elia, chairman of the Nevada Boxing Commission, who had pulled the strings to get Sugar the title shot with Fullmer, suddenly resigned after severe discord with his fellow commissioners. This meant that all the promises he had made to Sugar about reduced costs on hotel accommodations for the large contingent of African Americans slated to arrive to see the fight could not be met. Even worse, Dr. Elia's resignation left Sugar at the mercy of a local boxing promoter, Norman Rothschild. Sugar remembered Rothschild as a promoter from Syracuse who had handled some of Basilio's fights. "Any friend of Basilio was not a friend of mine," Sugar said.

Compounding this dilemma, another person associated with the fight had siphoned money from sixteen ringside seats, selling the $40 tickets for $1,000 each. This person told Sugar the profit, $960, would go to Sugar's favorite charity. "You're playing with my money," Sugar fumed. He insisted that since he was supposed to get 25 percent of the gate, and sixteen tickets had been sold for a total of $16,000, he had $4,000 coming.

There was another problem that had to be resolved. Sugar discovered that the ring was smaller than the regulation-size twenty square feet; it was sixteen feet and six inches. Moreover, the padding was too soft and thus an advantage for the plodding, slower Fullmer. Sugar relied on his speed, his ability to bounce around the ring—the larger the ring, the more room he had to roam. Yet another snag occurred when Sugar was told that they would not use the six-ounce gloves he'd expected. He had hoped for the smaller gloves in order to deliver that patented left hook that had dropped Fullmer for the full count in May 1957.

The prefight contention between Sugar and Fullmer almost ended with a laugh when they both wanted to wear white trunks, a choice belonging to Fullmer, the champ. Rothschild blurted that they both could wear white trunks. But a television producer yelled that wouldn't do. "Nobody will be able to identify them." Sugar and Fullmer looked at each other, both trying not to laugh. But Sugar's glee was short-lived. The next day a far more serious obstacle jeopardized the fight. The promoters wanted to delay the bout by a day so that it could be shown in South America. Once again Sugar was upset, realizing that such an arrangement would cut into the movie rights as far as South America was concerned. "The fight's off," Sugar told the promoters. To coax Sugar to their point of view, the promoters called Governor Grant Sawyer in Carson City. Sugar then spoke to the governor and explained the situation. Not only was he unhappy with the size of the ring and other details, but the promoters had also hired a referee who Sugar felt would not help his cause. "If I can get you a twenty-foot ring, will you fight?" the governor asked. Sugar said he would.

Things had been bad outside the ring for Sugar, but they were no better inside the ring against an aggressive Fullmer. The fight went the distance, with Sugar's face bruised and bashed almost as bad as it had been after the fights with Randy Turpin in the summer and fall of 1951. Fullmer got the verdict and Sugar left the arena physically and pridefully hurt. During the bruising third round, Sugar had taken more consecutive powerful blows than at any other time in his career.

Later, he found out that the ring had not been twenty feet after all. "The tape was at the twenty-foot mark," Sugar recalled, "but three feet had sheared out of the tape, and the two ends had been soldered together to fool George [Gainford] on purpose." Only in Las Vegas, Sugar exhaled.

There was comfort in the presence of Millie and some compensation in the check for nearly $85,000. Still, would this be Sugar's last title match? The night after the fight Sugar talked to Milton Gross of the *New York Post.* "He was still in bed," Gross reported. "His body still ached from the beating. His face seemed drained. He left me with the impression that nothing could coax him back into the ring again. But a man who lives the princely kind of life Sugar has must feed his fancy and fill his ego. There is more than one kind of hunger, but there is only one place where Robinson can appease it."[4]

· · ·

Sugar must have questioned himself at this time about the limits of the human body and how much punishment he could take. According to Dr. Ira Casson, an expert on boxing and brain damage, symptoms of brain damage "usually begin near or shortly after the end of a boxer's career. On occasion they are first noticed after a particularly hard bout. Symptoms develop an average of sixteen years after beginning the sport, although some cases have occurred as early as six years after becoming a boxer. Symptoms have been reported in boxers as young as twenty-five years of age. Although the disorder has been reported in amateurs, it is more common in professionals. It can occur in all weight classes but is seen most often in the heavier divisions, and champion boxers run as much risk of sustaining chronic brain injury as less skilled journeymen."

Sugar was no longer the resourceful and resilient young man of twenty-five, when he could laugh off a series of hard punches, answering them with his arsenal of blows. Repeated thuds against his head must have left some concussive damage. Edna Mae wrote that she began to notice the effect the punches were having on his memory and moods. If Sugar needed any warning signs, all he had to do was to remember what had happened to his idols, particularly Henry Armstrong. He had stayed in the ring far longer than he should have, practically battered into dementia. But with his usual bravado, Sugar shrugged off any notion of mental or physical decline. What he couldn't shake off was a blow to the inner heart, and Edna Mae was about to deliver one.

CHAPTER 24

MEXICAN DIVORCÉE

How much of the purse after the Fullmer fight actually belonged to Sugar is left to speculation, but a good percentage was usually required to take care of the crowd of well-wishers who, when they weren't applauding his every move, had their hands out for donations and monetary contributions. Edna Mae had more than a passing interest in the welfare of his income. He was often behind in his promised allotments to take care of their son, and with bill collectors pulling him every which way, the likelihood of his keeping his commitments were slim to none. Moreover, there was the abiding tax dilemma, which Edna Mae's records show she tried valiantly to fix. Then there were Gainford's salary and publicity costs, each just under fifteen thousand dollars.

When Sugar finally got back to New York, he went to see his wife and son. "He was totally miserable while he told me how happy he was," Edna Mae said. "He confided in me that he had started smoking marijuana and did not want his mother to know it." She was stunned by this revelation, since Sugar didn't smoke cigarettes or drink much. "I knew Sugar was in great emotional trauma to now be indulging in vices so detrimental to his health and career," she concluded.

Sugar prevailed on her even further, asking her to allow him to come to her house to smoke marijuana while their son was at school. He needed to calm his nerves, he told her. As usual when it came to Sugar's sweet talk, Edna Mae gave in. He would come to the house, get in bed (without her, at her insistence), and light up his joints, tossing the butts out the window, where they landed below the front door. One day Ray II came into the house with a handful of butts and showed them to his mother. He told her he had seen his father smoke those kinds of cigarettes. Sugar confessed to Edna Mae that Ray, then eleven, had seen him smoking a joint once before he left for school. She was furious, and that ended his privilege. But it was only the beginning of Sugar's fury.

When Edna Mae and Ray II returned home the next day after staying all night with her son's godmother, Sugar soon arrived and began ringing the bell and banging on the door. "Ray was in the bathtub, so I answered the door," she recounted. Sugar took one step inside the house and began calling her filthy names and smacking her upside the head, until she nearly passed out. Ray II came to the top of the stairs and started screaming for his father to stop hitting his mother. "You'll kill Mommy!" he cried. Sugar stopped, and went upstairs to his son to comfort him. Edna Mae used this moment to hurry to the kitchen to call for help. Aunt Blanche called Sugar's mother, who lived only four blocks away, and told her what was happening and threatened to call the police. Sugar's mother begged her not to do that, and promised she would be right over. She was there in a few minutes and quickly interceded, repelling another attack against Edna Mae by Sugar. While Sugar was in his mother's arms, Edna Mae grabbed Ray and hustled over to a neighbor's house.

Once Sugar left, his mother went to see about Edna Mae and Ray. She cringed at the sight of her daughter-in-law's face. Dr. Arthur Logan was summoned, and he took one look at her battered face and rushed her to the hospital for treatment and X rays. She was diagnosed with two concussions. After almost twenty years of marriage, infidelity after infidelity, years of abuse, and separation, she said, "I decided to get a divorce."

• • •

After losing to Fullmer, Sugar fought once a month over the last third of 1961. On September 25, the twentieth birthday of Ronnie, his oldest son, whom he rarely saw, Sugar won a ten-round decision over Wilf Greaves in Detroit. In October he outpointed Denny Moyer in New York City, and for the first time in his career, because of a less than exciting performance, he heard a chorus of sustained boos. "I was at the weigh-in for his first Denny Moyer fight," said fight authority Clint Edwards. "Sugar strolled in, bumped past everybody, stood on the scales, was weighed, and then turned to find out who he was fighting. When he looked back and saw it was Moyer, he commented, 'I'm fighting this baby-face kid?' It was another indication of how old he was getting."

"The contest with Moyer taught me many things," Sugar told Les Matthews of the *Amsterdam News,* who was popularly known as "Mr. 125th Street" because of the wide range of information he possessed about the community. "I will not forget them. Yes, the punches did hurt me. The only time a punch did not hurt me during my ring career was when I got under it or blocked it. I'm human." He wasn't exactly sure why his performance was so unusually blah. "My legs were in fine shape; so was my wind. I was in excellent condition. I must sharpen my punches. I was disgusted with myself when I missed. The boos never hurt me because I know the paying customers are always right. I love the cheers." [1]

The cheers returned in his next fight, against Al Hauser, whom he obliterated in Providence in November; then Sugar plastered Greaves again in December in Pittsburgh. Sugar had plummeted to the has-been circuit, hammering it out in almost meaningless bouts with nameless club fighters, many of them over the hill and, like him, trying to earn a buck without losing their teeth or their sanity.

It got so bad that one day when Sugar was training for a return match in February 1962 with Denny Moyer, whom he had defeated just months before, he was told he was no longer a special nonpaying customer at Harry Wiley's Gym. Sugar stared at the attendant incredulously with a you-gotta-be-kidding expression on his face. The next day Wiley patched up what Sugar had assumed all along—and fervently hoped—was a mistake. Indeed, according to actor Johnny Barnes, a longtime Harlemite who gave a realistic performance as Sugar in the movie *Raging Bull*, Sugar himself had bought the gym and then given it to Wiley in order to keep him from begging and pestering him for money. "Ray used it for tax purposes," Barnes explained, "and he allowed Harry to keep all the money paid through dues."

The courtesies he expected at Wiley's, Sugar also expected

each time he went by Edna Mae's under the pretext of wanting to see his son. She never denied him these opportunities, though she was ever on guard for an outbreak of his sudden anger. Sugar's mood, she said, could roll in like a thunderstorm, ripping apart everything in its path. That was one reason she never said much to him during these visits. Her hope was that he would come, spend some time with his son, and then leave peacefully.

Keeping the peace with Edna Mae didn't mean Sugar had to keep his peace with the IRS. He was still trying to recoup money owed to him from as far back as the first Basilio fight four years earlier in September 1957. Then, Sugar received a most miraculous windfall. The IRS sent him a check for $123,935.65.[2] The full amount seized had been $313,449.82, but Sugar had used it each time he needed it as credit on his taxes and the check the IRS sent was the amount left over.

Sugar wasted no time and hurried to the bank and cashed the check. "The money filled two large shopping bags, which he walked with down Seventh Avenue while carrying it back to the office," Edna Mae reported. Ray II was in Sugar's office the day the money arrived. "I was there at the office that day and saw my dad and a few of his friends holding duffel bags full of money," he recalled. "The manager of Chase Manhattan Bank had called them to say the government had made a mistake and there was a release on his money. And he wanted Dad to come in that day and pick up all the money owed to him. It was absolutely astounding to see all those duffel bags and shopping bags full of money, and there was no thought of anybody ripping them off or anything."

Now, Sugar's planned trip to Europe and his list of companions could be expanded, much to Edna Mae's chagrin. He had not divulged his good fortune to his wife, maintaining his woeful tale about being broke and destitute. But Sugar was in for a very rude awakening—and Edna Mae would be no better off: The money he received was taxable (of course, Sugar had never entertained that possibility). Edna Mae would be informed later that she was equally responsible for the indebtedness, though she never received any more than the stipulated support money during separation. With Sugar laying plans for a European sojourn in the fall of 1962, Edna Mae booked passage to Mexico, for a divorce.

· · ·

The summer of 1962 found Sugar in Los Angeles getting ready to tangle with the always tough Phil Moyer from Oregon. Back in February, Sugar had lost a decision to Moyer's brother, Denny; so giving Phil a shellacking would be a sort of revenge, he reasoned. But one Moyer was just as savvy and ring-wise as the other, and Phil too won a narrow decision over Sugar. Other than Millie and a few sweeties on the side who helped to salve his wounds, the only consolation in California was to be the company of Cassius Clay (not yet Muhammad Ali) and Joe Louis.

Photographer Howard Bingham caught the trio in a memorable pose one afternoon. Both Clay and Louis are wearing bow ties, while Sugar, seated between them, is informally attired in one of his typical striped knit short-sleeve sport shirts. It's a classic shot of three of the greatest boxers ever to step through the ropes. "It was during this time that I accidentally met Ali for the first time," said Bingham, who would become among the champ's most devoted and loyal friends, as well as his personal photographer.³ Clay was in Los Angeles to do battle with Alejandro Lavorante, who, by the fifth round, had been bludgeoned to the point of collapse. Only Doug Jones would go the route with Clay as he pranced inexorably to that memorable match with Sonny Liston.

. . .

En route to Mexico, Edna Mae reclined in her seat on the train and began reminiscing about how she used to travel with Sugar, holding hands, taking turns feeding each other, looking lovingly at each other with unbroken gazes. They were so much in love, she thought as the train raced toward Mexico, recalling how because of their mutual fear of flying, both of them preferred traveling long distances by train or boat. "As I rode across the weary miles and sat gazing out of my bedroom window on the train, I was reliving and remembering how much fun train rides had been for our immediate family—for me, Sugar, and little Ray. We would really turn the train into a hotel on wheels."

And then came a torrent of memories—Grand Central Station, darting redcaps, the streamlined *Twentieth Century,* the gallant porters standing at the head of each car, Penn Station and the cries of "All aboard!" "In those days we were often called the Robinson Caravan because of the large numbers of persons that traveled with us . . . Because of this we would have at least one whole car reserved for the Robinsons." In her reverie, she recalled the parade of celebrities who beckoned at their door—Jimmy Durante, Joan Crawford . . . all of them seeking autographs or asking if it would be all right to have a picture taken with the champ. "It seemed that we had so few private times together that we turned our travel times into hours packed with joy, love, and happiness. We hoped somehow that it could carry us through the times that were shorn of tenderness and caring by the pressures of his demanding life and profession. Now, here I was rolling into Juárez to put an end to our marriage."

Rather than sit in her room in the villa and sulk and cry, she decided to do the town with her lawyer and to see what sprawling Mexico City was all about. It was a splendid evening, she said, and everywhere they went they were serenaded by mariachi musicians dressed in colorful costumes and blessed with melodious voices. But despite the lavish dining, the dancing, and the touring of fabulous sites, there was no way she could dispel the marital trauma that gripped her. In the courtroom there was additional anxiety, since the entire proceeding was conducted in Spanish. Somewhere in the midst of the flurry of words she didn't understand, she was asked to raise her right hand and to repeat after the judge. Several minutes later she was escorted to another room, and her lawyer informed her she was a free woman.

Back in her room, with her lawyer still in tow, the hysteria was so intense that she ran to the bathroom and heaved between sobs. After taking some time to console her, the lawyer left and Edna Mae pulled herself together and sat relaxing in a large chair. She was jolted from her meditation by the jarring ring of the telephone. Somehow the press had caught wind that she was there, even though she'd checked in under an assumed name. The place was a known haven for divorcées, and the press always had informants on the scene to tip them off. (Two years before, in 1960, Hazel Scott had probably endured the same hounding when she was there ending her fifteen-year marriage to Adam Clayton Powell, Jr., and earlier in 1962, in January, Marguerite Mays had made the same trip to the same place to untie her seven-year knot with her husband, baseball great Willie Mays.) Uppermost in the newsman's mind was whether Sugar knew about the divorce, since he was then traveling in Europe. She told the reporter that Sugar was not aware that they were now officially divorced. By morning the news was everywhere: As of October 2, 1962, the Robinsons were no longer a unit.

CHAPTER 25

THE OTHER WOMAN

Sugar must have been somewhere between London (where he lost a decision to Terry Downes) and Vienna (where he was scheduled to fight Diego Infantes on October 17) when he heard the news. It would be weeks before he learned the details of the divorce—the grounds and other incidentals. A year before, when Edna Mae had been granted a legal separation, she was given custody of their child and Sugar was ordered to pay her two hundred dollars each week, maintain a checking account with a balance of at least six hundred dollars for household expenses, and make a number of other payments as well, based upon a percentage of his overall earnings. All these provisions remained in place in the final divorce settlement, and Sugar was also stuck with all of Edna Mae's legal fees, which totaled twenty-five hundred dollars. In the succeeding years she would be in and out of court trying to get her delinquent ex-husband to fulfill his obligations.

Another gnawing financial matter involved his agent, Joe Glaser. Glaser had brought nearly a $100,000 judgment against him based on Sugar's failure to pay off a loan. According to Glaser's attorney, Emil K. Ellis, Sugar had borrowed the money and used his property as collateral. Sugar's real estate firm, R.G.S. Realty Corporation, had defaulted in its payment on the mortgage by failing to meet installments that were due in July 1959. A foreclosure order was signed in Supreme Court in March 1962, and three of Sugar's buildings on Seventh Avenue had to be auctioned off in order to pay the debt. "Tenants living in the buildings, who have been paying rents to the receiver, attorney Harold Lipton, for several months, were notified . . . of the pending foreclosure sale to satisfy the judgment with costs and expenses." [1] Sugar had apparently embarked for Europe with this among the other burdens on his mind.

Among Sugar's troubling concerns, as he and Millie toured Vienna, was how to propose to her. They had become officially engaged on their way to Lyon. His victory over Infantes, whom he'd sent to the canvas for good in the second round, reassured Sugar and boosted his flagging confidence after he had for the first time in his brilliant career suffered back-to-back losses, to Phil Moyer in Los Angeles and Terry Downes in London. Oddly, Sugar didn't make an appearance in Paris during this trip. Months before he'd begun to plan this European tour, his resourceful promoter there, Charlie Michaelis, was drumming up a possible match for him with an opponent to be chosen by a poll and fought in Paris. The poll ran for weeks in a French paper, and did a good job of inflaming passions. There seemed to be a definite thirst for Sugar to return, no matter who would be selected to fight him. But nothing much came of this publicity stunt, and Sugar's next fight in France was eventually in Lyon.

In Lyon, on November 10, he knocked out Georges Estatoff in the sixth round. But Sugar's European conquests barely got a mention in the press, even in boxing magazines that had followed his movements like a bird dog. As Sugar's star began to wane, many boxing pundits turned their attention to other developments on the boxing horizon, in the heavyweight division. In one thudding round and after one thunderous punch in Chicago at Comiskey Park, Floyd Patterson was on his back as his conqueror, Sonny Liston, pranced and glowered nearby. It had taken the powerful Liston only 122 seconds to do away with Patterson, who was outweighed by more than twenty-five pounds. Two months later, on November 15, before more than 16,000 spectators at the Sports Arena in Los Angeles, twenty-year-old Cassius Clay smashed forty-eight-year-old Archie Moore with such menace and mayhem that the referee had to step in and call a halt to the evisceration. For once the cobra had bested the mongoose. The audacious Clay also had some fighting words for Liston, who was at ringside: "You go eight seconds with me and I'll give you the fight." The die was cast, the gauntlet thrown, and the pretty boy from Kentucky was ready to do some "bear hunting."

• • •

Freed from Sugar, Edna Mae returned from Mexico to face an avalanche of bills. The house note was overdue, the money she had expected each Friday as part of the divorce settlement had not come, and during a cold spell that gripped the city, there was no oil. When she called the oil company to find out why none had been delivered, she was told that the bill had not been paid. "I had to call my grandmother and have her send me money for house and living expenses," Edna Mae recorded in her notes. Ray II recalled how outdone his mother was about not being able to pay the bills and take care of herself. "One day my mother went to a major department store to make a purchase and was told that a stop had been placed on her credit card. Soon, even her charge cards at the food store were stopped; everything now had to be C.O.D.," he said.

Added to these bills, the landscaper wanted his back payment before he would do any more work around the house, and a sundry of other invoices jammed her mailbox. She had no money to defray any of them. In one way she was free of Sugar, but in another way he was very much on her mind and in her curses. There was no alternative but to take him to court. "After many months passed we obtained a thirty-thousand-dollar judgment against Ray in the Bronx court," Edna Mae wrote in her memoir. "But it was never paid."

Having to endure the humiliation of family court unnerved her; she looked at all the other battered women with crying children and almost walked out of the waiting room before picking up the necessary paperwork and meeting with a clerk. Her lawyer persuaded her to stay and confront Sugar, who arrived late and sashayed into the courtroom like he owned it, as Edna Mae recalled. The female judge asked Sugar why he hadn't been paying child support. Sugar said: "Darling, you must know that if I didn't pay it, I didn't have it." The judge bristled at the comment and responded: "Mr. Robinson, in the first place I'm not your darling, and you are entirely out of order." Sugar apologized immediately and was told he had a few hours to get the money and return to court. He obeyed the order and promptly returned with the money.

Meanwhile, much to Edna Mae's dismay, Sugar had put all of his businesses in his mother's name in order to protect his earnings from the court. Despite spinning deeper into debt, Sugar continued to live in the lavish way to which he had grown accustomed, directing bill collectors and the IRS to his ex-wife's door. To get some relief from her awful misery and to earn some money, Edna Mae enrolled in Wilfred's Academy of Hair and Beauty Culture to become a licensed cosmetologist. She was even able to convince Sugar to finance her in a business venture as a way to pay back some of the money he owed her. He agreed. But then came a major setback.

One day Edna Mae came home to find Sugar waiting at her doorstep. It was not a good sign, and it was even worse than she thought. As she entered the house, the mess she saw told her immediately what had happened: The house had been burglarized. "All my furs and jewels, plus all my son's jewelry, was gone," she said. Among her furs had been a full-length ranch mink coat, a Russian lynx coat, a Persian lamb broadtail coat, a platinum mink jacket, a platinum mink stole, and a silver-blue mink stole, in all totaling about thirty thousand dollars' worth of furs. "All the beautiful leather folding doors in our home had been slashed open and the thief had gone through them. The pity of that was that the doors were not locked." The valuable ermines and minks that she wore with such panache, glamorizing cocktail parties and nightclubs from coast to coast, were gone forever—even the mink she'd worn in 1951 when she was the cover girl on the premier edition of *Jet* magazine.

Gone too was the possibility of getting any compensation

from her insurance company, Lloyd's of London. "The renewal time came just after Ray and I had legally separated," she continued, "and he refused to renew my premiums, telling me that it made no sense to him to pay Lloyd's costly premiums when we were no longer together. I surely could not pay it, so the burglary was a total loss for me."

CHAPTER 26

ALI

Edna Mae was gone, his flamingo Continental had been sold, and his café had been closed for several months because of his inability to meet payroll. Everything was gone but Millie. And soon he realized that to keep her, he might have to try matrimony one more time. Yes, he had proposed to her in Vienna, but he'd planned on delaying the marriage as long as possible, while he concentrated on a series of fights from the end of January 1963 to May 5. Only Ralph Dupas in Miami Beach gave him any real trouble, lasting ten rounds but losing the decision. Ferdie Pacheco, popularly known as "the Fight Doctor," was invited by Sugar to work in his corner, and he noticed that though Sugar looked sensational, his boxing skills and reflexes had diminished. "It was almost immediately apparent that in the ring was a boxer who appeared identical to Sugar Ray Robinson but was an impostor," Pacheco related in his book. "I looked at Sugar Ray's trainer, who just shrugged. A feeling of sadness and despair crept over me. Robinson won that fight, although the outcome didn't really matter."[1]

Sugar may have been for many a mere shadow of his former self, but after Dupas he convincingly toppled three nondescript fighters like bowling pins without breaking a sweat. In June, however, he had a bout with tough Joey Giardello from Philadelphia. Giardello in his hometown could present a bloody problem for the aging Sugar. If he could get by Giardello, he thought, he had a chance to do what he had done five times before—regain the championship. To look past Giardello to get to Dick Tiger, who had taken the belt from Fullmer, was not very prudent of Sugar, but was a common practice for him. Boxing matches were like chess tournaments to Sugar: Giardello was just a meaningless pawn blocking the path to checkmating the king. It never dawned on him that he was washed up, that the party was over, that he was nothing more than a once glamorous champ who should have hung up his gloves several fights ago.

On June 24, Sugar stepped into the ring in Philadelphia against Giardello. Checking Giardello's record, Sugar must have felt a bit ambivalent about his chances. On the one hand he was encouraged to see that in a recent fight Giardello had lost to Ralph Dupas, whom Sugar had recently defeated. But on the other hand, Giardello had fought the tough Gene Fullmer to a draw (as of course Sugar had done in December 1960). Giardello, at thirty-three years of age, was a gritty, hard-nosed veteran who relished an opportunity to slug it out in the center of the ring. Sugar knew he was up against a real warrior and that he would be taking on a hometown favorite. Rocky Balboa was a fictional character, but if there was prototype for the film fighter's saga, Giardello's climb to the top, his life story would have been ideal. Sugar and Giardello banged each other with such ferocity that it was amazing that one of them didn't collapse from the accumulation of punishment. In the end, with both men standing, it could have been called a draw, but the decision went to Giardello. Sugar had known that he wouldn't stand much of a chance if the fight went the distance and it was left to the referee and the judges to make the call. To win he'd have had to put his opponent away, but Giardello's jaw was not made of glass, nor was he reluctant to trade punches with Sugar.

There was but one recourse for an ex-champion running out of top contenders in the States: head overseas—which Sugar did. "In the fall, I went to Paris, where Charlie Michaelis booked me," Sugar recalled. "In five fights, I didn't lose. Two of my victories were over Armand Vanucci." None of the fighters he met offered any real threat, and certainly not Vanucci, who according to Sugar was a guard for the painting *Mona Lisa* at the Louvre. This was Sugar's fourth tour of Europe, where his name had once been magic. There had been a time, whether in London, Paris, or Rome, when his appearance was guaranteed to draw thousands of spectators, each one of them clamoring to get near him, to luxuriate in the wattage of his iconic radiance, hoping it would brighten his or her own bleak life.

But after back-to-back defeats to Paul Pender in January and June of 1960, the excitement and surprise of his previous visits, when he was as much a rave as the jazz musicians had been during the twenties, was missing. He and his entourage were no longer besieged by the media; he had clearly lost some of the irrepressible charm that, at its peak, could leave his worshipers overcome by paroxysms of joy. The glitter and glamour that seemed inseparable from his special aura were diminishing with each fight, with each embarrassing decision to some unknown pug trying to make a name for himself.

Sugar's kinetic verve, especially to millions of Parisians, had rivaled that of the dazzling Josephine Baker, of another age. At the top of his game, he radiated a presence that suggested everything that was fresh, vital, audacious, and sexual. All the stereotypical connotations about the persona of the black "primitive," the animal sensuality, and the sheer power of his celebrity were enough to give him, in his prime, the appeal of a rock star or a Hollywood matinee idol. On the way home from possibly his last tour, he looked out over the ocean as the liner plied the Atlantic, and he had to know that it was getting near the end, that the final bell was about to sound.

Meanwhile, Edna Mae had completed her course work at Wilfred's. Now, with her license in hand, she was ready to open her own shop as a beautician. But Sugar welched on his promise to stake her once she finished the school and had her license. Unable to start her own business, Edna Mae considered working with another Wilfred graduate, but working a full-time job meant there would be no one to supervise her child. "I had to abandon that idea of being a beautician," she said. "I then desperately decided to try to return to the theater. I'd had such success with the leading role in *Born Yesterday* and believed that with help from the right source I could be on the Broadway stage again and be able to support my son and myself."

One option she toyed with was to contact Frank Sinatra. The crooner had once given her his private number and, at her suggestion, had been considerably charitable to the Links, a black women's organization that conducted fund-raising events to assist those in need. After several days of leaving messages for him, there was still no return call from Sinatra. Edna Mae concluded that he probably didn't want to jeopardize his relationship with Sugar, and therefore chose not to respond. Sinatra wasn't the only mutual friend the Robinsons shared who was forced to choose sides when they separated and eventually divorced. "Some feared losing their jobs," she assumed, "and others feared losing Sugar's friendship, which would mean being left out of the glamorous festivities that revolved around him or the distinct notoriety of being a close friend to one of the world's greatest champions."

. . .

For the first five months in 1964, Sugar took a sabbatical from battle, spending a good amount of his time with Millie or helping Cassius Clay get ready for his fight with Sonny Liston on February 25. He had not forgotten his first brush with Clay outside his café four years before when the "Louisville Lip" had been preparing for the Olympics. By now Clay had grown in stature, and his influence was no less seductive as he convinced Sugar to come to Miami and be in his corner, or at least by his side. During the weigh-in ceremony, Sugar was part of Clay's gaggle, which included trainer Angelo Dundee and Bundini Brown, who'd worked as a second in Sugar's corner for seven years. (Brown died in 1987 after a fall down the stairs of a cheap motel in Los Angeles. He was found paralyzed on the floor.) "Float like a butterfly, sting like a bee" was Bundini's advice, which Clay made famous. It took all of them and two or three others to keep Clay, whose pulse rate had climbed to 120, from tearing into his opponent. This bravado, which worked to intimidate his adversary and to cloak his own fear, would be standard fare for Clay. But on this early occasion, he was fined twenty-five hundred dollars for his taunting.

At the memorable fight, Sugar sat at ringside near Malcolm X and singer Sam Cooke. Sugar must have been pleased to see a replica of his fighting style and grace in a bigger man. Right down to the rapid prancing on his toes and the left hand hanging freely uncocked by his side, Clay had copied his idol. Sugar had told him to box Liston like he'd boxed LaMotta in their fights. He told Clay he had to be the matador to Liston's bull. "You can't match strength with Liston, just like I couldn't match strength with LaMotta. He was the Bull, but I was the matador and I outsmarted him. You can beat Liston the same way."

Clay followed Sugar's advice to perfection. His quick, snappy jabs kept Liston off balance and prevented him from unleashing his lethal power. At the end of round four, Clay was rubbing his eyes and complaining that they were burning and he couldn't see; his eyes were aflame with the ointment that had been used on Liston's cut. For half the fifth round Clay's vision was impaired, so he danced until he heard the bell.

When Liston heard the bell in the eighth round and remained on his stool, the referee signaled that the fight was over. Liston later said he had no feeling left in his left arm. Clay's feelings, meanwhile, were apparent to every spectator at the Miami Beach Convention Hall as he leaped for joy. "I shocked the world!" he screamed, pointing at all the sportswriters at ringside who'd had Liston beating him at seven-to-one odds. A bet on Clay that night would have resulted in a handsome pay-off; indeed, wise gamblers who bet on Clay—or Muhammad Ali, as he would announce himself to be soon after the fight— would end up on the winning side, and in the money, most of the time. At twenty-two, the colorful young fighter had shocked the boxing world and a few mumbling scribes—and it wouldn't be the last time.

In February 1964, shortly after dethroning Liston, Clay announced that he had converted to Islam. Sugar had seen Malcolm X with Clay in Miami, and it was rumored that he was going to join the Nation of Islam. Sugar presumed that Malcolm X had induced Clay to join the Nation, and since he'd never felt comfortable with Malcolm, Sugar decided to put some distance between himself and the two men. Ali had idolized Sugar as a fighter, but now he had a new hero, one who would give him greater cachet in the political realm.

CHAPTER 27

UP AGAINST THE MOB

Ever since the 1940s, when Sugar turned pro and demonstrated that he was championship material, the mob had been trying to get a piece of him. They had tried threatening and bullying him, and blocking his opportunities for major bouts, but they couldn't get him to bend to their will. Sugar was a hard nut to crack, they had conceded, though underworld types and bosses such as Frankie "Blinky" Palermo and Frankie Carbo were still after him right through the 1960s. Carbo, born in 1904, was a precocious criminal and already had an extensive rap sheet by the time he gained nationwide notoriety after being indicted for the slaying of a member of Murder, Inc. This information alone would have been enough to make most fighters break out in a cold sweat, but Sugar only laughed at such disclosures.

Even after it was widely known that Carbo virtually controlled the New York State Athletic Commission and promoter Mike Jacobs, Sugar was not impressed. Then again, he had to acknowledge that the mob's dominance of the fight game was killing his chances at climbing legitimately to the top of the ranks. There were rumors that even his longtime associate, Joe Louis, had become "friendly" with the mob. To be sure, the mob was circling him like rabid wild dogs, but that was about as close as Sugar would allow them.

"Sugar always liked to be surrounded by a bunch of gangsters and members of the mob," said actor Johnny Barnes, who at fifteen began dreaming of one day playing Sugar in a movie and got his wish in 1979, trading fake punches with Robert De Niro in *Raging Bull*. "He liked their company, but he never got involved with them, and he was never arrested or convicted of any wrongdoing. Furthermore, Sugar Ray infuriated the mob and promoters because he insisted on negotiating his own contracts. The lawyers who accompanied him were only there to read the contract and to make sure everything he wanted was enclosed; that was their only purpose. Ray said he could talk for his own money. When it came to money, Ray was a hard bargainer. If you wanted to interview him or take his picture, more than likely you had to pay."

Because he was his own man when it came to cutting a deal with promoters, Sugar was ostracized for almost six years in New York City, Barnes said. "That's why he had so many of his fights in Chicago from about 1941 to 1947," he added. And once the owners and promoters at Madison Square Garden— Jim Norris and Mike Jacobs—"blacklisted" Sugar, all the other arenas followed suit. [1] This was not completely true. Between 1942 and 1946, when he fought Tommy Bell and defeated him for the vacated welterweight title, Sugar had more than ten fights in New York City, though his appearances at the Garden were indeed limited.

Still, Barnes was not mistaken about Sugar's negotiating his own contracts and demanding to be paid whenever he thought he had something coming. "I want to tell you," Sugar told reporter/author Peter Heller, "if I was due a dollar, I felt I wanted that dollar. If I could help a man make a dollar, I thought I deserved a part of it. And I took a stand to get that, and if they didn't pay me I didn't fight." [2] According to writer Jack Newfield, Sugar was "the Curt Flood of fighters," in that he was difficult to negotiate with and drove a hard bargain to get what he wanted before signing a contract. "It was this determination that led him to demand a cut of the film, radio, and television money . . . to get the money up front," Newfield said.

• • •

There wasn't much money for Sugar to get up front in his bout with an unknown Art Hernandez in the summer of 1964 in Omaha. That nobody in boxing circles had heard of Hernandez and that the fight was taking place in Omaha and not one of the major arenas was indicative of Sugar's plight. He had fallen off the charts, and there was no point in his applying the hard negotiating tactics that had made him such a pain in the neck to the big-time promoters in New York City. Getting Hernandez to ink a contract took little cajoling; he was just as eager to get a payday as the star of the main event. But although it was a breeze to get Hernandez's name on the dotted line, it proved much tougher to line him up for one of his patented hooks, Sugar learned. They fought to a draw.

With few lucrative fights on the horizon, Sugar had to look

beyond it all the way to Europe. Beginning in the fall of 1964, he lined up several fights, most of them fodder and thus commanding very little payoff. Even so, it was better than anything on paper in the States.

• • •

As he prepared to venture to Europe for the fifth time, this time with a scaled-down retinue, Edna Mae had just about wilted under a blitz of financial woes. The setbacks had come one right after the other, each one more devastating, like Sugar's deadly blows. The coup de grace came when she learned that both of the banks she did business with—Carver Federal Savings and Loan Association and Manufacturers Trust Company—had been ordered by the U.S. Treasury Department and the IRS to secure $267,724.11 from her accounts. The notice of levy from the IRS indicated that income tax owed covered a four-year period from 1957 to 1961, excluding 1958. Taxes owed in 1959 were particularly startling, totaling $122,203.97.

"My God!" she exclaimed. "We had no such amounts, but our accounts were emptied and given to the IRS and the accounts closed out. I was in total shock for days. I remembered that a similar seizure had been done to Joe Louis's children." And like the Louis family's, her lifestyle was altered dramatically. She was no longer able to maintain even a semblance of her former life—the trips across the country were curtailed; the seemingly unlimited shopping at the major stores, the dining at luxurious restaurants and clubs and not having to worry about the cost were a thing of the past. Her son began to blame her for the changes in their life after she divorced Sugar. "I'd never confuse him by talking against his dad," she said. "The child was already beginning to show deep-seated hostility to me."

When Sugar returned from Europe toward the end of November 1964, having vanquished most of his opponents—compiling a record of five victories, one defeat, and one draw—he arrived just in time to celebrate Christmas, and there were even some presents for his ex-wife and child. After the visit, Ray II accompanied his father to the car, with Edna Mae watching them from the window as they walked along holding hands. She had lost her husband; now she pondered if she was losing her son, too. When Ray returned to the house and walked in the door, he didn't say a word to his mother. The remaining days of the holiday season were glum for Edna Mae. There was now more than enough time to rethink the moves she had made, to reexamine her relationship with Sugar's mother, who, she heard through the grapevine, was no longer resentful of her, telling whoever would listen how kind and good-mannered Edna Mae was. "Her appreciation of me had come too late," Edna Mae wrote.

During Sugar's last trip to Paris, there were news clips of him with Millie and his sister, Evelyn, who had recently joined Sugar's ever-shrinking crew. To see Sugar and the women being smothered by an adoring mob of Parisians only made Edna Mae more miserable, and she would do all she could to avoid such reports. But the photos in the newspapers and magazines would sometimes catch her by surprise, as it must have in 1985 when Sugar came to New York to be honored along with other boxing legends. A photograph of Sugar and Millie, her arms draped over his shoulders, appeared in the *Daily News,* and it was later found among Edna Mae's collection of memorabilia. Nowhere in her notes or memoir does she discuss how these moments made her feel.

Caught in a time warp, reminiscing her days and nights away, she tried dating to break out of the doldrums and to end the loneliness. "I began to have invitations to so many lovely affairs from eligible males that my ego was greatly improved at the thought that I was being so sought after," she said. At last, she began to enjoy her new freedom, especially when she was invited out to go ballroom dancing, which she loved so much. Because Sugar had visiting privileges to see his son, he would frequently drop by the house, often unannounced. There were several occasions when he confronted one of Edna Mae's suitors, and inevitably that would end the courtship, most of the men choosing not to be the victim of Sugar's venom or fists. She also had to endure the pleadings of her son, and his demands that she not go out with other men. He didn't want Edna Mae to go out again "because if you do then my daddy can never come back home." To salvage her relationship with her son, she put off for the moment any serious dating, fearing that to do so would only anger her son and increase the possibility of permanent rupture between them. "The trauma and heartbreak of losing one parent had been frightening to our son," she confessed to herself.

There was little time for Sugar to contemplate what was going on between his ex-wife and their son, when he thought of them at all. Toward the end of his autobiography, they began to slowly fade from the pages, as Millie assumed a greater importance in his life. She kept his mind focused on the remaining few fights of his career, providing the mental support that Edna Mae had once provided. One fight he was particularly focused on was the one with Jimmy Beecham, slated for March 1965 in Kingston, Jamaica. This was the third time he would fight in the Caribbean, but the first time in Jamaica. Getting a good fight anywhere was becoming harder and harder for the ex-champ, no matter that he was the once glorious and glamorous Sugar Ray Robinson.

Having lost some of his appeal in the ring, Sugar felt compelled to reconcile with Muhammad Ali, asking him to serve in his corner as a second. With Ali by his side, he hoped, more spectators would be attracted to the fight. Sugar knocked Beecham out in the second round. Ali was so busy trying to get his new wife, Sonji, to adjust to the lifestyle prescribed by the Nation of Islam that in his autobiography, *The Greatest,* he talks more about his fights with her than about Sugar's bout.

It got so bad between the couple that Sugar had to come to Sonji's rescue. Upset that Sonji's miniskirt kept crawling up her leg during a party for Sugar at some large estate in Kingston, Muhammad snatched her by the arm and marched her off to a bathroom, where he locked the door and released all his hostility. He pulled on her dress; but in his trying to stretch it, it tore. This fueled Sonji's resistance, and they became so loud that Sugar came to the door to see what was happening. "This is my wife and this is my business, so get away from the damn door," Ali screamed to Sugar. But Sugar said he wasn't going anywhere until he found out what was going on. "Listen, I'm gonna open this door in a second, and if you ain't gone, I'm gonna whip you good," Ali warned. "You ain't nothing but a middleweight, so go on, mind your own business." Sugar heeded Ali's command, realizing that if he were to knock the door down and confront Ali, it might be a worse mismatch than his fight with Joey Maxim. When Ali finally opened the door, the couple came out sheepishly, embarrassed by the incident. This was the beginning of the end for them as a pair, and in a few days, Sonji slipped away from Ali as he prepared for his return bout with Liston.

CHAPTER 28

A BLOODY BRIDEGROOM

Sugar and his team knew it was time to put together an impressive string of victories over worthy opponents if he were to get another championship shot. There were three more fairly convincing victories for the aging fighter. "I had turned forty-four," Sugar stated. "If my chance came, I had to be ready. I arranged a trip to Honolulu, for a fight with Stan Harrington." Harrington was of Irish, Hawaiian, and English ancestry, and his face, it was reported, resembled ten miles of rough road. "On the way, I had another one (fight) scheduled in a bull ring in Tijuana, Mexico, with a Mexican mailman, Memo Ayon. The dust from the dirt streets is in the air in Tijuana. As I sweated, I felt the grime forming on me." Sugar was so concerned about keeping the dust from caking up the pores of his body that he paid little attention to Ayon's banging away at his head. When it was over, Ayon was given the decision. Sugar believed the decision was one of the most unfair and one-sided of his career.

After the fight, he and Millie left town immediately, driving all night to Los Angeles. Their destination was Millie's apartment, where she lived upstairs over her uncle and aunt. But Sugar suddenly changed his mind. "We're going to Las Vegas," he told her. It was time for them to get married, he insisted. They drove to the Los Angeles International Airport and got the next flight to Las Vegas. From McCarren Field, they took a cab downtown to the marriage license bureau. With the license in hand, their next stop was the chapel near the Sands Hotel. Sugar wore his sunglasses to conceal his identity; he didn't want any publicity. On May 25, 1965, they were married.

Rather than proceeding on to Honolulu as they had planned, the newlyweds flew back to New York City. Sugar had something else on his mind: his son. Edna Mae was no longer living in Riverdale. Not only was she unable to keep the maintenance on the house—and even worse, her garden—but the burglary had spooked her and she was afraid to be there after dark. "It was then that I decided to move out of the area," she said. "Sugar's lawyer encouraged me to do so by offering to find a good man to act as agent for me to find a buyer for the house. Manhattan College owned the property next to me and they wanted my property in order to expand their school's advanced science programs."

But there was a snag in the process: Sugar's agent, who was mainly there to protect his client's interest. Whatever money Sugar could siphon from the deal would help defray his enormous tax debt. When one of Edna Mae's real estate friends heard the property was for sale, he made her an offer larger than the one proposed by Manhattan College. Sugar was bitter when he was told of the new arrangement, which threatened to cut his agent, and thereby his commission, out of the deal. His bullying tactics succeeded, and Edna Mae signed the papers with his agent to negotiate the sale of the house. "When the sale was completed," she continued, "the IRS, mortgage holders, and the agent were paid, and all that was left for me was a little over $23,000." As if she hadn't gone through enough heartache, Sugar's lawyer summoned her to his office and snatched an additional five hundred dollars for his services and to provide a small bonus for the tax agent.

Edna Mae was devastated. "It was like robbery without a gun," she said. With very little time to sell her furniture from the patio, the yard, and the bar, she alerted all of her friends to hurry on over and take what they wanted. They came in droves, even pulling up the immaculate shrubbery and other plants decorating the estate.

Edna Mae found a large apartment on the west side of Manhattan with three bedrooms, a large kitchen and pantry, a spacious living room, and a hall that could serve as an additional room. In this way, she was able to keep most of her furniture, and more important, the large apartment would make it easier for her son to adjust to the new living quarters. "I still had my car," she said with a sigh, "but I learned that if I tried to renew my license and registration the Tax Department would seize it also for tax payments, so I sold it for only a thousand dollars, to our chauffeur. Sugar had insisted that if I sold it, to paint it another color to prevent anyone from having his famous flamingo color. I didn't have a dime to waste and thought our loyal employee deserved the car. Anyway, a local Harlemite had already copied the color and would brazenly park it right in front of Sugar's café, so I decided one more couldn't hurt."

Others have noted that whenever Sugar traded for a new car, he paid to have the old one painted another color so that whoever purchased the used car could not be mistaken for him.

Back from the West Coast, Sugar dropped by the apartment to inform his son that he had remarried. Ray II, now seventeen, was very upset by the recent developments. Their home had been sold, he had left behind his friends in Riverdale, and now his father had broken the news that he'd remarried. Perhaps to appease his heartbroken son, Sugar came back to the apartment a few days later and asked Edna Mae if Ray could go with him to Honolulu. "For a moment I was speechless," she remembered. "If I said no, the child would never forgive me. I answered of course I'd let him go." Besides, she had been taking Ray to the beach so that he could practice surfing. Now, he could demonstrate his skills on the giant waves of Hawaii. In a few days they were off, and Edna Mae was a bundle of mixed feelings, happy and sad at the same time. It would not be the last time she would be so intensely conflicted.

What little honeymoon the newlyweds had coming took a backseat to Sugar's bout with Stan Harrington in Honolulu. Sugar had to enjoy the picturesque landscapes and cobalt blue oceans through puffed-up eyes. Harrington was a lot more than Sugar had expected. "He busted me up over the eye, with a butt, and he got the decision. I was a bloody bridegroom," he said.

CHAPTER 29

POUND FOR POUND

Edna Mae had just waved good-bye to her son and watched him ride off with his father en route to the airport when she got a phone call from one of Sugar's former associates. He was irate and blabbering all kinds of nonsense about Sugar and what he was going to do to him if he didn't get the money he was owed. "He was very distraught," she stated. "He said he had gone to Sugar's office and asked for some of his money. He told Sugar that his bills were piling up, yet whenever Sugar traveled, he would inevitably have an entourage. He knew that was costing Sugar big money, but that he also needed money, and immediately." He told her that Sugar spoke to him like he was nothing but a piece of trash. The angry associate felt he had been used and abused by Sugar.

"I went back later that night and I saw him go into his office alone," Edna Mae said the man told her. "I followed him into the office and locked the door. I forced him at gunpoint to open the safe, but there was no money in it. I told him that if anyone else had treated me like he did and spoken to me like he did that day, I'd have killed them." He said that he kept the gun pressed against Sugar's head, while he begged for his life. Sugar's life was spared, but as soon as he left the office, Sugar called the police.

The man told Edna Mae that he knew Sugar was going to the airport to take a flight to Hawaii, "but the plane will never get off the ground." After he hung up the phone, she called the airport to see if Sugar and Ray had boarded and if the plane was in flight. They were still waiting to board when she reached her ex-husband. Sugar told her that the flight had been delayed because of a report that there might be a bomb on the plane. She was a nervous wreck until the plane finally landed safely in Hawaii.

Sugar rarely mentions any of his sparring mates in his autobiography, but much of his sharpness in a fight can be attributed to a stable of fighters who often took a beating to get him ready. "Two of them stand out in my mind," said boxing aficionado Clint Edwards of the sparring partners who helped Sugar sharpen his skills and plot his moves. "Dino Woodard and Danny "Bang Bang" Womber. They could throw plenty of leather. Bang Bang eventually ended up working in Sugar's barbershop, the Golden Glover. He was the process man who 'gassed' the hair of all the pimps and players who came through. Duke Ellington, B. B. King, a number of big-name entertainers with a 'do' patronized Sugar's shop. And there was Gene Burton, who was not a sparring partner but Sugar's stablemate. They banged each other around in several exhibition bouts. Naw, he wasn't like the other 'opponents' who padded Sugar's resume."[1]

Author Joyce Carol Oates views "opponents" thusly: "An 'opponent' is known in the boxing trade as a man who loses, and is dependable," she explained. "Matched with a younger, promising boxer with financial backing he will give a decent showing . . . He may have dreams of winning a title but his value to the trade is that he helps build up . . . another boxer's record. His career is a foregone conclusion: He has none." In short, she notes, "he is a human punching bag."[2] The flip side of an opponent was a "policeman." Jake LaMotta was a policeman, a concept he explains in great detail: "In boxing a 'policeman' is a top fighter who, for one reason or another, can't get a crack at the title. So the only fights he can get to make any money are with the real tough kids on the way up—the ones the champ himself would just as soon duck. Archie Moore was a policeman for years, and Rocky (Graziano) used to like to use the tag with me because I was knocking off guys he would like to give a miss to."[3]

Given this definition, Sugar was, from 1940 to 1946, a patient policeman waiting to be called.

• • •

Upon their return from Hawaii in June, Sugar and Millie moved into one of the bedrooms at his mother's house. Since they planned to be on the road a lot, the living arrangements were only part-time, and would eliminate the cost of renting an apartment. And this made a lot of sense for a fighter who was living part of the time in California and the rest in New York City.

In addition, their troubled financial state had been further damaged a month before, when the Justice Department filed suit asking Sugar to return a tax refund of $123,935.65 that he had received on May 13, 1963. The suit was presented in the nick of time, because in two days the statute of limitations would have expired. Attorney General Nicholas Katzenbach said the case involved the amount of taxes Sugar owed on earnings from a middleweight title fight with Carmen Basilio on September 23, 1957. In April, the United States Tax Court had backed Sugar by ruling that he did not owe as much as the government claimed. However, it did not stipulate how much he did owe. The decision brought to a close a situation that began when Sugar thought he had made a deal with the IRS on past taxes. Sugar, according to the government, which had rejected his installment payment plan, should have reported the full income from the fight in 1957, rather than the $139,600 he disclosed as 1957 earnings. [4] Once more Sugar was in desperate need of cash, which meant more blows in the ring with opponents who could not guarantee substantial gate receipts.

On June 24, 1965, Sugar was in Richmond, where he won a ten-round decision over Young Joe Walcott (no relation to Jersey Joe Walcott, whose real name was Arnold Cream). Young Walcott would take two more plasterings from Sugar, in Richmond on July 27 and in Philadelphia on September 23. Walcott was Sugar's opponent in three of his last nine fights, and they were often tune-ups for something bigger down the road, such as Sugar's bout with Joey Archer, a stick-and-jab boxer, in Pittsburgh, the two finally contracting for the winter. In the meantime, Sugar was on his way back to Honolulu by August.

He had just returned from Hawaii, after experiencing another loss to Harrington, when the Watts riots erupted, once again stemming from a clash between the black community and white police officers. It took 13,000 National Guardsmen to halt the five-day outburst, which left 34 dead, some 900 injured, and more than 3,000 arrested and which caused property damage of $225 million. According to Edna Mae, Ray II, who had been with his father and stepmother since their trip to Honolulu, "had already called me and asked to come home because his father had struck him twice. Sugar had also struck several other people, including members of his staff and family. His striking his son really had me puzzled, because at home he could not even stay in the room with us if I ever attempted to discipline the child." Now, she said, things had obviously changed, and so had Sugar.

One very demonstrable change in Sugar was his immersion in the political arena. Jazz trumpeter Freddie Hubbard said that Sugar campaigned for New York City mayoral candidate John Lindsay in the summer of 1965, not too long after Lindsay threw his hat in the ring in May. "When Lindsay came to Brooklyn to campaign for mayor, he brought Sugar Ray Robinson and [they] went to the biggest Baptist Church in Brooklyn." This was probably Concord Baptist Church, then pastored by the venerable Reverend Dr. Gardner C. Taylor.[5]

Sugar's relationship with Lindsay eventually soured, when the ex-champ was unable to get an audience with the mayor during his first few months in office. The falling-out, according to Woody Klein, Lindsay's press secretary during his first administration, in his memoir *Lindsay's Promise: The Dream That Failed,* can be blamed primarily on the mayor's over-scheduling. Klein recalled that Sugar had campaigned for Lindsay throughout the summer and made an appointment to see the mayor one afternoon in February. "Lindsay was already two hours behind in his schedule by the time Robinson's turn came," he said. "A secretary asked him to wait even longer.

Robinson became insulted and stormed out of City Hall. This was not an unusual occurrence. Others were angry at the Mayor for failing to keep appointments on time. But Ray Robinson was a 'name' and the press knew about his visit that day. The result: a story in the morning *Herald Tribune* headlined: SUGAR RAY QUITS LINDSAY TEAM. It pointed out that Robinson, who had also accompanied the Mayor on his daily morning walks to City Hall from midtown during the transit strike, had turned down an offer from the Mayor to become a member of the city's new Sports Committee, consisting of fifteen famous athletes. 'I don't want any job,' he was quoted as saying. 'I'm not a politician. The man [Lindsay] seems to have changed since he got elected. I hope I don't regret that I campaigned for him.' " Sugar proved somewhat prophetic, because Lindsay would in 1969 switch his allegiance from the Republican Party, after he failed to win its primary in a reelection bid, to the Liberal Party.

• • •

Sugar had two fights in October, and he won them both. He had to win these tune-up matches in preparation for a more difficult challenge from Joey Archer, the fancy-dancer, slick boxer from thw Bronx with hardly any dynamite in his punch. At forty-four, Sugar was in the best condition he had been in years, perhaps feeling that his advanced age required additional sparring sessions and roadwork. He was serious about this fight, and serious about another shot at the middleweight title. A title bout would bring in more money, much more than the $790 he had earned beating Peter Schmidt in Johnston, Pennsylvania, on October 1, and far more than the $500 that was his take after stopping Rudolf Bent in Steubenville, Ohio, in the third round on October 20.

The bout with Archer was set for November 10, and Sugar was as enthusiastic about the encounter as he was when he'd first turned pro 201 fights before. "Archer was supposed to have a tough chin," Sugar mused. "He had only been down once in his career. But nobody had a tougher chin than Fullmer, and I took him out with my left hook." One factor that Sugar failed to consider, however, was age. At twenty-seven, Archer was almost eighteen years Sugar's junior, and while he may not have possessed a knockout punch, neither had he ever been knocked out. Sugar would have to conjure up some of the magic of old to overcome the odds.

It was a good thing the fight was in Pittsburgh, and not in New York City. The night before the fight, Manhattan, like other cities in the Northeast corridor, was pitch black. The blackout was the result of power lines from Niagara Falls to New York City operating near their maximum capacity. At about five-fifteen a transmission line relay failed. Now there was insufficient line capacity for New York City. The power grid wasn't prepared to handle this overload.

Nor was Sugar ready for Archer's maximum capacity.

Two rounds into the fight with the younger Archer, Sugar was up on his toes and bouncing with confidence, jolting him with crisp and effective combinations. However, when Sugar landed what he thought was his best punch, Archer blinked a bit but shook it off. That was not a good sign. In the fourth round, Sugar feinted with his left, but his legs got tangled, and Archer unleashed a solid right hand that plunked Sugar on the top of the head. Since Sugar was already off balance from a series of feints and tangled feet, the punch put him flat on his behind. Although the punch was not that effective, Sugar decided to take a nine count and catch his breath. But Sugar was much more fatigued than he thought, and found it difficult to get back his previous sharpness. "At the final bell, I just wanted to get out of the ring. Disappear. Vanish." As the decision went to Archer, Sugar searched the audience for Millie, who had been screaming words of support throughout the fight. "That's all right, honey," she yelled now at Sugar. "You didn't get hurt."

Sugar wasn't in pain physically, but emotionally he was a wreck, and embarrassed as never before. Jazz great Miles Davis was equally embarrassed by Sugar's futility. Pete Hamill, the columnist-novelist, was sitting next to Davis that night. "I remember Miles standing up, and there were tears welling his face to have seen this because I think he believed Robinson was going to get knocked out." After the fight, Hamill recalls, Davis went to the dressing room, leaned over Robinson, lying on a rubdown table, and said, "Ray, you're packing it in." Robinson nodded his head and said, "You're right."[6]

Sugar felt a little better later on when Archer came over to congratulate him on a splendid fight and to say how much he admired him. One fan told Sugar he was just like the Sugar Ray Robinson of old, but to Sugar he was just *old* Sugar Ray Robinson. Would there be a return match? Sugar's manager, Gainford, shook his head in disgust, insisting the fight should have gone to his man. He denounced the officials and promised that if there were another bout with Archer, it wouldn't be in Pittsburgh.

That evening in his hotel room, Sugar decided it was time to have a heart-to-heart talk with Millie about his career. "I'm not going to have any more fights," he promised. "No more comebacks." Millie was elated, and told him that was her wish too. His career would end with a defeat, but he had compiled an enviable record, one that any fighter would be proud of, that few could equal, and no one could take that away from him.

From the Archer bout, Sugar had enough money to rent an apartment on Riverside Drive. He didn't want to risk having his relationship spoiled because of his mother, who he believed had interfered in his relationship with Edna Mae.

Not too long after the fight he got a call from John Condon, chief of publicity at Madison Square Garden, and a man Sugar greatly respected. He wanted Sugar to come down to his office; there was something special he wanted to discuss with him. What Condon proposed was a special tribute to Sugar, to be scheduled December 10, exactly a month after his last fight. This would be an opportunity for his fans to see him one more time, in a ceremony honoring his illustrious career. Condon told him that the Garden would be featuring a welterweight title fight between Emile Griffith and Manuel Gonzalez. A half hour before the fight the arena would be darkened, Condon explained; then the four guys he defeated for the middleweight crown would be summoned to the ring and introduced to the crowd before proceeding to neutral corners of the ring.

There was only one proviso: Sugar had to promise that there would be no more fights, no comebacks, lest it look like the whole idea was a setup to bilk folks out of money. Sugar had a proviso as well: If RKO-Television was going to televise the event, then he would have to be paid. The television producer was also at the meeting, and was momentarily taken aback. "But we thought you would consider it good for boxing if it was on," he pleaded with Sugar. "I want it good for Sugar Ray, too," the boxer responded. Though in the twilight of his long career, Sugar was still finding ways to be a pacesetter. It was not the first time he had demanded extra compensation for television rights, but this time others were paying attention, and in a few years it would be a standard clause in a fighter's contract.

To avoid paying Sugar, his ceremony was scheduled a half hour before the ten o'clock fight and would be over by the time the televised championship bout began. (However, the entire ceremony was filmed, and is included in a documentary by Bill Cayton on Sugar, titled *Pound for Pound*.) When Sugar was introduced to the crowd, he half strolled, half trotted to the ring apron, bounded up the steps, bent through the ropes, and danced around the ring in a knee-length white terry cloth robe. His hair was glistening under the Garden lights. The thunderous applause was a good sign that those fans who were rankled by Sugar's dismal recent performances were willing to forgive, and to remember instead the thrills he had provided in the ring over the last score of years. "They cheered him wildly, frantically, affectionately, with unconcealed emotion and enthusiasm," wrote *New York Times* sports reporter Joe Nichols. Ring announcer Johnny Addie then introduced Sugar's former opponents: Bobo Olson, Gene Fullmer, Carmen Basilio, and Randy Turpin. Each of them entered the ring attired in boxing gear and robes, embraced Sugar, and departed to a corner. The embrace from Turpin was especially warm and genuine. Even Basilio, who had very little affection for Sugar and often referred to him as an "arrogant son of a bitch," appeared gracious and sincere. "LaMotta was there too," Sugar reminisced, "but the State Athletic Commission wouldn't permit him to be introduced in the ring because he had confessed to fixing his fight with Billy Fox."

LaMotta remembered the event this way: "The Garden promoters brought in, at their expense, all the former middleweight champions that Robinson had fought . . . they even brought Randy Turpin in from England. Who was the only former champ they excluded? Jake LaMotta, that's who! . . . I was the only former champ who could have walked to the Garden! I lived ten blocks away. I still ask myself, what the hell did I do so wrong that deserved such treatment?"

Former mayor Vincent Impellitteri was given the honor of presenting Sugar with a huge trophy that was inscribed "The World's Greatest Fighter."

Sugar was never much for words, particularly in such a large setting as this. But after a moment of stammering he said what was in his heart: "This is the first time I've had an experience such as this. I don't know whether to be happy or sad, but it fills me full. I'm not a crybaby, but it just gets to me. I know it's not good-bye, but it is farewell." Then came one of his favorite French phrases, which he had learned during his European tours: *"Tout à l'heure"* (I'll see you later). The Garden, with more than twelve thousand in attendance, erupted with deafening applause, more deafening even than when he had beaten the four men now gracing the corners during seven title fights—four men who now triumphantly hoisted him on their shoulders.

As Sugar enjoyed the moment, singer/actor Gordon MacRae began singing, "Should auld acquaintance be forgot . . . ," and Sugar recognized this as his cue to take his final bows and to exit the ring, lugging a giant-size trophy to an apartment that he claimed didn't have a decent table to hold it. Before he left the ring, however, there was one last glance around the arena, where nearly all the spectators were on their feet, whistling and cheering, their hands banging together.

Two hours later, at a sit-down dinner at Mamma Leone's, Sugar was toasted again. Joining the fighters and dignitaries from the ceremony were Mayor John Lindsay, whom Sugar had helped to win the election, and Muhammad Ali, whom Sugar insisted on calling Cassius Clay. Clearly, Sugar had set aside his past grudges against the two men. For more than a couple of hours the fighters swapped memories about past fights, each topping the other with anecdotes and tall tales. But soon the party was over. And repeatedly Sugar and Millie heard fans and friends cry out, "You were the best, Sugar Ray. Pound for pound, you were the best."

CHAPTER 30

LORD OF THE RING

It was probably fitting and proper that Sugar's fortune would rise and fall with Harlem's. At the peak of his earning power, Harlem flourished too, and there was a vital connection between his enterprises and the community; they fed off each other. Sugar provided jobs and inspiration to other aspiring entrepreneurs. "The most interesting thing about the whole phenomenon known as Sugar Ray Robinson was his presence in Harlem," his son observed. "Everywhere he went he would drive his car, and this made him automatically conspicuous. If it was parked outside a building, they knew he was there. The man didn't care; he had girls all over town. He got to know doormen all over the city, and they would watch his car while he was upstairs taking care of his business. He was a combination of a goodwill ambassador and a sex god. He was keeping everybody happy." This may have been true, but many younger Harlemites also saw him as a role model, someone from their neighborhood who had made it big, and thus made it possible that *they* could also make a name for themselves and give back to the community. And in 1965, Harlem needed a lot of giving back.

Psychologist Kenneth Clark's *Dark Ghetto* drew in sharp relief some of the social, political, and economic problems besetting Harlem at that time. He'd had a chance to witness the depressing aspects up close during his tenure at HARYOU-ACT (Harlem Youth Act), from which he resigned in the summer of 1964. Now, unencumbered, he could turn his keen perceptions on the social and racial realities plaguing a community he had adopted, especially its youth. He and his wife, Mamie, had earned their standing in the scientific community a decade earlier with their pioneering work on *Brown vs. the Board of Education.* They had also established a child development clinic, in the belief that black children were educable and not refuse to be discarded on society's dung heap. His anger was barely suppressed in statements such as this one from an interview he gave *Newsweek* in 1964: "They send hundreds and hundreds and thousands of cops (into Harlem). They would do better to send one-third as many building inspectors, or a thousand sanitation workers, or just an attempt at proper schooling . . . But you know what I think we're going to get? 'Quiet the natives, then go on with business as usual.'" Business as usual was spreading squalor, increased police brutality, soaring rents in dilapidated housing units, more homeless people in the streets, and continued unrelieved unemployment. Attorney Hope Stevens, one of Harlem's most highly respected leaders, asked, "How is the economy of the people of Harlem to be described? We may begin by referring to the capital accumulation evidenced in the segregated community. We talk of purchasing power of the colored people in New York City and arrive by simple multiplication at figures running in the billions of dollars representing their market potential. This is true only if we assume that by and large, the total income of the average black wage earner is spent to meet his needs and satisfy his wants. But in this assumption there is no room for savings. And capital can only be accumulated through retained savings."[1]

This description was also a summary of Sugar's condition at the time. By now, his once fabulous café was called the Gold Lounge, and under new ownership. The place where his office, Sugar Ray Robinson Enterprises, used to be was now Mr. Benbow, a women's dress shop. Perry's Cleaners and the Playboy's Barber Shop stood where his cleaners and barbershop had once thrived. On the corner at 124th Street, a beauty parlor, the House of Beauty, was busy, with women under hair dryers sitting where Edna Mae's lingerie items had once been displayed. Today, this block is taken up by the Ennis Francis apartments. To the right of the front door, embedded in the brick wall, is a plaque that commemorates Sugar's magnificent feats in the ring. Some friends and family members are still waiting for the sign to go up on the corner in his name.

Sugar had no savings, few prospects, and with each succeeding week was becoming more and more destitute and desperate. He began to borrow money from friends and associates, even hitting up the former mayor Impellitteri, now a judge, for a few thousand dollars. His rent alone, at $365 a month, kept him on the prowl for handouts and loans. Sugar had established an extravagant lifestyle, and he felt compelled to keep his "front up," to use the vernacular of the day. Keeping his hair processed, his suits cleaned and pressed, and his station wagon—the days behind the wheel of a flamingo Caddy or Lincoln were a fading memory—gassed up were once chump-change expenses but were now things he could hardly afford.

"My father was good at knocking people out in the ring, but as a businessman, well, he left a lot to be desired," Ray II has offered. "He accumulated a lot of money and he bought things. He bought his mother a house; he bought Mom a house; he liked being on Seventh Avenue, so he bought a bar; he liked getting his hair done so he bought a barbershop; since he had acquired some real estate he opened a real estate office; he had to have his clothes cleaned, so he bought a cleaners; and to keep my mother busy, he bought her a lingerie shop. True, he was a self-made man, and I don't want to downplay that, but he didn't have money sense."

Sugar considered going back in the ring, which would have meant going back on his word, but he concluded that fighting exhibitions wouldn't be the same as taking on professional bouts. Gainford, who like trainer Harry Wiley had been with Sugar throughout his boxing days, shot the idea down. And the "Emperor" was right again: It would not be fitting to see this glorious gladiator hauled from the arena on his shield.

With few options available to him, he went back into show business. He still had his looks, those great legs, and a decent singing voice. He decided to produce another album, as he had done back in the early sixties. His second one was appropriately titled *I'm Still Swinging* and was completed in 1964, according to an article in a Harlem weekly .[2] It was recorded on the Continental label, whose president was Donald H. Gabor; Continental also produced albums by Charlie Parker and trumpeter Hot Lips Paige. Featured on the album are tunes composed by Don Gernigan, and the music was arranged by Danny Small and Jack Hansen for a twelve-piece band. If the

"Robinson" listed on the compositions is Sugar, then he helped write some of the lyrics, which aren't bad, but not exceptional, either. Trumpet master Kenny Dorham and trombonist Benny Green are listed among the performers, though neither offers a solo. "Sugar, working in his undershirt and pants in the hot (Regent) studio, had a large clientele with him who nodded with approval at the playbacks. His biggest fan was, as usual, his sister, Evelyn."[3]

"There wasn't a wide distribution of the album," said Ray II. "I have no idea how many were printed or whether it was ever reviewed." Sugar's vocal range was limited, but he had a relaxed style, which worked best on snappy, up-tempo numbers like the album's title song. The liner notes by Pete Hamill say little about the recording date or the musicians, so there is no verification that Dorham or Green was in the band.

Sugar also tried his luck in Hollywood. He picked up a few bucks from acting in a number of television dramas starring Ben Gazzara, Danny Thomas, Mickey Rooney, Tony Randall, or Gary Crosby, mainly cameo roles. "When the movie *The Detective* was shot on location in New York, Frank Sinatra got me a bit part as a cop," he said. He had a much larger role with Robert Conrad in a *Mission: Impossible* segment that focused on the underworld's grip on boxing, a fitting theme for the ex-champ. Ed Asner was one of the stars of *The Todd Killings* in 1971, and if you didn't pay attention you might have missed Sugar's spot. In *Candy,* a 1968 film based on a book by Terry Southern, and featuring such actors and musicians as Richard Burton, Marlon Brando, James Coburn, and Ringo Starr, Sugar makes a brief appearance at the film's beginning, where he is Burton's chauffeur. Burton plays a poet who sweeps onto campuses like a pied piper and lures away infatuated female students, including a naive Candy. Sugar is his aide-de-camp, and is named "Zero," which just about sums up his performance. Thankfully, the brevity rescues him from the embarrassment the others endured in this campy, spoof-driven sexcapade. Sugar had gone from being virtually a matinee idol, a cherished icon, to becoming a second-rate bit player in B movies. Once more his life mirrored the misfortunes of his longtime friend Joe Louis, who during this same period of time was wearing a uniform outside Caesars Palace in Las Vegas, greeting high rollers and big spenders.

· · ·

Ironically, a fighter who had probably fought and raised money for more charities—the Cancer Fund, the Infantile Paralysis Foundation, the B'nai B'rith, et al.—than any other boxer was now in need of assistance himself. His situation resonated with the same sadness as that of Joe Louis, who through exhibitions had raised so much money for the government during the war years, only to later have millions of dollars stripped from him by the IRS.

To help pay some of the bills, Millie took a job as a receptionist at the National Broadcasting Company. Sugar was so upset at seeing his wife struggling to work through a terribly cold winter that he insisted she quit. He was able to borrow some more money and they tucked away a few dollars, so much so that one day Millie surprised Sugar with a piano she had purchased at bargain rates. (Years before, Edna Mae had also surprised him with the gift of a piano.)

Once upon a time, when the cash was almost literally leaping out of his pockets, Sugar would see something he liked, nod his head, point, and instruct the merchant to charge the item to him and ship it to his home. Now, there were moments of solitude and reflection when he would try to calculate how much he had fretted away; it must have been more than four million dollars, he surmised. The cost of taking a group of people to Europe several times had left a gaping hole in his savings, he reflected. But there had always been more money on the horizon. Now the spigot was tight, the Midas touch had turned to pewter. But, as he said on many occasions, there were no regrets. "If I had a chance to do it all over again, I'd do it the same way . . . To be a champion, you have to believe in yourself when nobody else will."

"The same way" would mean 202 total bouts; 109 knockouts; 65 victories by decision; 6 draws; 18 losses by decision; 1 defeat by a technical knockout; 1 no-decision and 1 no-contest. "He created a new place for the imagination of a fighter," said Jack Newfield in the HBO special he produced in 1998 on Sugar's life, *Sugar Ray Robinson: Bright Lights and Dark Shadows of a Champion,* "the way Louis Armstrong or Frank Sinatra or Marlon Brando opened a new room in their art form." Another distinction for Sugar was being named *Ring* magazine's Fighter of the Year almost ten years apart, in 1942 and again in 1951. No other "lord of the ring" can make such a claim.

• • •

Sugar was eventually diagnosed with a number of crippling ailments, including diabetes, hypertension, arteriosclerosis, and Alzheimer's disease. Each illness had its own way of ravaging his once glorious body, robbing him of his strength, curtailing his prodigious appetite for life, even removing the memory of his greatest triumphs before thousands of cheering fans.

There is no way to determine the degree to which Sugar was aware of his steady physical decline, how he dealt with the irony of his name and the debilitating diabetes, and the arteriosclerosis, which hardened vessels that used to supply the blood flowing to his magnificent legs, destroying their once enviable elasticity. And he may have been spared any full realization of the Alzheimer's, given its slow but steady erosion of one's faculties.

Despite the setbacks, in later years there were a number of significant triumphs for a man who was used to basking in the spotlight, to being the main attraction. In 1967, he was elected to the Boxing Hall of Fame in Canastota, New York. The moment must have been ironic for Sugar, since this was the hometown of Carmen Basilio. After he and Millie moved to Los Angeles in 1969, he founded the Sugar Ray Robinson Youth Foundation, and, on occasion, when he felt up to it, he would drive over to its Main Street Gym and spar a few rounds with Danny Lopez, Armando Muniz, or Carlos Palomino, just to keep his trim figure toned. Each year since its inception in 1969, the Foundation has provided thousands of underprivileged youth in the Los Angeles area with social, sports, and other recreational activities. However, the Foundation sponsors no boxing programs.

Working out at the gym was an ingrained habit to Sugar—so was his womanizing, which he continued until his physical deterioration made it no longer possible. In 1981, when Gainford died, Sugar took a trip to New York for the funeral. Millie wasn't with him, and he was accompanied by a bodyguard. "After the funeral service," author Ralph Wiley wrote in an article for *Sports Illustrated*, "Ray met Edna Mae and suggested they go to his hotel together. 'I told him I couldn't do that; we weren't married anymore. He got very upset. I had to tell his bodyguard to please take him away, because I didn't want to get hurt.' Robinson remained a womanizer until the diabetes, hypertension, and Alzheimer's began to take their toll." But this would be the last time he and Edna Mae would ever see each other.[4]

• • •

For her part, Edna Mae applied her usual energetic resolve to a number of activities—a little acting, some charitable work, a monthly round of civic and social affairs. In the middle and late eighties she made frequent appearances on various television talk shows. She was a guest on David Susskind's show in 1985 with Vikki LaMotta and the wives of two other boxers. In contrast to the bitterness between their ex-mates, Edna Mae and Vikki were quite cordial as they recalled their lives with Sugar and the Bull. "They looked forward to fighting each other," Vikki said. "They were perfect for each other." Among Edna Mae's most telling comments was one regarding the horde of hangers-on who swarmed around Sugar at every opportunity. "Sugar thought it was better to give them a job than a handout," she said.

A few years later she and Kitty Carlisle Hart were among several senior women on Joan Rivers's show. And when Edna Mae was asked what made her feel most glamorous, she said it was when she could get all dressed up in her furs. "Especially my chinchillas." The worst thing about getting old, she said, was "memory, both the good and the bad parts." Indeed, memory would be something lost to both Sugar and Edna Mae in their final days. She often spoke of how painfully aware she was of Sugar's rapidly changing mental status, but how she'd never thought it would grow so severe and one day claim his life. Nor did she think Alzheimer's disease would also claim hers, as it did.

Several performances kept her spirits up and her hopes alive. In 1994, Edna Mae was a featured performer with David

Margulies, Anne Pitoniak, Jerry Stiller, and Fritz Weaver in a musical program entitled *In Words and Music*. The program was sponsored by Stanley Eugene Tannen's FREE Theatre Project and was held at the Fifth Avenue Presbyterian Church. Tannen later would rent a room from her in her spacious apartment on 90th Street. [5]

"My mother was involved in all kinds of social and political activities, including fund-raising campaigns during the civil rights movement," Ray II recalled. "She once worked with Carly Simon's mother, raising money for various political causes. It was perhaps from all of this activity that we ended up participating in the March on Washington in 1963."

As she struggled to keep her sanity, she wished the same for Sugar. "I suppose I wanted to really believe that the former days of plenty were going to return to Sugar," Edna Mae reflected toward the end of her memoir, "so I ignored the obvious decline of his empire and kept praying and hoping God would remember how Ray had always loved Him and thought of Him as number one, with himself a little lower. At least he now was away from all the problems and pain of this merciless town (Harlem) that had raised him to its pinnacle and graced him with unlimited power and fame. Sugar had always led the parade while thinking he was clothed in brilliant and costly robes."

But now, she lamented, the party was over: "Suddenly there was no more applause and all doors were closed to him."

All doors except those to boxing immortality.

THE FINAL BELL

Between his last appearance at Madison Square Garden in 1981 and the time when he was saluted in 1988, Sugar and Millie settled into a quiet life in Los Angeles, with occasional trips to Las Vegas to attend a big fight at Caesars Palace. He also spent some time at his Foundation, mainly to meet and greet celebrities and potential donors. A number of organizations and institutions invited him to participate in their events, capitalizing on his power to still attract crowds. During these appearances he was rarely ever to do more than wave to well-wishers, given the degenerative impact of Alzheimer's.

The last few months of his life found him in seclusion, save for the presence of family and close friends. When he was in public, he was impeccably dressed and always managed to summon that famous smile. Toward the final days of his life, Sugar's battle against several ailments, including diabetes and hypertension, escalated. It was as if for every lethal punch he'd delivered, he was getting back two in return. That matchless stamina of his was finally down to the last breath.

Eight days after Sugar Ray Robinson died on April 12, 1989, more than two thousand mourners attended the memorial service for him at the West Angeles Church of God in Christ in Los Angeles. It would be the first and last time they would see Sugar flat on his back and not getting up. Whether it was an accumulation of punches, diet, or old age, the coroner's report said Sugar had succumbed mainly to arteriosclerotic cardiovascular disease, compounded by Alzheimer's, hypertension, and diabetes. The Reverend Jesse Jackson delivered a eulogy that captured the pathos and bathos of Sugar's adventurous life. "He was part of the American quilt," Jackson said of him. "His patch of the quilt had nonnegotiable integrity. He was born on the bottom but he left on the top. He went from guttermost to uttermost." The erudite minister's reflections caused even Edna Mae to shiver, remembering the good times she'd shared with Sugar. She had been reluctant to attend the funeral, but did at the insistence of her son. In a distant pew from Sugar's "immediate" family, she grieved silently, absorbing the eulogy in a private fashion.

Even a fighter/celebrity as coddled as Sugar had been for more than a quarter of a century would have called a halt to the flow of postmortem encomiums, which rivaled even the cluster upon cluster of flowers that crammed the church. To Mike Tyson, then the heavyweight champion, Sugar was an inspiration. "I had the opportunity to meet him once," he told Michael Connelly of the *Los Angeles Times*. "He had a great impact on me with very few words."

Tyson had never stood toe-to-toe with Sugar, but Joey

Giardello, who held the middleweight title from 1963 to 1965, had. "He was really a great puncher," he told Phil Berger of the *New York Times*. "A sharp puncher. His hand speed was out of the ordinary. He had smartness and quickness. He was a legend." Bobo Olson agreed. "He was the greatest boxer to ever step into the ring," he said. "He was the best. I tried to copy his style a few times but I couldn't do it. He was too good."

"When Sugar Ray stepped into the ring," said music mogul Berry Gordy after the funeral, "he was swift, elegant, magnificent and deadly. This man was unique."

Author and sports historian Kenneth Shropshire summed up Sugar this way: "Although not without his faults, Sugar Ray Robinson is one important athlete to look to. He understood the commodification of the black performer in the sports and entertainment industries and made the system serve his own needs, all the while displaying remarkable pride, power, and grace. Many athletes have taken Sugar Ray's name, but few, if any, will be able to live up to all that he embodied."

"I will never forget the pointers he gave me when we trained together at the gym on 137th Street and Broadway," said Jackie Tonawanda, the first woman to be licensed to box in the State of New York. "He was always so generous and patient with me. I have a picture of us that I will always cherish."[1]

"He was the greatest," said Max Schmeling, who fought Joe Louis in two memorable contests. "A distance fighter. A half-distance fighter. An infighter. Scientific. He was wonderful to see."

"He was a fistic genius," said the dean of fight trainers, Ray Arcel. "He had grace and rhythm. He could hit and not get hit. You got such pleasure watching him; people used to go to the gym just to see him shadowbox."

"A lot of people say there was a comparison between Sugar Ray Robinson and Sugar Ray Leonard," said Leonard. "Believe me, there was no comparison."

Trainer Al Silvani concurred. "Sugar Ray Robinson had two hundred seventy-four fights," he began, exaggerating the total number of professional fights Sugar had. "How could you put them in the same category? . . . Sugar Ray Robinson fought the toughest guys in the world continuously. . . . And don't forget, he fought fighters like Jake LaMotta six times—at that time you couldn't pick your own opponent."[2]

In the end, in the twilight of his life, he was but a shadow of his former self, and could not be comforted by the victories of the past. "He didn't even remember me," Gene Fullmer said at Sugar's funeral. And then Fullmer added: "But they all remembered him."

Filmmaker/comedian Woody Allen remembered Sugar this way: "I was so crazy about Ray Robinson, who was an amazing fighter. I had a chance to have dinner in his house and to spend some time with him, and so I have a very positive feeling about him as an athlete and a man. He was someone I idolized and then met, and who lived up to my feelings about him. Many don't live up to your expectations. I won't say who, but the ones who did are Robinson, Stan Musial, and Groucho."

These expressions from celebrities and fight authorities are part of a consensus on Sugar's lofty place in the boxing pantheon, and his legend seems to increase each year, given the mediocrity of the current crop of fighters. Because of changing social conditions, particularly the expanded opportunities for black men in America, we may never produce another home-grown champion of Sugar's caliber. He was a dazzling personality of incomparable athletic ability. It was hard to believe that someone with such playboy good looks could be so deadly lethal in the ring. And he was indubitably the ringmaster, subduing a "Tiger," a "Bull," and a Buffalo.

The final bell of Sugar's life has sounded, but as long as old men gather in musty gyms and reminisce about the good old days, their tales will invariably linger on memories of Sugar. "After Sugar, they threw away the mold," said ninety-four-year-old Langley Waller, who was a witness to Sugar's life in and out of the ring. "He was the original, the one and only."

EPILOGUE

Pound for pound, punch for punch, Sugar was deemed beyond comparison in the ring. "Sugar Ray Robinson, without a doubt, was a great fighter and would have been a great fighter in any era," boxing historian Herb Goldman told Katherine Dunn of the Internet's Cyber Boxing Zone.[1] And while there have been imitators, they are mere holograms when it comes to rivaling the genuine article. You can combine all the more recent and notable "Sugars"—Ramos (54–7–4); Ray Seales (56–8–3); Ray Leonard (36–3–1); and Shane Mosley (39–3)—and collectively they have had only twelve more professional fights and exceeded Sugar's victory total by a slight margin of ten (though Mosley, as of this writing, has yet to hang up his gloves, despite two miserable recent performances, against Vernon Forrest and Winky Wright). There was Sugar nonpareil and then there were the near-great pretenders, who have nothing to be ashamed of in their failure to match up to the original's majesty, or to come close to his legend. Perhaps Jeff Ryan of *Ring* is right—the other Sugars ought to "apologize for their conceit."

The other Sugars may not have an argument about Sugar Ray Robinson's supremacy, but there are many boxing historians and authorities who vigorously disagree about the "pound for pound" designation, particularly those advocates of Muhammad Ali. As the old axiom contends, any comparison is odious, and to extend one across time and beyond weight categories is even more problematic. If it were a matter of ring record, then Rocky Marciano's forty-nine victories without a defeat is the standard, despite his conquests over Louis, Walcott, Charles, and Moore when they were all far beyond their prime. For sheer punching power, it's hard to think anyone hit any harder or more effectively than Joe Louis. Jack Johnson was a defensive wizard, and few could match Jack Dempsey as an infighter. When it comes to ring prowess and cunning, then Ali, Sandy Saddler, and Joe Gans pop into mind. And no one could take a punch like Jake LaMotta. Of course then again, Sugar had a sizable portion of all these skills.

In 2003, *Boxing Monthly*, a British publication, began running a sports series entitled "Judge and Jury," in which sports experts offered their choices about who was the greatest performer in his or her particular field. In the boxing category, Ali and Sugar were the final choices. Of the first four experts to weigh in on the issue, two were in favor of Ali and two were for Sugar. How four experts compare with five hundred sportswriters who voted Ali the best of all time in 1976 is something to ponder.

In any case, it was left to Neil Allen, a former boxing correspondent of the *Times* (London) and the *London Evening*

Standard, to break the deadlock. "It's Gotta Be Sugar," the headline of Allen's article declared in a pink that would have rivaled Sugar's Caddy. Allen made his case based on two important factors. For one, the global population of people Sugar's size surpassed that of the population of people—and potential boxers—of Ali's size. "Even today, when youngsters are bigger and taller than their predecessors half a century ago, flyweights and heavyweights can be regarded as a comparative minority," Allen proposed. Flyweights and heavyweights comprised the ends of a perfect bell-shaped curve, and the welter- and middleweights made up the majority, where Sugar was king. "He had thousands of potential opponents compared with the hundreds" in the other weight divisions, Allen noted.[2]

Moreover, he continued, during the time in which Sugar went to battle in the world's arenas, the men were in much better shape, given the large number of ex-servicemen. Allen's third point, that the competition Sugar faced on average was better than Ali's, is less convincing. Can a case be made based on a comparison between the likes of Sonny Liston, Jimmy Ellis, Joe Frazier, Ken Norton, Floyd Patterson, George Foreman, Leon Spinks, and Larry Holmes, who pulled on the gloves against Ali, against Fritzie Zivic, Tiger Jones, Artie Levine, Randy Turpin, Carmen Basilio, Gene Fullmer, Bobo Olson, Rocky Graziano, Kid Gavilan, and the six grueling standoffs with Jake LaMotta that Sugar had to face? Was Joe Frazier equivalent to LaMotta? How did Zivic compare with Ken Norton? It's hard to say.

Also, when you place Ali's and Sugar's records side by side—the latter had more knockouts than the former had fights—consideration has to be given to the different eras in which they fought. We can never know how well bare-knuckled fighter Tom Molineaux, born in captivity in 1784, would have fared against the relatively modern fighter Sam Langford, and there is no way to determine the outcome of a bout between a fighter from one generation challenging another of comparable skills from another. And Sugar against Ali? Sugar wouldn't have stood a chance, given the weight difference. Or would he have?

Archie Moore, the exceptional light heavyweight, believed that Ike Williams, Sugar's contemporary, was the best welterweight he ever saw. But Williams believed Sugar was the best in the business. "I wouldn't fight Sugar Ray because I never could have beaten him, the greatest fighter ever," he told a reporter at *Boxing Monthly*. "When I mentioned the possibility of such a fight to my wife she grinned and said: 'Ike, that's one fight I don't want to see.' I didn't either."

• • •

This brings me to the end of my biographical bout with the great Sugar. In the ring, Sugar was easily apprehended; it was simply a matter of enjoying his wizardry and understanding the skills he combined to make him one of boxing's immortals. He possessed an exquisite jab that snapped the bull-like neck of Jake LaMotta. His left hook, no matter the trajectory, was invested with poetic power. Then there was his potent right cross, which often followed the former punches. Few fighters had the quickness to elude this combination or the stamina to withstand a series of such blows.

But as a man he was complex, with many intriguing contradictions. While he gathered about him an ensemble of well-wishers, he often ignored his immediate family. One can criticize his lavish lifestyle—the houses, clothes, cars, and parties—but he also contributed thousands of dollars to charitable organizations. More than one informant spoke of his gentleness with children; but then, there are the reports of his abuse of the women in his life.

Ultimately, Sugar was a gladiator, a warrior in what many have seen as the cruelest sport. He was not a minister, an intellectual, a politician, or a community leader professing the highest principles of integrity.

After gathering the books, magazines, microfilms, films, newspapers, and interviews about him, I am undiminished in my admiration for Sugar the boxer. He remains the indisputable pound-for-pound greatest fighter who ever lived. We may be disappointed that he was not of sterling character and was flawed, as we all are, but what he did with most of the moments of his life led to his reaching the pinnacle of his profession. And perhaps, as the poet John Keats said about truth being beauty and beauty truth, that is all we need to know.

. . .

Sifting the gems from his second wife Edna Mae Robinson's memoir and listening to her son, I gained another perspective on Sugar, that dark side of his personality that controlled the retinue surrounding him like a benevolent dictator. The more the sycophants around him vied for his attention, the more he ignored them. He could be as generous to strangers as he was penurious with friends and relatives. While there are many moments in his autobiography where he appears to be absolutely forthcoming, too often he is elusive and extremely selective in what he chooses to recall. It is difficult to get to the man beyond the smoky arenas and shadowy dressing rooms. Paradoxical? Bipolar? Dual personalities? A dissembler?

These are some of the words with which Sugar has been labeled, but they may be too simple and neat to define the man's complexities. After three years of my plying through books, articles, photos, memorabilia, and interviews, Sugar remains a cipher, defying a writer with the same darting moves, the same clever feints he employed against fighters on the prowl.

But even an icon is at the mercy of nostalgia and market forces. Recently, I was stunned to see Sugar's image on billboards advertising Nintendo, in which he can be seen delivering a devastating blow to an opponent on his way to the canvas. This photo was taken from an actual fight, probably in the late forties when he was busy defending his welterweight championship. The Nintendo game, however, is a simulated one, in which Sugar can be matched with such powerful contemporary heavyweights as Lennox Lewis or Evander Holyfield, and depending on your ability to control the joystick or the remote, it becomes possible for the smaller Sugar to knock out the bigger fighter.

Toward the end of his life, Sugar was asked what he thought of computerized fights that matched him against the likes of Muhammad Ali, Jack Johnson, Rocky Marciano, or any other fighter from boxing's pantheon. He dismissed it as pure nonsense. And he probably would have felt the same about the recent rash of simulated fights on game platforms. As good as some of these games are, imaginary bouts wherein contestants control the movements of their favorite fighters are a poor approximation of ring reality.

Whether animated or simulated or real, there was only one Sugar Ray, only one fighter who many of the other greats claimed was "pound for pound" the best fighter ever. Even

Muhammad Ali, who declared he was the "greatest," was willing to concede that Sugar might have been even greater than he was.

. . .

There was no perfect fighter, no consummate master of the "sweet science," but Sugar comes as close as any to that ideal. He possessed all the attributes of a great fighter: stamina, speed, resilience, balance, versatility, savvy, mathematical rhythm, and punching power—"poetry with a punch." In a recent *Ring* collectors' special of the one hundred greatest punchers of all time, Sugar was ranked eleventh, behind heavyweight Earnie Shavers and in front of Ruben Olivares. "He could hit you just as hard backing up as coming forward," boxing historian Bert Sugar has often remarked.

Sugar's left hook was perhaps his most lethal weapon. He could launch it from so many different geometric angles, with the authority to leave its recipient in every position but perpendicular; it could come at you like a bolo or from a wide, arcing angle, or from as close as a few inches away, with devastating power. Ask Gene Fullmer. It could come as a lead, a counterpunch, or it could dig into an opponent's gut, following a jab or a right cross. When Sugar got you in trouble, he was a menacing, deadly finisher. If you had a weakness as a fighter, he would eventually find it and exploit it unmercifully. Ask Jimmy Doyle and Flash Sebastian. There were very few styles he didn't figure out in his prime; sometimes it might take a couple of fights, but he was a shrewd craftsman with the moves of a chess master in the squared circle. Ask Randy Turpin and Carmen Basilio. And ask Joe Louis, who knew him longer and better than almost anyone else in the world, and who called him "the greatest fighter ever to step into the ring."

Who the best fighter of all time was will be debated until the sport's final bell, and even then there will be no consensus. There may have been fighters who were faster, stronger, smarter; who punched harder, were more resilient, and were perhaps even prettier. But none combined these attributes with such verve and flamboyance—and success—as Sugar Ray Robinson.

SUGAR'S RING RECORD

Amateur Fights—85 victories (69 KOs—49 in first round), 0 defeats

Professional Fights—175 victories (109 KOs), 19 defeats (1 KO), 6 draws, 1 no-decision, 1 no-contest

---

1940

Oct 4	Joe Echeverria	New York	KO 2
Oct 8	Silent Stafford	Savannah	KO 2
Oct 22	Mistos Grispos	New York	W 6
Nov 11	Bobby Wood	Philadelphia	KO 1
Dec 9	Norment Quarles	Philadelphia	KO 4
Dec 12	Oliver White	New York	KO 3

1941

Jan 4	Harry LaBarba	Brooklyn	KO 1
Jan 13	Frankie Wallace	Philadelphia	KO 1
Jan 31	George Zengaras	New York	W 6
Feb 8	Benny Cartegena	Brooklyn	KO 1
Feb 21	Bobby McIntire	New York	W 6
Feb 27	Gene Spencer	Detroit	KO 5
Mar 3	Jimmy Tygh	Philadelphia	KO 8
Apr 14	Jimmy Tygh	Philadelphia	KO 1
Apr 24	Charley Burns	Atlantic City	KO 1
Apr 30	Joe Ghnouly	Washington, DC	KO 3
May 10	Vic Troise	Brooklyn	KO 1
May 19	Nick Castiglione	Philadelphia	KO 1
Jun 16	Mike Evans	Philadelphia	KO 2
Jul 2	Pete Lello	New York	KO 4
Jul 21	Sammy Angott	Philadelphia	W 10
Aug 27	Carl Red Guggino	Long Island City, NY	KO 3
Aug 29	Maurice Arnault	Atlantic City	KO 1
Sep 19	Maxie Shapiro	New York	KO 3
Sep 25	Marty Servo	Philadelphia	W 10
Oct 31	Fritzie Zivic	New York	W 10

1942

Jan 16	Fritzie Zivic	New York	KO 10
Feb 20	Maxie Berger	New York	KO 2
Mar 20	Norman Rubio	New York	KO 8
Apr 17	Harvey Dubs	Detroit	KO 6
Apr 30	Dick Banner	Minneapolis	KO 2
May 28	Marty Servo	New York	W 10
Jul 31	Sammy Angott	New York	W 10

Aug 21	Ruben Shank	New York	KO 2
Aug 27	Tony Motisi	Chicago	KO 1
Oct 2	Jake LaMotta	New York	W 10
Oct 19	Izzy Jannazzo	Philadelphia	W 10
Nov 6	Vic Dellicurti	New York	W 10
Dec 1	Izzy Jannazzo	Cleveland	KO 8
Dec 14	Al Nettlow	Philadelphia	KO 3

1943

Feb 5	Jake LaMotta	Detroit	L 10
Feb 19	Jackie Wilson	New York	W 10
Feb 26	Jake LaMotta	Detroit	W 10
Apr 30	Freddie Cabral	Boston	KO 1
Jul 1	Ralph Zannelli	Boston	W 10
Aug 27	Henry Armstrong	New York	W 10

1944

Oct 13	Izzy Jannazzo	Boston	KO 2
Oct 27	Sgt. Lou Woods	Chicago	KO 9
Nov 17	Vic Dellicurti	Detroit	W 10
Dec 12	Richard "Sheik" Rangel	Philadelphia	KO 2
Dec 22	George Martin	Boston	KO 7

1945

Jan 10	Billy Furrone	Washington, DC	KO 2
Jan 16	Tommy Bell	Cleveland	W 10
Feb 14	George Costner	Chicago	KO 1
Feb 23	Jake LaMotta	New York	W 10
May 14	Jose Basora	Philadelphia	D 10
Jun 15	Jimmy McDaniels	New York	KO 2

Sep 18	Jimmy Mandell	Buffalo	KO 5
Sep 26	Jake LaMotta	Chicago	W 12
Dec 4	Vic Dellicurti	Boston	W 10

1946

Jan 14	Dave Clark	Pittsburgh	KO 2
Feb 5	Tony Riccio	Elizabeth, NJ	KO 4
Feb 15	O'Neill Bell	Detroit	KO 2
Feb 26	Cliff Beckett	St. Louis	KO 4
Mar 4	Sammy Angott	Pittsburgh	W 10
Mar 14	Izzy Jannazzo	Baltimore	W 10
Mar 21	Freddy Flores	New York	KO 5
Jun 12	Freddy Wilson	Worcester, MA	KO 2
Jun 25	Norman Rubio	Union City, NJ	W 10
Jul 12	Joe Curcio	New York	KO 2
Aug 15	Vinnie Vines	Albany, NY	KO 6
Sep 25	Sidney Miller	Elizabeth, NJ	KO 3
Oct 7	Ossie Harris	Pittsburgh	W 10
Nov 1	Cecil Hudson	Detroit	KO 6
Nov 6	Artie Levine	Cleveland	KO 10
Dec 20	Tommy Bell	New York	W 15
	(Wins Vacant World Welterweight Title)		

1947

Mar 27	Bernie Miller	Miami	KO 3
Apr 3	Fred Wilson	Akron	KO 3
Apr 8	Eddie Finazzo	Kansas City, MO	KO 4
May 16	George Abrams	New York	W 10
Jun 24	Jimmy Doyle	Cleveland	TKO 9
	(Retains World Welterweight Title)		
Aug 21	Sammy Secreet	Akron	KO 1

Aug 29	Flashy Sebastian	New York	KO 1
Oct 28	Jackie Wilson	Los Angeles	KO 7
Dec 10	Billy Nixon	Elizabeth, NJ	KO 6
Dec 19	Chuck Taylor	Detroit	KO 6
	(Retains World Welterweight Title)		

1948

Mar 4	Ossie Harris	Toledo	W 10
Mar 16	Henry Brimm	Buffalo	W 10
Jun 28	Bernard Docusen	Chicago	W 15
	(Retains World Welterweight Title)		
Sep 23	Kid Gavilan	New York	W 10
Nov 15	Bobby Lee	Philadelphia	W 10

1949

Feb 10	Gene Buffalo	Wilkes-Barre, PA	KO 1
Feb 15	Henry Brimm	Buffalo	D 10
Mar 25	Bobby Lee	Chicago	W 10
Apr 11	Don Lee	Omaha	W 10
Apr 20	Earl Turner	Oakland	KO 8
May 16	Al Tribuani	Wilmington, DE	Exh 4
Jun 7	Freddie Flores	New Bedford, CT	KO 3
Jun 20	Cecil Hudson	Providence	KO 5
Jul 11	Kid Gavilan	Philadelphia	W 15
	(Retains World Welterweight Title)		
Aug 24	Steve Belloise	New York	KO 7
Sep 2	Al Mobley	Chicago	Exh 4
Sep 9	Benny Evans	Omaha	KO 5
Sep 12	Charley Dotson	Houston	KO 3
Nov 9	Don Lee	Denver	W 10
Nov 13	Vern Lester	New Orleans	KO 5

| Nov 15 | Gene Burton | Shreveport, LA | Exh 6 |
| Nov 16 | Gene Burton | Dallas | Exh 6 |

1950

Jan 30	George LaRover	New Haven, CT	KO 4
Feb 13	Al Mobley	Miami	KO 6
Feb 22	Aaron Wade	Savannah	KO 3
Feb 27	Jean Walzack	St. Louis	W 10
Mar 22	George Costner	Philadelphia	KO 1
Apr 21	Cliff Beckett	Columbus, OH	KO 3
Apr 28	Ray Barnes	Detroit	W 10
Jun 5	Robert Villemain	Philadelphia	W 15
	(Wins Pennsylvania Middleweight Title)		
Aug 9	Charley Fusari	Jersey City	W 15
	(Retains World Welterweight Title)		
Aug 25	Jose Basora	Scranton	KO 1
	(Retains Pennsylvania Middleweight Title)		
Sep 4	Billy Brown	New York	W 10
Oct 16	Joe Rindone	Boston	KO 6
Oct 26	Carl "Bobo" Olson	Philadelphia	KO 12
	(Retains Pennsylvania Middleweight Title)		
Nov 8	Bobby Dykes	Chicago	W 10
Nov 27	Jean Stock	Paris	KO 2
Dec 9	Luc Van Dam	Brussels	KO 4
Dec 16	Jean Walzack	Geneva	W 10
Dec 22	Robert Villemain	Paris	KO 9
Dec 25	Hans Stretz	Frankfurt	KO 5

1951

| Feb 14 | Jake LaMotta | Chicago | KO 13 |
| | (Wins World Middleweight Title) | | |

(Vacates World Welterweight Title)

Apr 5	Holly Mims	Miami	W 10
Apr 9	Don Ellis	Oklahoma City	KO 1
May 21	Kid Marcel	Paris	KO 5
May 26	Jean Wanes	Zurich	W 10
Jun 10	Jan deBruin	Antwerp	KO 8
Jun 16	Jean Walzack	Liege, Luxembourg	KO 6
Jun 24	Gerhard Hecht	Berlin	NC 2

(Robinson disqualified by referee for a kidney punch.
Commission later changed it to a no-contest.)

Jul 1	Cyrille Delannoit	Turin, Italy	KO 3
Jul 10	Randy Turpin	London	L 15

(Loses World Middleweight Title)

Sep 12	Randy Turpin	New York	KO 10

(Regains World Middleweight Title)

1952

Mar 13	Carl "Bobo" Olson	San Francisco	W 15

(Retains World Middleweight Title)

Apr 16	Rocky Graziano	Chicago	KO 3

(Retains World Middleweight Title)

Jun 25	Joey Maxim	New York	KO by 14

(For World Light Heavyweight Title)

Dec 18	Announces Retirement	

1953

Did not fight

1954

Oct 20	Announces Comeback		
Nov 29	Gene Burton	Hamilton, Ontario	Exh 6

1955

Jan 5	Joe Rindone	Detroit	KO 6	
Jan 19	Ralph "Tiger" Jones	Chicago	L 10	L
Mar 29	Johnny Lombardo	Cincinnati	W 10	
Apr 14	Ted Olla	Milwaukee	KO 3	
May 4	Garth Panter	Detroit	W 10	
Jul 22	Rocky Castellani	San Francisco	W 10	
Dec 9	Carl "Bobo" Olson	Chicago	KO 2	
	(Regains World Middleweight Title)			

1956

May 18	Carl "Bobo" Olson	Los Angeles	KO 4
	(Retains World Middleweight Title)		
Nov 10	Bob Provizzi	New Haven, CT	W 10

1957

Jan 2	Gene Fullmer	New York	L 15	L
	(Loses World Middleweight Title)			
May 1	Gene Fullmer	Chicago	KO 5	
	(Regains World Middleweight Title)			
Sep 10	Otis Woodard	Philadelphia	Exh 2	
Sep 10	Cosby Linson	Philadelphia	Exh 2	
Sep 23	Carmen Basilio	New York	L 15	L
	(Loses World Middleweight Title)			

1958

| Mar 25 | Carmen Basilio | Chicago | W 15 |
| | (Regains World Middleweight Title) | | |

1959

| Dec 14 | Bob Young | Boston | KO 2 |

1960

Jan 22	Paul Pender	Boston	L 15	L
	(Loses World Middleweight Title)			
Apr 2	Tony Baldoni	Baltimore	KO 1	
Jun 10	Paul Pender	Boston	L 15	L
	(For World Middleweight Title)			
Dec 3	Gene Fullmer	Los Angeles	D 15	
	(For NBA Middleweight Title)			

1961

Mar 4	Gene Fullmer	Las Vegas	L 15	L
	(For NBA Middleweight Title)			
Sep 25	Wilf Greaves	Detroit	W 10	
Oct 21	Denny Moyer	New York	W 10	
Nov 20	Al Hauser	Providence	KO 6	
Dec 8	Wilf Greaves	Pittsburgh	KO 8	

1962

Feb 17	Denny Moyer	New York	L 10	L
Apr 27	Bobby Lee	Port of Spain, Trinidad	KO 2	
Jul 9	Phil Moyer	Los Angeles	L 10	L
Sep 25	Terry Downes	London	L 10	L
Oct 17	Diego Infantes	Vienna	KO 2	
Nov 10	Georges Estatoff	Lyon, France	KO 6	

1963

Jan 30	Ralph Dupas	Miami Beach	W 10
Feb 25	Bernie Reynolds	Santo Domingo	KO 4
Mar 11	Billy Thornton	Lewiston, ME	KO 3
May 5	Maurice Rolbnet	Sherbrooke, Canada	KO 3
Jun 24	Joey Giardello	Philadelphia	L 10
Oct 14	Armand Vanucci	Paris	W 10
Nov 9	Fabio Bettini	Lyon, France	D 10
Nov 16	Emile Sarens	Brussels	KO 8
Nov 29	Andre Davier	Grenoble, France	W 10
Dec 9	Armand Vanucci	Paris	W 10

1964

May 19	Gaylord Barnes	Portland, ME	W 10
Jul 8	Clarence Riley	Pittsfield, MA	KO 6
Jul 27	Art Hernandez	Omaha	D 10
Sep 3	Mick Leahy	Paisley, Scotland	L 10
Sep 28	Yolande Leveque	Paris	W 10
Oct 12	Johnny Angel	London	KO 6
Oct 24	Jackie Caillau	Nice, France	W 10
Nov 7	Baptiste Rolland	Calen, France	W 10
Nov 14	Jean Beltritti	Marseilles, France	W 10
Nov 27	Fabio Beltini	Rome	D 10

1965

Mar 6	Jimmy Beecham	Kingston, Jamaica	KO 2
Apr 4	Ray Basting	Savannah	KO 1
Apr 28	Rocky Randall	Norfolk, VA	KO 3
May 24	Memo Ayon	Tijuana	L 10
Jun 1	Stan Harrington	Honolulu	L 10

Jun 24	Young Joe Walcott	Richmond	W 10
Jul 12	Fred Hernandez	Las Vegas	L 10
Jul 27	Young Joe Walcott	Richmond	W 10
Aug 10	Stan Harrington	Honolulu	L 10
Sep 15	Bill Henderson	Norfolk, VA	NC 2
Sep 23	Young Joe Walcott	Philadelphia	W 10
Oct 1	Peter Schmidt	Johnston, PA	W 10
Oct 20	Rudolf Bent	Steubenville, OH	KO 3
Nov 10	Joey Archer	Pittsburgh	L 10
Dec 10	Announces Retirement		

INTERVIEWS

Johnny Barnes, December 7, 2002
Howard Bingham, November 30, 2002
Sylvia Dixon, December 17, 2002
Clint Edwards, November 2, 2002; December 7, 2002
Howie Evans, September 4, 2003
Kelly Howard, March 15, 2003
Delilah Jackson, September 25, 2002
Carl Jefferson, November 26, 2003
Max Roach, July 24, 2003
Hilly Saunders, February 23, 2003
Roger Simon, March 12, 2002
Percy Sutton, January 17, 2003
Jackie Tonawanda, May 1, 2003
Langley Waller, November 4, 2002; July 2, 2003
Rev. Dino Woodard, May 8, 2002
Sigmund Wortherly, December 27, 2002

NOTES

CHAPTER 1: FROM RED CLAY TO BLACK BOTTOM

1. Gene Schoor, *Sugar Ray Robinson* (Paris: Hachette, 1952), p. 1.

2. Donald L. Grant, *The Way It Was in the South: The Black Experience in Georgia* (New York: The Carol Publishing Group, 1993), p. 307.

3. Coleman Young with Lonnie Wheeler, *Hard Stuff: The Autobiography of Mayor Coleman Young* (New York: Viking Press, 1994), p. 20.

4. Sunnie Wilson with John Cohassey, *Toast of the Town* (Detroit: Wayne State University Press, 1998), p. 43.

5. Ibid. p. 47.

6. Joe Louis with Edna and Art Rust, Jr., *Joe Louis: My Life* (New York: Harcourt Brace Jovanovich, 1978), p. 24.

7. Schoor, p. 6.

CHAPTER 3: A HOME IN HARLEM

1. Schoor seems to believe they were on relief during their days in Detroit. There is no confirmation of this in any of the other material about Sugar's formative years. It appears that his mother always worked.

2. Schoor, p. 15.

3. Schoor relates a similar incident but he names the boy Sonny Leacock.

4. Sugar calls him "Booksiegel" in a *Sport* magazine article by Ed Fitzgerald in June 1951.

CHAPTER 4: THE CRESCENT'S STAR

1. Interview with Sigmund Wortherly, December 27, 2002.

CHAPTER 5: THE MAN WITH THE GOLDEN GLOVES

1. Ronald K. Fried, *Corner Men: Great Boxing Trainers* (New York: Four Walls Eight Windows, 1991), p. 80.

2. Interview with Langley Waller, July 2, 2003.

3. Sometimes Kurt and sometimes with one *n* in his last name.

CHAPTER 6: PUNCHING FOR PAY

1. Kathleen A. Hauke, *Ted Poston: Pioneer American Journalist* (Athens: University of Georgia Press, 1999).

2. Barney Nagler, *Brown Bomber* (New York: World Publishing, 1972), p. 27.

3. Sugar Ray Robinson, with Dave Anderson, *Sugar Ray: The Sugar Ray Robinson Story* (New York: Da Capo Press, 1994), p. 80.

4. Ibid., p. 87.

CHAPTER 7: SUGAR RAY AND EDNA MAE

1. Robinson, p. 94.
2. David Dean, *Defender of the Race: A Biography of James Theodore Holly* (London: Carlson Publishing, 1978), p. 195.
3. Howard Brotz, ed., *African American Social and Political Thought: 1850–1920* (New Brunswick, N.J.: Transaction Publishers, 1996).
4. Interview with Delilah Jackson, September 25, 2002.
5. Interview with Clint Edwards, November 2, 2002.
6. Interview with Sylvia Dixon, December 17, 2002.
7. *Sport,* June 1951, p. 84.

CHAPTER 8: THE MATADOR AND THE BULL

1. Nick Tosches, *The Devil and Sonny Liston* (New York: Little, Brown and Company, 2000), p. 80.
2. Robinson, p. 107.

CHAPTER 9: FROM SILK TO OLIVE DRAB

1. Robinson, p. 115.
2. John Peer Nugent, *The Black Eagle* (New York: Bantam Books, 1971).
3. Robinson, p. 123.
4. Arnold Rampersad, *Biography of Jackie Robinson* (New York: Alfred A. Knopf, 1997), p. 102.

CHAPTER 10: CHAMPION AT LAST!

1. Althea Gibson, *I Always Wanted to Be Somebody* (New York: Harper and Brothers, 1958).
2. Richard Bak, *Joe Louis: The Great Black Hope* (New York: Da Capo Press, 1998), p. 237.

3. Robinson, p. 133.

4. Bob Roth, Internet.

5. Robinson, pp. 137–38.

CHAPTER 11: A DREADFUL DREAM

1. Robinson, p. 141.

CHAPTER 12: A BROWN BABY AND A PINK CADILLAC

1. *New York Times,* February 4, 1949.

2. *Ring—Boxing the 20th Century,* p. 86.

3. *New York Times,* July 12, 1949.

4. Interview with Hilly Saunders, February 23, 2003.

5. *Daily Worker,* August 26, 1949.

6. Robinson, p. 150.

7. James Haskins and N. R. Mitang, *Mr. Bojangles: The Biography of Bill Robinson* (New York: William Morrow, 1988).

8. *Ring,* February 1951, p. 6.

9. Robinson, p. 152.

10. Rampersad, p. 266.

11. *Amsterdam* News, September 1950.

CHAPTER 13: "LE SUCRE MERVEILLEUX" IN PARIS

1. *The New Yorker,* September 29, 1951.

2. Interview with Langley Waller, November 4, 2002.

3. Interview with Roger Simon, March 12, 2002.

4. *Jet,* April 1, 1954.

5. Tyler Stovall, *Paris Noir: African Americans in the City of Light* (Boston: Houghton-Mifflin, 1996), p. 68.

6. *New York Times,* January 3, 1951.

CHAPTER 14: THE ST. VALENTINE'S DAY MASSACRE

1. David Remnick, *King of the World* (New York: Vintage, 1999), p. 46.

2. Jeffrey T. Sammons, *Beyond the Ring: The Role of Boxing in American Society* (Urbana: University of Illinois Press, 1988), p. 142.

3. Jake LaMotta, with Joseph Carter and Peter Savage, *Raging Bull* (Englewood Cliffs, N.J.: Prentice-Hall, 1970), p. 148.

4. Fried, p. 302.

CHAPTER 15: IT'S TURPIN TIME

1. Jean-Claude Baker and Chris Chase, *Josephine: The Hungry Heart* (New York: Random House, 1993), p. 298.

2. *Our World,* August 1951, pp. 40–44.

3. In his autobiography Sugar may have inverted the dates, believing his moment with the president's wife occurred before the fight. He also contradicts newspaper accounts when he said he wore a pink Lou Viscusi tie to match his pink Cadillac.

4. *New York Times,* June 16, 1951, p. 5.

5. *New York Times,* June 29, 1951, p. 23.

6. *Sunday Express,* March, 16, 1969.

7. *New York Times,* August 3, 1951.

8. *New York Post,* May 18, 1956.

9. *Our World,* November 1953, pp. 71–74.

10. Robinson, p. 210.

CHAPTER 16: BUMPY, BOBO, AND ROCKY

1. *Ebony,* April 1954.

2. Gerald Early, *The Culture of Bruising: Essays on Prizefighting,*

Literature, and Modern American Culture (Hopewell, N.J.: The Ecco Press, 1994), p. 106.

CHAPTER 17: TAKE IT TO THE MAXIM
1. Interview with Carl Jefferson, November 26, 2003.
2. Grantland Rice, *Sunday Mirror,* June 29, 1952, p. 52.
3. LaMotta, p. 188.
4. Stanley Weston and Steven Farhood, *The Ring—The 20th Century* (BDD Illustrated Books, 1993).

CHAPTER 18: TOP HAT AND TAILS
1. *New York Times,* October 14, 1952, p. 41.
2. Art Taylor, *Notes and Tones* (New York: Da Capo Press, 1993), p. 119.

CHAPTER 19: RETURN TO THE RING
1. *Tan,* March 1955, p. 49.
2. A. Rampersad, *The Life of Langston Hughes, Volume II: 1941–1967, I Dream a World* (New York: Oxford University Press, 1988).
3. *The Daily News,* November 4, 1951.
4. *Sunday Post,* September 23, 1962.
5. Robinson, p. 267.
6. Roger Kahn, *The Flame of Pure Fire: Jack Dempsey and the Roaring '20s* (New York: Harcourt, Brace and Company, 1999), p. 358.
7. Muhammad Ali, *The Greatest* (New York: Random House, 1975), p. 96.
8. Ali, p. 280.
9. Sammons, p. 138.

10. *New York Times,* May 19, 1956, p. 15.

11. Ibid.

CHAPTER 20: THE PERFECT PUNCH

1. *Grand Rapids Express,* January 5, 1957, p. 32.

2. *New York Times,* May 3, 1957, p. 33.

3. Ibid.

CHAPTER 21: BROKE!

1. *New York Times,* March 13, 1958, p. 37.

CHAPTER 22: SUGAR'S DILEMMAS

1. *New York Post,* April 16, 1959.

2. *New York Times,* October 24, 1959.

3. *New York Post,* August 7, 1959.

4. *Amsterdam News,* November 28, 1959.

5. *Amsterdam News,* January 21, 1961.

6. Interview with Max Roach, July 24, 2003. (Edna Mae may have been a couple of years off in her memory of the concert and the incident. Roach's memory is hazy about the whole affair, but he seems to feel it occurred in the early sixties, which would be consistent with his black militancy phase.)

7. Charles Nichols, ed., *Arna Bontemps/Langston Hughes Letters, 1928–1967* (New York: Dodd, Mead & Co., 1980).

CHAPTER 23: MILLIE AND THE MORMON

1. Conrad Lynn, *There Is a Fountain* (New York: Lawrence Hill, 1979).

2. In her preparation notes for her memoir, Edna Mae calls the woman Maxine.

3. Interview with Kelly Howard, March 15, 2003.
4. *New York Post,* September 27, 1961.

CHAPTER 24: MEXICAN DIVORCÉE
1. *Amsterdam News,* October 28, 1961, p. 28.
2. She may have been a few months off in her recollection of the refund, which the IRS said was received on May 15, 1963.
3. Interview with Howard Bingham, November 30, 2002.

CHAPTER 25: THE OTHER WOMAN
1. *Amsterdam News,* March 10, 1962.

CHAPTER 26: ALI
1. Ferdie Pacheco, with Jim Moskovitz, *The 12 Greatest Rounds of Boxing: The Untold Stories* (Toronto: Sport Classic Books, 2003), p. 73.

CHAPTER 27: UP AGAINST THE MOB
1. Interview with Johnny Barnes, December 7, 2002.
2. Peter Heller, *"In this Corner": Forty World Champions Tell Their Stories* (New York: Simon & Schuster, 1973).

CHAPTER 29: POUND FOR POUND
1. Interview with Clint Edwards, December 7, 2002.
2. Joyce Carol Oates, *On Boxing* (Hopewell, N.J.: Ecco Press, 1994), pp. 33–34.
3. LaMotta, p. 154.
4. *New York Times,* April 15, 1965, p. 22; May 15, 1965, p. 17.
5. Art Taylor, *Notes and Tones* (New York: Da Capo Press, 1993), p. 203.

6. Pete Hamill, quoted in *Sugar Ray Robinson: The Bright Lights and Dark Shadows of a Champion.* HBO, November 10, 1998.

CHAPTER 30: LORD OF THE RING
1. John Henrik Clarke, *Harlem USA* (New York: Seven Seas Press, 1964), p. 183.
2. *Amsterdam News,* July 22, 1962.
3. *Amsterdam News,* July 22, 1962.
4. *Sports Illustrated,* July 13, 1987.
5. *New York Beacon,* April 4, 1994.

THE FINAL BELL
1. Interview with Jackie Tonawanda, May 1, 2003.
2. Fried, p. 304.

EPILOGUE
1. *CBZ Journal,* April 2001.
2. *Boxing Monthly,* July 2003, p. 17.

BIBLIOGRAPHY

Ali, Muhammad, with Richard Durham. *The Greatest: My Own Story*. New York: Random House, 1975.

Bak, Richard. *Joe Louis: The Great Black Hope*. Dallas: Taylor Publishing, 1996.

Baker, Jean-Claude, and Chris Chase. *Josephine: The Hungry Heart*. New York: Random House, 1993.

Bernard, Emily, ed. *Remember Me to Harlem: The Letters of Langston Hughes and Carl Van Vechten, 1925–1964*. New York: Alfred A. Knopf, 2001.

Blumenthal, Ralph. *Stork Club*. New York: Little, Brown & Company, 2000.

Clark, Kenneth B. *Dark Ghetto: Dilemmas of Social Power*. New York: Harper Torchbooks, 1965.

Clarke, John Henrik, ed. *Harlem USA*. New York: Seven Seas Press, 1964.

———, ed. *Malcolm X: The Man and His Times*. Trenton, N.J.: African World Press, 1990.

Dodson, Howard, Christopher Moore, and Roberta Yancey. *The Black New Yorkers: 400 Years of African American History*. New York: John Wiley and Sons, 2000.

Early, Gerald. *The Culture of Bruising: Essays on Prizefighting, Literature, and Modern American Culture*. Hopewell, N.J.: Ecco Press, 1994.

Fried, Ronald K. *Corner Men: Great Boxing Trainers*. New York: Four Walls Eight Windows, 1991.

Goldman, Peter. *The Death and Life of Malcolm X*. Urbana and Chicago: University of Illinois Press, 1979.

Grant, Donald L. *The Way It Was in the South: The Black Experience in Georgia*. New York: Carol Publishing Group, 1993.

Graziano, Rocky, and Rowland Barber. *Somebody Up There Likes Me: My Life So Far*. New York: Simon & Schuster, 1954.

Haskins, James, and N. R. Mitang. *Mr. Bojangles: The Biography of Bill Robinson*. New York: William Morrow, 1988.

Hauke, Kathleen A. *Ted Poston: Pioneer American Journalist*. Athens: University of Georgia Press, 1999.

Hauser, Thomas, with the cooperation of Muhammad Ali. *Muhammad Ali: His Life and Times*. New York: Simon & Schuster, 1991.

Heller, Peter. *In This Corner: Forty World Champions Tell Their Stories*. New York: Simon & Schuster, 1973.

Johnson, Jack. *Jack Johnson: In the Ring—and Out*. Introductory articles by Ed Smith, "Tad," Damon Runyon, and Mrs. Jack Johnson; with special drawings by Edward William Krauter and other illustrations. Chicago: National Sports Publishing Company, 1927.

Kahn, Roger. *The Flame of Pure Fire: Jack Dempsey and the Roaring '20s.* New York: Harcourt, Brace and Company, 1999.

LaMotta, Jake, with Joseph Carter and Peter Savage. *Raging Bull: My Story.* Englewood Cliffs, N.J.: Prentice-Hall, 1970.

Louis, Joe. *The Joe Louis Story.* New York: Grosset and Dunlap, 1953.

———, with Edna and Art Rust, Jr. *Joe Louis: My Life.* New York: Harcourt Brace Jovanovich, 1978.

Mailer, Norman. *The Fight.* Boston: Little, Brown and Company, 1975.

Malcolm X, with Alex Haley. *The Autobiography of Malcolm X.* New York: Ballantine Books, 1964.

Nagler, Barney. *Brown Bomber.* New York: World Publishing, 1972.

Nugent, John Peer. *The Black Eagle.* New York: Bantam Books, 1971.

Oates, Joyce Carol. *On Boxing.* Hopewell, N.J.: Ecco Press, 1994.

Pacheco, Ferdie. *The 12 Greatest Rounds of Boxing: The Untold Stories.* Toronto: Sport Classic Books, 2003.

Parks, Gordon. *Voices in the Mirror: An Autobiography.* New York: Doubleday, 1990.

Remnick, David. *King of the World: Muhammad Ali and the Rise of an American Hero.* New York: Vintage Books, 1999.

Robinson, Jackie, with Alfred Duckett. *I Never Had It Made.* New York: G. P. Putnam's Sons, 1972.

Robinson, Sugar Ray, with Dave Anderson. *Sugar Ray: The Sugar Ray Robinson Story.* New York: Da Capo, 1994.

Sammons, Jeffrey T. *Beyond the Ring: The Role of Boxing in American Society.* Urbana and Chicago: University of Illinois Press, 1990.

Schoor, Gene. *Sugar Ray Robinson*. Paris: Hachette, 1952.

Sugar, Bert Randolph, ed. *The Ring: 1981 Record Book and Boxing Encyclopedia*. n.p.:Ring Publishing Corporation, 1981.

Tosches, Nick. *The Devil and Sonny Liston*. New York: Little, Brown and Company, 2000.

Wiley, Ralph. *Serenity: A Boxing Memoir*. New York: Henry Holt, 1989.

Wilson, Sunnie, with John Cohassey. *Toast of the Town: The Life and Times of Sunnie Wilson*. Detroit: Wayne State University Press, 1998.

Young, Coleman, with Lonnie Wheeler. *Hard Stuff: The Autobiography of Mayor Coleman Young*. New York: Viking, 1994.

INDEX